U0491841

2019年度东南大学科研启动经费资助项目“基于平行文本语料库和网页文本定时提取技术的中国企业英文网站文本语料库开发与应用研究”（项目编号：3217009202）结题成果

2020年度东南大学高校基本科研业务费专项资金资助项目“美国西部小说中的女性形象研究”（项目编号：3217002001B2）结题成果

2021年度中央高校教育教学改革专项资金资助项目“《英语演讲与辩论》课程思政智慧教学设计研究”（项目编号：5217002124A）成果

2022年度中央高校教育教学改革专项资金资助项目“东南大学“课程思政”校级示范课改革试点——《审辨思维与交流技巧》”（项目编号：5217002201A）成果

江苏高校品牌专业建设工程二期项目（英语）（项目编号：1117000186）学术成果

| 光明社科文库 |

中美组织机构英文网站比较与课程思政应用

刘　彬◎著

光明日报出版社

图书在版编目（CIP）数据

中美组织机构英文网站比较与课程思政应用 / 刘彬著. -- 北京：光明日报出版社，2023.5

ISBN 978-7-5194-7270-2

Ⅰ.①中… Ⅱ.①刘… Ⅲ.①英语—阅读教学 Ⅳ.①H319.37

中国国家版本馆 CIP 数据核字（2023）第 096175 号

中美组织机构英文网站比较与课程思政应用

ZHONGMEI ZUZHI JIGOU YINGWEN WANGZHAN BIJIAO YU KECHENG SIZHENG YINGYONG

著　　者：刘　彬

责任编辑：郭思齐　　　责任校对：史　宁　李佳莹

封面设计：中联华文　　　责任印制：曹　净

出版发行：光明日报出版社

地　　址：北京市西城区永安路 106 号，100050

电　　话：010-63169890（咨询），010-63131930（邮购）

传　　真：010-63131930

网　　址：http://book.gmw.cn

E - mail：gmrbcbs@gmw.cn

法律顾问：北京市兰台律师事务所龚柳方律师

印　　刷：三河市华东印刷有限公司

装　　订：三河市华东印刷有限公司

本书如有破损、缺页、装订错误，请与本社联系调换，电话：010-63131930

开　　本：170mm×240mm

字　　数：287 千字　　　印　　张：16

版　　次：2023 年 10 月第 1 版　　　印　　次：2023 年 10 月第 1 次印刷

书　　号：ISBN 978-7-5194-7270-2

定　　价：95.00 元

前 言

回顾网络发展的历史，我们可以发现，网站见证了网络走向广泛民用的开端，网络带来的丰富世界是从 1989 年 3 月的欧洲核子研究中心（CERN）开始的。物理学家蒂姆·伯纳斯-李（Tim Berners-Lee）向欧洲核子研究中心递交了一份建议书，建议采用超文本技术（Hypertext）把中心内部的各个实验室连接起来，在系统建成后，将可能扩展到全世界。当时，超文本技术刚刚出现，国际超文本学术会议频频举行，每次都有大量论文涌现。但是，除了蒂姆，几乎没有人想到将超文本技术引入计算机网络。1989 年的夏天，蒂姆开发出了世界上第一台网络服务器和第一台网络客户机。1989 年 12 月，蒂姆为他的发明正式定名为“万维网”（World Wide Web），即人们熟悉的“WWW”。1991 年 5 月，万维网首次应用于互联网（Internet），由此揭开了互联网新纪元，网上冲浪成为人们生活不可或缺的一部分。

Info. cern. ch 是世界上有史以来第一个网站和网站服务器，运行在欧洲核子研究中心的 NeXT 计算机上。访问者可以了解更多有关超文本技术的信息，建立网页的技术细节，以及如何进行网络搜索。我国境内最早的门户网站是常青藤网站，成立于 1997 年，曾推出国内最早的中文搜索引擎之一，汇集了当时中国、新加坡等 10 万余条中文地域网络地址。

今天，有数以亿计以上的网站，以及数以十亿计的用户，发布传播的信息更是不可计数，如今人们购置的电脑手机基本都需要联网使用。与网站相比，微信公众号、小程序、微博等传播媒体基于移动终端设计，“随时随地无处不在”传播方式更有效，影响力更大。作为历史最“悠久”的网络产物，网站似乎已成为网络时代最“传统”的传播途径。与其他网络传播模式相比，很多现代语言习惯能够在网站上形成在一段时间内相对固化的状态，由于网络快照功能可以记录某一时刻的网站内容，所以我们有机会研究网站语言文本随时间演变的过程，揭示网络时代现代语言的发展规律。

根据大众传播的不同需求，网站有不同类型，大致分为以下几种：以信息展示为主的展示类网站、以售卖服务或物品为主的商城类网站、以平台入驻，提供服务为主的服务类网站、以某些目的、功能为核心建立的功能类网站、以交流信息、交换资源为主的论坛类网站。其中，以信息展示为主的展示类网站还可进一步细分为门户类网站、产品类网站、企业官网类网站和营销类网站。本书介绍的实证研究主要关注包括企业官网在内的组织机构官网类网站。

从数量上看，企业官网在组织机构官网中占据主导位置，它是企业在互联网上进行网络营销和形象宣传的平台，相当于企业的网络名片，利用网站来进行宣传、产品资讯发布、招聘等。其他组织机构官网也承担着类似的对外宣传的作用。

在日常社会生活中，名片虽然概念“过时”，但因其固有的介绍社会身份和交际工具的属性，并未完全退出历史舞台。和名片一样，网站虽然已经属于网络传播媒体中的“前浪”，但可以预见，在相当长的一段时间内，组织机构网站仍然会像名片一样，继续发挥其展现对外形象和网络交际平台的作用。

网站对社会生活而言具有重要意义，而文字语言在信息有效传播过程中占据着无可取代的核心地位。有鉴于此，本研究主要关注全球化背景下的我国组织机构英文网站的文本语言特征，将美国同类组织机构的官网作为语言在不同社会使用的客观参照系而非“绝对正确”的标杆，有助于为英语全球化现象和中国英语变体的社会语言学研究提供参考。此外，以此研究主题为契机，本书还探索了将网络作为辅助英语课程思政教学的语料库和自主学习素材库的可能性，引介了面向义务教育阶段至大学阶段的英语教育全学段的学生自主探究式项目教学案例，这些案例以学生为主体，以鼓励学习者使用语言和训练语言输出能力为目标，主要形式是学生在教师指导下完成自主学习研究，通过团队合作完成项目要求。通过对这些案例的评析，本书讨论了项目式教学与英语课程思政理念的具体结合方式。能力所限，展现的网络语料库辅助英语课程思政教学的广阔前景不及万一，本书作为引玉之砖，期待不同学段的英语教育实践者以及英文网站内容建设者和研究者，共同探索网络语料库辅助英语课程思政教学的新路径和新方法，共建英语课程思政教学研究共同体。

刘彬

2022 年 5 月 28 日　南京

目 录
CONTENTS

第一章

导　论

第一节　网站本地化与国内外相关研究

本地化自诞生伊始，就与翻译紧密交织在一起，成为多语信息生产和管理的重要组成部分。本书从面向产品结果的角度看待本地化，对选定的中美组织（包括商业和非营利组织）的本地化和非本地化英文网站进行了文本规约分析。皮姆（Pym 2011）曾断言，源语言为中文且本地化目标语为英文的网站文本通常会保持其原始的体裁规约，本书介绍的比较研究希望为此观点提供实证证据，从而用实例证明，中国组织文化以特有的电子交互方式，丰富了以英语为媒介的网络空间。作为开篇，本章阐述并介绍了网站本地化研究的关键概念和基本思路，特别是本地化网站的文本规约分析，然后确定相关文献的空白以及后续章节中要讨论的研究主题。

本研究的总体假设是，与非本地化的英文网站相比，本地化的英文网站在宏观和微观结构层面都表现出独特的文本语言特征。为了实证检验这一假设，本文将分别比较选定的本地化网站与可比的非本地化网站的导航文本和内容文本（比较研究的具体内容和方法见第二章和第三章）。本章的主要作用是为实证研究奠定理论基础。第一章第一节为当前研究涉及的相关主题做好理论准备；第一章第二节划定本研究的范围，介绍了本书涵盖的研究主题。

作为介绍当前研究背景的第一步，本节首先阐明研究网站文本规约（convention）的意义。然后从行业和学术的角度阐述了本地化和翻译之间在概念上的关联，再讨论在翻译研究的背景之下研究网站本地化这一“新翻译模式”（Jiménez-Crespo 2009：79）的可行性。笔者认为，翻译研究现有的知识体系可以为网站本地化的理论和实践提供重要指导。

一、"最传统的数字化体裁"——网站

规约包括网站规约，可以被视为文本体裁的基本构件，规约分析有助于加深对特定文体（genre）的理解。米勒（Miller 1984）所定义的文体是指基于大规模修辞行为典型化的规约性话语类别；作为一种行为，文体从情境和产生情境的社会背景中获得意义。对体裁的这一通用定义强调了动作和情境对理解体裁的重要性，但哈提姆和梅森（Hatim，Mason 1990）对体裁的概念阐释与翻译研究最为相关："一种常规化的文本形式，它反映了特定社交场合所涉及的功能和目标以及参与者的目的。"这呼应了包括目的论在内的功能和社会文化视角的翻译方法。在翻译研究中，规约被定义为隐含或默认的非约束性行为规定，"基于常识和交流双方对于彼此在某种特定情形下采取何种行为的期望"（Nord 1991a：96）。按照这样的思路，网站规约在翻译研究中可以被视为网站产品特别是网站文本所体现出的非约束性特征，以期实现网站的预期目的。

网站规约兼具稳定性和灵活性。尽管技术有起有落，但网络规约可以在网络环境中稳定下来，帮助人们更好地理解网络媒介传播，同时网络规约也具有灵活多变的特点，促进对技术如何随时间推移影响网络媒介的动态理解。作为一种以网络为媒介的数字化体裁，网站通过创建对交互形式和内容的共同期望来构建传播，进而通过规约性特征减轻生产和解释的负担。

此前出版的文献已经凭直觉或实证研究认可了作为一种数字化体裁的网站的整体规约化，其中包括本节标题中引用的研究（Jiménez-Crespo 2011：5）。目前的研究将此类讨论扩展到本地化的背景下。研究发现了网站内容组织或内容结构越来越相似的发展趋势，将这种规约化归因于信息架构和网站设计的标准化行业实践（Symonenko 2007：29）。至于网站内容本身，网页设计指南或其他出版物通常指定网页写作需要采用轻巧的风格（使用简单句，用简短词汇组织话语）、简洁性（需要读者处理的信息较少）、每段一个要点、倒金字塔风格（先写主要信息，再写细节）以及便于跳读的排版特征（Carrada 2000）。当前研究选择了其中具有可操作性形式的特征作为研究对象，旨在以文本语言学的视角探索本地化组织网站的规约。

网站本地化的行业实践需要从业者在掌握参考信息的情况下体现更大的灵活性，这充分说明实证探索网站本地化中的文本规约的重要性。可以说，将文本结构调整为目标话语社区所期望的原型是对任何网站进行本地化的关键考虑因素，特定网络体裁的预期术语和措辞规约也是如此（Nord 2014）。希门尼斯-克雷斯波（Jiménez-Crespo 2010：187）认为，文本体裁原型结构的跨文化差异

是大多数翻译过程中的常见问题，因此对参与本地化的翻译人员提出了挑战。本地化实践中的另一个挑战是，技术与翻译交织在一起，通常会迫使翻译人员保留数字文本的固定的上层和宏观结构，即底层的后端编码结构及其屏幕呈现。

哈提姆和梅森（2014）构想的三个通用维度——形式方面（规约化形式）、社会文化方面（社交场合）和认知方面（参与者的目的），对于理解不同语言和文化中的网站复杂性非常重要（Borja，Izquierdo，Montalt 2009：62）。网站的形式方面或规约化形式在文化上是中立的吗？换言之，不同国家和语言起源的网站是否会表现出相同的规约化特征？是否有任何因素导致或影响已发现的规约化或偏差？因此，本地化已成为开展此类跨文化比较的重要场景，可以通过比较以相同语言呈现的本地化和非本地化网站，为上述问题提供初步解答。

人们认为文化、语言、文本类型和体裁改编是传统语言、交际和功能主义方法的核心概念，而技术适应则被视为本地化的一个决定性特征（Jiménez-Crespo 2013：16）。然而，在网络本地化中，维护质量的主要是非技术组件，因为非技术领域存在着更广泛的文本、话语和交流问题。希门尼斯-克雷斯波（2013：106）将此归因于网络体裁中存在的大量文本类型和体裁，这种情况需要采用更接近于其他翻译类型和模式的研究方法。在以网络为媒介的传播中的这种体裁嵌入也强调了体裁分析是网络本地化研究和教学的坚实基础（Jiménez-Crespo：2013：3）。

在开始讨论网站本地化之前，回顾本地化的概念发展历程是很有必要的。

二、网络空间背景下的本地化与翻译

本地化（有时简称为“L10n”）在语言服务领域的历史相对较短。它的出现可以追溯至1980年代的首次软件翻译（Esselink 2000：5），肇始于美国大型跨国软件商希望为自己的产品开拓新的市场（Schäler 2007：120）。爱尔兰本地化产业的发展历史表明，一个国家拥有大规模本地化产业，可能是考察其经济和社会发展状况的决定性因素（Schäler 2007）。

在既往的学术文献中，已有很多学者给出了本地化的定义。希门尼斯-克雷斯波（2009：79）认为，本地化是“一种技术、文本、交流和认知过程，通过这一过程，交互式数字文本经过调整，可以在不同的文化和语言接收环境中使用”。希门尼斯-克雷斯波将本地化视为过程，文本视为对象，与这一关注重点不同，谢勒尔（Schäler 2006：3）主张对本地化进行更广泛的乌托邦式定义，即“数字产品或服务的语言和文化调整，以满足外国市场和跨全球数字信息流的多语言管理的需求”。

凯迪尔科斯和艾思林柯（Cadieux, Esselink 2002）则考虑到本地化所处的背景，力图构成紧密的概念域，他们提出用公式化的方式表述全球化总体环境，使用了一个重新定义的术语——GILT，其中 G 代表全球化（Globalization），处于该概念系统中的最高层级，意思是将一个事物调整后推向多个市场；I 代表国际化（Internationalization），包括所有有助于后续本地化的准备工作；L 表示本地化（Localization），含义是使该事物适应特定市场的需求；最后，T 代表翻译（Translation），从一种语言转换成另一种语言。在这个等级化概念体系中，翻译（T）是本地化（L）的一部分，本地化（L）与国际化（I）一同构成了全球化（G）。

本研究旨在从翻译研究的角度解答网站本地化问题，本地化和翻译正在共同发展，有必要简要讨论二者术语概念之间的关系。在数字产品开发的产业环境中，翻译被视为本地化过程的一个组成部分。这主要是因为本地化需要一定程度的技术适应，对输出的译文通常用于纸质出版物制作的传统孤立翻译行为而言，这种技术适应是较为陌生的。为全面了解现代创作和本地化环境中的内容创建，莱特（Wright 2004：589）引入了一种面向技术的工作流范式，其中传统的文档制作顺序链被迭代和增量过程所取代。这种范式转变使产品信息生命周期中的译员角色发生了显著改变。

以技术为导向的本地化工作流程催生了新的专业和岗位，例如，本地化译员、质量控制专家、软件开发人员和工程师，每个人都在一个庞大的团队中发挥作用，并增添了本地化行业的活力，引入除翻译以外的其他学科（Tennent 2005：103），翻译正越来越紧密地融入整个文档制作过程（Bowker 2002：139）。

由上述讨论可知，如果翻译是本地化的一个组成部分，用山德里尼（Sandrini 2005）的话来说，这意味着本地化专业人士掌握指挥权，而译者只负责输出目标语文本。然而，从翻译研究的角度看，翻译过程既涉及语言转移，也涉及文化转移，译文达成预期的交际意图或功能非常重要。因此，翻译总会涉及对文本本身或与文档相关的其他项目（如图形等）的某种形式的改编。归根结底，翻译是一项享有数百年历史的人类任务，而本地化则是自 30 年前发展起来的一种现象，也许只是一个新名称，一种特定类型的翻译。从这个意义上说，翻译应该被视为比本地化更广的概念。

此外，马祖尔（Mazur 2009：352）主张，在仅开展文本分析时，本地化也可以被视为翻译的一部分。如果本地化是调整文本以使其适应当地（目标文化）的语言和文化规范和惯例，那么这似乎已经是翻译研究和实践中非常成熟的观点了。相关详细讨论可参见奈达的动态对等（Nida 1977）、诺德的工具性翻译

(Nord 1991b)、豪斯的隐蔽翻译（House 1977）或韦努蒂的归化（Venuti 1986）。总而言之，本地化和翻译的关系的解读差异源于不同的立场。

尽管本地化和翻译的概念异同在未来一段时间内仍将是工业界和学术界争论的话题，但某些行业趋势表明这两个概念可能会融合。萨根特和雷（Sargent，Ray 2010：2）观察到资源包使标准翻译工具和流程更容易处理软件字符串，在某种程度上消除了本地化和翻译之间的区别。另一方面，艾思林柯（Esselink 2003a：85）在探讨整个行业的发展前景时认为，本地化公司曾经通过专注于软件应用程序的翻译、工程调试和测试而区别于传统翻译公司，现在大多数本地化公司正在迁移到 Web 本地化解决方案。艾思林柯（Esselink 2003a：85）进一步预测了可能的行业动态：本地化行业将慢慢融入翻译行业，形成“多语种出版行业”或“多语言解决方案行业”；大型本地化公司则不断向上游移动并提供内容创建和产品支持解决方案。

总体而言，关于本地化和翻译的理论讨论长期以来一直围绕着一批常见问题，这些问题突出了技术、自动化、标准、互操作性和效率的作用（Van Genabith 2009)。正如谢勒尔（2010：213）指出的那样，其原因是关于本地化问题的讨论和研究一直被本地化行业务实的商业思路所主导，跨国数字出版商希望借助本地化，在开发数字内容方面实现短期投资回报最大化。

目前流行的以行业为中心、技术驱动的技术路径强调除文本和语言以外的维度。有鉴于此，为开拓当前主流本地化活动以行业为导向的发展重点，本书介绍了一项文本语言研究，旨在从翻译研究的角度加深对网站本地化的理解。

如果从实现本地化产品总体目标的角度看，网站本地化可以定义为根据客户提出的目标，针对特定市场修改网站的过程，其中“市场”是指一群人（一个地区、一个国家或一个语言社区），共享一种语言、一种书写系统和可能需要一个单独版本的产品的其他属性（Yunker 2002：17)。网站本地化的细节（Pierini 2007）“涉及所有页面的翻译，包括所有纯语言元素——词汇（图形分隔的文字块）、替代文本、链接和支持文档。必要时，还包括对源文本的改编，以确保产品在当地市场的接受和成功，例如，日期、重量、度量和货币的改编；通过省略与目标接收者无关的信息、添加额外信息或对源文本进行摘要式翻译来修改内容；采用目标文化中常用的写作风格，改变源文本风格。”

由于就本地化定义难以达成统一共识，本研究中的“非本地化的英文网站”特指选定的美国组织的英文网站，而“本地化的英文网站”特指选定的中国组织的英文网站，二者均针对英语市场。由前文讨论可知，“本地化”一词有两个关键特征——技术导向性和市场导向性。然而，本地化和翻译过程中的技术集成水平不断提高，仅从技术上区分本地化和翻译几乎是不可能的。此外，当涉及源自其他语言的英文数字产品时，“目标市场”这一概念往往难以定义。鉴于定义方面面对的挑战，目前的研究将网站本地化视为将中文网站引入英语文化和语言环境，同时突出与语言和文本相关的产品特定功能的一项工作。

网站本地化的问题不仅限于对文化差异和技术影响的考量。该领域已发表的研究似乎以规范性框架和评估为主，然而合格网站“应该”具备的要件尚未形成共识。皮姆（2010：12）指出，将网站传播与跨文化营销理论联系起来的专著倾向于强调文化适应的必要性，而在网站中发现的趋势则更多地与新的创意文化社区的形成有关。有人认为，本地化在努力跟上技术发展步伐的同时，并未充分受益于翻译相关的理论概念，而这些理论概念有助于以更有效的方式塑造许多本地化过程，就像规约概念一样（Jiménez-Crespo 2009：80）。为了通过真实世界的证据深刻体会学术理论与实际网络生态系统之间差距，本文通过对源自中文的本地化英文网站的规约进行描述性分析，强调了本地化产品的自主性。从这种意义上看，承认并理解本地化和翻译研究之间的联系可以提供一种新的研究范式。

三、用翻译学地图探索网站本地化的疆域

关于本地化和翻译研究如何相互关联和相互作用的概念性讨论，已发表的文献已经提出了一些有力的观点。希门尼斯-克雷斯波（2010：287）认为，本地化专家将翻译理解为“专注于传达词句的含义和信息”（Lommel 2007：7）或“只是语言问题”（Brooks 2000），这样的想法已经过时了，这种简单化的定义忽视了现代翻译理论和范式最根本的交流、语用、功能主义、认知和社会语言学方面。按照夫拉伦（Folaron 2006：5）的说法，在学科历史发展过程中，翻译研究一直在批判性地处理与语言、文化和社会密切相关的问题，并探索社会类别（种族和性别）、社会概念（权力和意识形态）以及社会历史时期（古典主义、结构主义和后现代主义）。正如夫拉伦（Folaron 2006：5）所言，要提升翻译技术和本地化技术的学科解释力，应当超越对特定工具、程序和应用程序的观察或描述，探究塑造当下全球传播实践的多重复杂动态。为了实现这样的提升，翻译研究可以采用并调整经过历史检验的洞见、模型和方法，扩展其话语空间，接纳在以技术为媒介的数字世界中通过翻译进行的跨文化交流。遵循同样的思路，本书关注本地化网站这种技术（计算机和互联网）和翻译融合而成的数字产品。

有些对翻译研究的一般性介绍已经尝试将网络产品本地化领域包括在内，

但结果相当有限（Sandrini 2005：3）。威廉姆斯和切斯特曼（Williams，Chesterman 2014）确定了以下研究领域："厘清当下实际做法，从微观和宏观层面调查网站约束和用户需求对译者决策的影响，评估产品，探索使用受控语言设计网站以方便翻译的可行性。"本研究关注网络传播产品，旨在通过分析面向使用英语的访客的中国营利性和非营利性组织网站来更广泛地了解本地化。

在开创性著作《翻译和网络本地化》（2013）中，希门尼斯-克雷斯波对网络本地化研究的现状和未来发展进行了全面审视。该书确定并讨论的研究主题有网络本地化中"文本"概念的重新界定、基于网络的体裁分析、网络本地化的质量、在该领域开展实证研究的指导原则、本地化能力以及专业化和众包的影响。其中，文本语言特征的体裁分析与当前的本地化网站研究关系密切。

第二节 本书的研究目的与主要内容

继第一节阐明关键术语和概念之后，本节重点介绍当前研究解决的主要问题。一方面，本研究通过分析一些流行议题，查漏补缺，填补了网站本地化的文献空白。另一方面，通过探索行业和源语言对本地化网站的文本语言特征的影响，开辟了新的研究领域。

一、丰富当前网站本地化研究的视角

在既往已发表的网站本地化研究中，有两个主要研究趋势需要重新评估。首先，过分强调语言外的维度尤其是视觉设计而忽视了语言问题。这主要是因为既往研究经常重点关注网站的非文本元素，以期将这种多模态媒体与其他传统媒体（如纸质印刷品和电视）区别开来。其次，网站本地化的评估很大程度上受到一条行业准则的影响，即本地化文本应该看起来"好像原本就是在目标市场中开发的"（LISA 2003：11）。在实践中，这意味着对本地化网站是否符合目标市场或文化的规约进行评估，任何偏差都会被简单地视为本地化错误或失败。然而，正如先前的研究已经证明的那样，本地化的网站文本不一定与原本产生于目标市场的文本共享相同的规约集合（Jiménez-Crespo 2009）。

（一）文本语言问题被技术和语言外问题所掩盖

作为一个利润丰厚、充满活力和跨专业的领域，网站本地化通常涉及营销、设计和软件工程以及语言过程（Pym 2010：1）。拉克（Lako 2012：358）指出，

对网站本地化过程的重要元素可以分为前端（“网站访问者在网站界面上看到的内容”）和后端（“幕后发生的事情”）。其中，导航结构和内容管理系统（CMS）是常规文本翻译从未涉及过的元素。前者是前端元素，由导航菜单和页面层次结构表示；后者是后端元素，允许对本地化内容进行控制以便实时更新。正如皮姆（Pym 2010：1）所说，网站的本地化在识别可翻译元素、非线性、所需的文本处理工具、准备和协调翻译过程的方式，以及可能涉及的改变程度等方面均不同于非超文本翻译。

尽管学术界和工业界在对网站开发和本地化的总体认识方面存在分歧，但双方都认同网页设计最起码应与其语言内容一样重要的想法，应该以适合屏幕阅读的方式排版。正如皮姆（Pym 2010：1）指出的那样，与印刷品页面不同，网页应该是为了使用而构建的，而不仅仅是为了阅读。然而，学术研究中对设计而非内容的普遍强调，似乎已经到了掩盖文本和语言问题的地步。

大多数已发表的网站本地化研究都属于信息系统（IS）和市场营销领域，密切关注除了网站文本之外的所有内容。文献综述（Chiou 2010）显示，信息系统领域的相关研究聚焦技术导向因素，如可用性、可访问性、可导航性或信息质量，而市场营销领域的相关研究主要评估广告、促销、在线交易、订单确认或客户服务。这两种研究视角都强调了网站的语言外维度，这是可以理解的，因为与内容相比，形式更能让网站与传统大众媒体区分开来。

然而，以语言和文本为代价突出颜色、设计和功能的情况似乎越来越多，以至于诸如这样的陈述并不罕见：“在适当的情境和风格中使用本地语言只是本地化工作的一小部分。公司还需要考虑调整颜色、图标、标志、网页布局、数字格式、日期格式……”（Singh 2004：3）。具有讽刺意味的是，这位作者同时也承认了网站本地化中语言适应的复杂性（然而“微不足道”）：“语言不仅在字符、语法规则和标点符号方面有所不同，而且在其起源、对历史和传统的强调、方言的使用和修辞风格方面、符号和隐喻的使用甚至说服策略的使用也有所不同。”（Singh 2004：3）

在进一步讨论文本和语言对本地化的意义时，加西亚解释了对文本的贬低以及翻译者角色的降级对质量的影响：

在本地化中，文本纯粹被视为一种商品，除了可用性之外几乎没有内在价值。译者与其说是处理文本整体属性的熟练工匠，不如说是处理具有受控语言特征的句段的流水线工人……在出版环境中，翻译者的工匠身份和文本的稳定属性在某种程度上可以暗示质量；在本地化中，质量只是许多需要衡量的维度中的一个（Garcia 2008：51）。

事实上，传统的文本语言特征对于在线呈现是必不可少的，虽然网络与传统大众媒体的呈现偏差是在网站评估中值得注意的重要因素，但“文本仍然是网页中的关键信息资产”（Sandrini 2005：2）。与任何本地化计划一样，网站本地化的主要目标是将最终产品（在本书中为网站）的可用性扩展到更广泛的用户群，对目标用户群来说，语言和相关的区域问题是客户体验的关键要素（DePalma 2012：2）。在埃森伯格（引自 Singh 2005：23）看来，网络发展已经历了四个阶段：技术阶段（专注于 gopher 信息查找协议和网络论坛）、设计阶段（专注于设计有吸引力的网站）、营销阶段（一个营销支出不受限制的时期，几乎不关心收入和利润）以及今天的业务阶段（强调网络投资的回报）。随着科技产品如雨后春笋般发展的尘埃落定，是时候反思文本和语言，以确保有的放矢，获得开销合理的网络成功。

（二）过分遵从目标市场规约，导致具有创造性和创新性的偏差消失

除了平衡文本和非文本因素这一难题之外，网站本地化人员在提升网站有效性方面也面临着从众与保持独特性的两难境地。维护一个有效的网站对于企业加强客户关系和提高市场份额至关重要（Law，Buhalis 2010：1）。在德穆伊（De Mooij 2004：206）看来，广告和营销的永恒困境是遵循目标文化中产品类别的规约，还是与众不同以提高知名度并在人们的记忆中占有一席之地。使用独特性吸引注意的风险在于可能会不契合消费者的既有认知图式，被弃之不顾。例如，习惯于符号、信号和间接交流的高语境文化受众处理信息的方式不同于习惯于解释、有说服力的文案和修辞的低语境文化受众（De Mooij 2004：206）。因此，营销人员通常不愿通过冒险走出消费者的舒适区来释放独特性的力量。

此外，学术文献长期以来一直将具有文化一致性的网站视为最佳实践，因为这可以提高网站的可用性，从而引导访问者对网站抱有较为积极的态度并最终增加商业机会（Chun，Singh，Sobh，Benmanmoun 2015；Vyncke，Brengman 2010）。网站访问者可能会从不同层面认识到不同程度的文化一致性，包括语言、功能（网站人体工程学、功能和技术规范）和图形设计（典型的文化标记，如颜色、国家标志、符号和英雄）（Bartikowski 2014）。在这三个层面中，网站语言在学术文献中受到的关注最少。在一项针对本地化网站的研究中（Singh，Kalliny 2012），提议的评估框架只有一个文本语言变量“翻译质量”，未做进一步细分；评估者（两名双语学生）浏览了每个研究网站的 50 个网页，并根据总体印象使用李克特五点量表进行评分。

在网站开发的研究方法方面，学术界和工业界并没有太大区别。网站设计和网络规约行业分析的流行指南似乎尽一切努力实现普遍性和普适性，很少考

虑可能存在的国家或语言特定差异。这可以通过融合理论（引自 De Mooij 2004：51）来解释，该理论提出，尽管各国拥有不同的文化和历史遗产以及多种多样的政治经济体系，但在工业化和现代化的影响下，国家正变得越来越相似。

然而，正如麦克卢汉（McLuhan，引自 De Mooij 2004：255）所言，技术创新仅仅是人类的增强或扩展。它们通常被人们用来增强当前的活动，并不会改变人们的价值观或习惯。随着技术专长作为差异化因素的增值作用逐渐减弱，文化专长作为收入来源和独特卖点的影响将与日俱增（Sargent, Ray 2010：2)。

因此，本书介绍的实证研究旨在细化网站本地化的文本语言规约分析，进而修正“无法辨识出来源地即是本地化成功”的普遍看法。在日益全球化的社会中，出版商、营销商和广告商对“奇怪”特质和刻板印象善加利用（Schäler 2006)。

通过对选定组织网站的文本语言特征的探索，接下来的分析处理影响本地化网站识别特征的两个主要因素：行业和源语言。

二、探索特定行业对本地化网站的影响

目前的研究将进行行业内和跨行业分析，以确定组织网站的文本特征是否受到特定行业的影响。解读不同行业之间的差异不仅对行业分析师很重要，对组织网站本地化从业者也很重要。本书介绍的比较研究的结果有助于更好地理解组织网站所体现的行业部门形象，从而有助于理解不同行业和专业的网络写作风格。

除了差异和偏差之外，本研究还将探索特定行业部门的本地化和非本地化英语网站的文本语言相似性，从而为网络内容的译者和作者提供现实世界的参考（研究方法论见第三章)。

本研究选择了来自五个行业部门——教育机构、政府、旅游目的地、电子商务和语言服务公司的组织网站样本开展先期研究。在不久的将来，随着行业多元化程度不断加深，预计将在更多的行业领域开展进一步的工作。萨根特和海智（Sargent, Hegde 2012：25）对行业部门的多元化给出了以下解释：

随着国家从资源发展转向信息发展，著名的本土公司自然而然地体现出行业部门的多样性。这是因为虽然老行业的现有业务可能会整合，但对资源、制造和服务公司的需求并没有消失。与此同时，在经济发展的下一阶段，新公司正在形成，如服务或信息，在该国的经济基础内创造了更大的多样性。

三、在网络组织话语中探寻书面英语变体以及源语言对本地化网站的影响

一般而言，多语版本的组织网站是随着国际商务和传播需求的增加以及网络技术的发展而产生的。皮姆（2009：139）描述了本地化行业中的语言层次结构以及由此产生的方向性：

> 一些语言（笔者补充）是中心化的，用于生产，还有一些是半中心化的，对消费有很强的约束作用，另外一些实际上被排除在生产、消费和翻译的关系之外。在这个层次结构中，翻译趋向于从中心化生产转向半中心化消费。这通常意味着从英语转向世界上所有主要语言。因此，本地化具有很强的方向性，从中心语言转向更外围的语言。这种方向性如此之强，以至于向另一个方向的运动被称为“反向本地化”（Schäler 2006）……随着经济全球化的加剧，我们可以预期反向本地化现象将变得更加重要。

当前对从简体中文到英文的本地化网站的研究，不仅是对上述引文所定义的反向本地化的发展的关注，而且力求揭示反向本地化的另一层意义，即“保留或有意将语言或文化的陌生感引入面向特定目标市场的数字内容，目的是有意将数字产品或服务与该市场的主导文化区分开来”（Schäler 2006：12）。本地化的最终目标是发布可被视为在当地制作的产品的本地化文本（LISA 2003：5），但据观察，本地化过程中的独特约束导致目标文本具有独特的语言特征（Jiménez -Crespo 2009：97）。此外，人们认为陌生感可以促成商业成功，不是让数字内容适应目标国家的文化和语言，而是通过完全相反的方式来开发可能最具吸引力的卖点（Schäler 2006：11）。因此，如何在适应目标文化和保有“陌生感”之间找到平衡，这个问题向网站本地化的从业者提出了挑战，同时也给予他们启发。

如果目标文化从网站本地化中接受一些偏离“正统”的新输入是可取的，那么目标语言没有理由不从善如流，从陌生的营销魅力中受益。一些学者长期以来一直主张承认世界英语现象，即英语作为通用语（ELF）或全球英语，他们认为在英语母语国以外的国家使用和发展的英语不应被简单地视为误用或错误的英语，而应被视为英语的不同变体，以促进国际和跨文化交流（有关相关文献的最新回顾评述，请参阅 Jenkins 2015）。因此，也可以从同样积极的角度看待源语言不同的本地化英语，以期丰富而非阻碍网络媒介传播（有关已发表

的简体中文源语的本地化英文网站研究的更多详情，请参见第三章）。

通过为本地化培训和实践提供经验证据，本书介绍的面向产品的描述性案例研究契合翻译研究的“实用转向”（Wilss 1987；引自 Snell-Hornby 1988：67）。这一转向指的是社会语言学和跨文化研究的兴起助力翻译研究学科发展，此类研究认为语言具有无限的可变性，与文化和传播密不可分。

第三节　本书结构

本书共分七章。作为总体介绍，第一章给出了网站本地化研究的基本背景，阐释了相关的关键术语和概念，梳理了国内外相关研究，并介绍了本书所涉及的研究主题，最后规划了本书的结构。第二章通过简要讨论具体的研究问题并提出相应的假设，界定了此次网站本地实证研究的范围，此外还探讨了研究的意义。第三章介绍了本书所依据的实证研究方法和描述性研究方法，随后描述了研究数据的收集和汇编程序，并介绍了研究所采用的多维度比较分析框架。第四章展示并分析了研究对选定的本地化和非本地化英文组织网站的分析结果，对当前研究的问题给出了解答。第五章总结了此次实证研究的主要发现，确定新出现的研究主题和问题，同时为组织网站翻译/本地化方面的语言管理和培训提供具体影响和建议，并讨论研究的局限性和潜在的未来调查途径。第六章探索将不同行业英文网站的研究发现和结论应用于英语教学实践的可能性，将英文组织网站视为英语教学的真实语料，为我国小学、中学和大学不同学段的英语课程思政教学设置了不同学习目标、不同训练难度层次的教案示例。第七章对全书内容进行全面概括总结。

第四节　本章小结

本章首先介绍了本书的关键术语和概念（第一节），并简要指出了当前对网站本地化的研究将如何解决现有研究中存在的一些不足之处（第二节）。具体而言，本书从翻译研究的视角研究本地化，将把焦点放在此前以技术为中心的研究很少关注的“传统”文本语言方面。此外，关注网站本地化的文本语言维度，将在一定程度上消解已发表的研究过分强调语言外元素（如颜色和设计）的总体趋势。其次，对本地化和非本地化网站进行描述性比较分析，将通过经验证据检验流行的规范性网站设计指南和对网页设计和内容写作的评估，从而说明：本地化网站实际上是通过突出而不是消除陌生感取得营销成功的。另外，比较研究将通过分析选定行业部门的网站文本来探索特定行业对组织网站文本规约的影响。最后，目前对简体中文本地化的英文网站的研究将探索书面英语变体是否存在，从而更好地掌握全球英语的动态发展情况，并通过对本地化和翻译如何影响接受市场和文化的正面描述，来丰富对英语作为通用语言（ELF）的理解。第三节简述全书各章内容，第四节总结全章。继本章的一般性介绍之后，第二章将通过阐明本研究要回答的研究问题来划定当前研究的范围，并针对本书涉及的各个研究主题梳理相关文献。第二章还就相关研究问题给出简要的研究假设。

第二章

基于语料库方法的组织网站比较研究范畴与意义

本章在第一章阐释的网站本地化理论基础上，概述了语料库研究方法，回顾了语料库相关研究，通过阐明研究问题和相应的基本假设，明确了研究的范围，然后说明了当前研究的意义。最后，介绍了本书的结构，对本章进行总结。

作为一种在商业推广方面占据主导地位的本地化模式，网站本地化随着对基于网络的本地化环境的需求不断扩大而蓬勃发展（Bahri，Mahadi 2015：33）。网站文本与网络上的任何其他文本一样，通常会与互联网的传播动态相互影响，而互联网本身可以被视为文化转型的工具。然而，在互联网促进全球传播的同时，国家或语言特定的差异并未完全消除，应予以考虑（ECDGT 2009：29）。正如第一章第三节所讨论的，以前的研究倾向于运用 IS、市场营销或企业传播理论来探讨企业网站的主题和设计。另一方面，对网络传播的组织话语的语言学探索还不够充分，尤其是从中国的角度。此外，在网站本地化的背景下，很少有研究从定量、语言和分析的角度审视组织网站（Shan，Wang 2017：1171）。这种世界范围内“对语言问题的兴趣缺乏”（Gâţă，Praisler 2015：129），也是网站管理员和/或网站设计师的常态，这种现象可以在促销类本地化场景中普遍存在的不译策略中找到部分解释，例如，将在不同国家推出的同一广告的本地化（Rodríguez 2016：135）。宣传类翻译经常保留大部分甚至全部的原文不译，这通常是为了保留源语言和文化的象征价值。然而，翻译包括广告在内的宣传材料不仅是为了传达产品价值，还要传达品牌价值和文化价值，或提供有关价格、用途或所提供服务的信息（Rodríguez 2016：140）。文本内容对实现这些目标做出了重大贡献，翻译在传递品牌和文化的相关价值方面发挥根本性作用，在需要时操纵文本材料以充分传达营销活动的本质（Rodríguez 2016：140）。

翻译研究这一学术领域在某种程度上和本地化行业一样，在研究本地化网站时忽视了语言和文本问题。翻译研究文献很少讨论网站文本的翻译，尽管有学者认为网站文本翻译涉及几个不同翻译层面的问题和决策，包括文化适应、超文本片段的信息排序和语言使用（Nauert 2007：1）。

只有几个英文发表的本地化网站研究和本研究一样关注文本语言层面，其中，对石油和天然气公司网站的研究（Umoh 2015）提供了全面的网站本地化文献综述，对本地化网站进行多维分析，包括粗略检查网站被译成目标语言的内容所占比重。此外，希门尼斯-克雷斯波对本地化和非本地化西班牙语网站的比较研究（2012、2011a、2011b、2010、2009 和 2008）大多遵循同一种方法论框架，本书的实证研究借鉴了这一框架并加以改编。基于这些关键参考文献以及其他已发表的提出一般性假设和分析以供进一步检验的相关研究，第一节和第二节提出了四个研究问题并做出了相应的基本假设。

第一节 本书的研究问题和基本假设

数字文本已被认定为占据主导地位的英语向世界各地传播规约的主要工具之一（House 2001）。另一方面，“反向本地化”的出现和发展（该术语的定义和讨论见第一章第三节）表明，不同语言话语社区日益增长的数字文本生产和使用可能导致了独特规则出现（Jiménez-Crespo 2009：80）。因此，为了探讨中国机构的本地化英文网站中存在这种趋势的可能性，本书将首先回答一个关于网站最常规组件——导航文本的问题，以研究网站文本的常规特征（研究方法的具体细节见第三章）：

一、在本研究涉及的本地化网站中，导航术语和短语的标准化程度如何？

根据文献（Price，Price 2002：45；引自 Jiménez-Crespo 2009）的分类，网站文本可分为界面文本和内容文本。希门尼斯-克雷斯波（2013：32）对这两种文本的定义如下：

界面文本是将网站各部分联结在一起并为超文本和网站提供全局连贯性和粘连性的所有文本交互片段，例如，导航菜单、对话框或聊天中的控件。这些片段在属于同一类型的网站中都是相似的，其中包括注册选项、帖子的评论、在全局超文本中导航或上传个人资料图片。内容文本与界面文本不同，可以定义为让每个网页都成为一个超文本单元的特定文本。

希门尼斯-克雷斯波在其发表的大部分本地化网站实证研究中均关注网站具有交互性的部分，当前的研究同样如此。界面文本包括菜单、按钮中呈现的文本和/或实现导航目的的链接，为了回答第一个研究问题，本研究专门考察了界面文本类别中的导航文本。这些导航版块被视为涉及网站上最常规文本的区域（Nielsen，Tahir 2002）。探索该区域的文本规约有助于确定在本地化过程中，源文本（中文）规约是否已被目标文本（英文）规约所替代。在此提出的假设是，尽管大多数导航词汇单元已与非本地化英文组织网站保持一致，但本地化的英文网站仍在一定程度上保留了中文源语言的规约。

下一个主要研究问题从最常规的导航文本转向不太常规的内容文本，调查本地化网站的文本语言特征。除了其他潜在因素，如具有展示性的网络语境以及计算机技术促成的本地化过程，这些文本语言特征主要受到中文源语言的影响。

二、本地化的网站文本在多大程度上体现了特定语言的特征？

书面内容的本地化对于日期、货币和计量单位等方面的恰当迁移以及传达正确的组织形象都是非常重要的（Bahri, Mahadi 2015：36）。本研究将本地化英语网站不同交际版块的内容文本与可比的非本地化对应版块的内容文本及其中文原版进行比较，以确定源自英语目标语言或中文源语言的常规特征。

回顾已发表的文献可以发现，尽管有大量研究比较了不同源语言（含中文）和文本类型的原版和英译版，但迄今为止，很少有英文出版物关注源语言为中文的本地化英文网站。从文本语言学的角度来看，大多数源语言为中文的本地化和非本地化英文网站的比较都是规定性的错误分析，主要目的是评估翻译质量（参见本章第二节和第三章的比较研究相关概述）。目前研究的一个关键的不同点是通过描述性文本分析来加深对中国组织机构英语网站规约的理解。对当前研究问题所做的假设是，本研究涉及的本地化内容文本能够反映源语言（在本研究中是中文）的影响，不过，要确定这种影响的程度尚待进一步研究。

那么，如果不考虑本地化场景和源语言，还有什么因素会影响本地化与非本地化英文网站之间存在的差异呢？下一个研究问题深入研究行业影响力的存在。

三、本地化网站是否有任何行业特定的常规特征可区别于来自不同行业的其他网站？

随着经济全球化的快速发展，对我国的商业或非营利组织而言，要增强产业和国家核心竞争力，实施“走出去”战略，最关键的是在海外树立正面形象，发展世界知名品牌。因此，中国组织和机构应当重视建立和维护自己的网站，在实现便利、自主和互动的同时，应对跨文化挑战（Shan, Wang 2017：1170）。

此前，关于本地化组织网站的大多数研究都集中在某一个行业的商业公司，特别是电子商务。与其他类型的网站相比，商业网站改编较少，因为它们几乎没有文化相关元素（Sierro Fernández 2016：83）。然而实际上，网站改编，或者更确切地说是网站本地化，对于公司在充分了解客户需求的情况下借助网站平台接触目标客户是非常重要的，适当的本地化将向潜在客户证明，公司理解并尊重他们的语言和文化（Bahri，Mahadi 2015：35）。最近发表的唯一一篇从文本语言学的角度研究中国公司的本地化英文网站的英文文献是对中国能源公司网站所体现的品牌个性的研究（Shan，Wang 2017）。本书将采用并调整该研究提出的方法框架，选择五个行业——语言行业、电子商务、高等教育、政府和旅游目的地，探讨行业对组织网站的影响（选择标准和抽样策略见第三章）通过行业内和跨行业比较来回答行业影响这一研究问题，目前的假设是同一行业内的本地化和非本地化网站都存在某些行业特定的特征，但由于行业间界限始终处于模糊和变迁之中，这些行业相关特征会随着时间的推移变得不确定。

除了差异和偏差之外，本研究还将确定选定行业部门的本地化和非本地化英文网站所共有的文本语言相似性，从而为实证研究的知识储备添砖加瓦，为英文网页翻译和写作实践提供信息（进一步分析和讨论见后续章节）。为了对在回答上述三个研究问题过程中收集的所有线索进行更加深入的反思，下一个也是最后一个研究问题具有总结作用，探讨了在本地化网站中存在书面英语变体的可能性。

四、中文本地化的网站是否存在英文变体?

大量令人信服的讨论围绕着英语作为全球化、国际交流、科学和娱乐行业语言的压倒性影响展开（Zafiu 2010：16）。全球英语在全球化批判理论中得到广泛定义，表明英语作为一种加强跨国社会、经济、文化和政治关系的手段的传播和使用，应用场景如全球英语媒体、信息技术和国际专业语言（Russo 2012：9）。关于英语作为一种全球语言的研究已经从不同的角度证明，语际和语内翻译往往没有保留英语语言变体的特殊性和差异性，取而代之的是全球性代码所代表的同质化或标准化，然而，关注全球英语的跨地域和跨文化方面，可能有助于重新定位当前的研究思路。具体而言，关注不同种类的英语语言和其他语言如何流动传播，进而影响全球英语（Pennycook 2007）。此外，人们认为英语的重心将会转移，美英旧式的母语英语模式将让位于主要受亚洲影响的多中心英语模式（Pennycook 2007：110）。

与其他非英语国家一样，中国组织的英文网站很难确定目标读者（参见 Limon 对斯洛文尼亚网站的分析；2008：3）。不太可能只针对以英语为母语的用户（可能只代表访问网站的一小部分人）；目标受众可能是全然不懂中文的网络用户，他们中有许多人很可能会定期用英语与中国组织开展商务交流。一般来说，当代英语应被视为一种跨文化交流的媒介，主要供非母语者之间交流使用，有时是非母语者和母语人士之间，偶尔是母语人士之间。

有人认为，与中国有关的英语目前所处的发展阶段比那些外圈国家（如印度和新加坡）早得多（见 Kachru 提出的三个英语圈；1992）。而且这种英语不是通过中国英语使用者之间的交流而发展起来的，因此它不太可能被视为传统意义上的一个单独的英语种类（Jenkins 2015：161）。在此提出的初步假设是，本研究涉及的网站文本能够体现某些特征，使本地化网站中使用的英语有别于非本地化网站。

本节构建四个研究问题并做出匹配假设之后，接下来的第二节按照与第一节中提出的四个研究问题完全相同的顺序，阐明当前研究的意义。

第二节　运用语料库方法研究组织英文网站的意义

文本语言的比较分析是本书研究本地化英语文本的基础，最终目的在于通过实证研究证实，随着英语的广泛使用和改编，非母语使用者至少应该和母语使用者一样，享有如下英语语言使用权：

> ……［T］进行创新，每一个不同于某种母语国家标准英语的差异不会自动标记为“错误”。这就是语言国际化的意义——它传播各地并成为一种全球通用语，造福所有人，而不是为了促进与母语使用者的交流而传播（Jenkins 2015：53）。
>
> 创新的主要问题是需要确定观察到的语言使用特征何时确实是创新，何时仅仅是错误。创新被视为可接受的变体，而错误只是谬误或未受过教育的不当使用。如果创新被视为错误，那么一种非母语国家使用的语言种类将永远不会得到认可（Bamgbose 1998：22）。

此外，不能仅仅因为某个语言特征与美英等核心圈使用者使用的方式不同，就简单地视之为错误，它可能是一个创造力偶发和适应新环境的例子，甚至反映了语言接触和正在发生的变化（Jenkins 2015：41）。因此得出的结论是，在全球范围内，所谓英语能力欠缺的现象“可能是基于身份、创造力以及语言和文化接触的重要社会语言学现实的差异问题”（Bolton，Kachru 2006：11）。有鉴于此，本书分析了中文源语言的本地化英语的语言特征，以探索非母语使用者产生某种英语变体的可能，这种英语变体的地位并不一定低于母语英语。

具体而言，第二节的每个小节都与第一节的小节一一对应，进一步阐明了本书探索这四个息息相关的研究问题的重要性。

一、为本地化实践和评估提供语言和文化方面的参考

之前关于网站本地化的大多数学术研究越来越多地关注本地化非语言方面的问题，意图将本地化与传统意义上处理“单模态”文本的翻译区分开来。因此，语言和文本通常被视为“浅表层的文化差异”（Purwaningsih 2015：3）。由于“文化”一词涵盖的范围通常不仅限于将文本转换为目标语言的语言问题（Bahri，Mahadi 2015：34），而翻译学界非常熟悉语言文本问题，因此本地化涉及语言和文本的问题往往会被边缘化。为了强调本地化将新的视角引入翻译，本地化被视为网络信息的“文化化”（O'Hagan，Ashworth 2002：66-78）。商业信息如产品或品牌名称的翻译，需要商业领域的专业知识，包括国际市场研究和多元文化广告宣传（Bahri，Mahadi 2015：36）。这些商业领域通常会就非常多样化的问题而不是“简单的翻译问题”提供建议（O'Hagan，Ashworth 2002：73）。

为了抵消语言和文本逐渐被技术和流程掩盖的研究趋势，有学者（Torres del Rey，Rodríguez Vázquez 2017：3）批评了本地化研究中普遍存在的语言和文本问题边缘化，具体观点如下：

> 来自非翻译导向领域的企业界（或公众舆论）往往从语言学的角度理解本地化从业者的工作，认为本地化就是将一种语言的文本字符串替换为另一种语言的问题，一个找到正确等价物的“简单”问题。这样的观点没有考虑到现实传播和语言服务于特定目的的基本原则：（一）具有至关重要的意义是环境——地点、时间、参与者、具体状况和围绕语言的生产和接受或使用的参与者共享知识，即情景语境；伴随我们想要交流的语言的文本和符号，它们共同构建意义，即协同文本；（二）在人们面对和处理每种文本体裁的方式中期望和常规所发挥的关键作用，一般而言，没有过多的认知负担，没有外部互补资源的帮助，在每一种交流和互动的方法和媒介中，参与者的期望和常规都会产生很大的影响。不同语言和文化的这两个关键方面——环境和常规——可能存在很大差异，这给跨语言文化传播构成了巨大挑战。

在大多数情况下，缺乏适当的语言和文化输入会影响网站本地化项目的效果（Bahri，Mahadi 2015：35）。因此，对任何类型的本地化和网站本地化的从业者、评估者和培训师而言，文本规约应该是关注重点。按照谢勒尔（2006）的说法，即便对网络上的数字内容进行本地化的技术问题如今原则上已经得到解决，但如何使目标文化接受这些内容的问题尚未得到解答。本书的第一个研究问题对最常规的网站文本——导航文本进行了规约分析，可以看作是深化对组织网站本地化的理解的起点。

二、解码本地化网站语言，丰富互联网应用语言学研究

互联网是一个依赖于语言（Crystal 2011：92）的领域，无论是书面语还是口头语，即使是在网站仅包含图像的情况下，语言也作为元数据的一部分，存在于页面的基本内容规范中。互联网的语言特征或方面（facet）分为技术方面和社会方面。“方面”这一术语出自知识管理领域，技术方面和社会方面的定义（Herring 2007）如下：

技术方面表征媒介，由相关的计算机硬软件以及管理各种输出的协议的特性决定。社会方面则表征媒介使用者的数量、关系和行为，他们交流的内容和目的，以及他们使用的语言。

作为一种表征网站的社会方面，此类网络组织传播的参与者所认可的语言约定或语言规约①是本书的研究重点。笔者期望目前对本地化和非本地化英文组织网站的文本语言学研究能够丰富互联网语言学应用方向的发展。互联网语言学这一新兴学科领域的主要倡导者克里斯托尔（Crystal 2011：2）将其定义为对电子媒体中所有语言表现形式的科学研究。克里斯托尔提议（Crystal 2011：3），互联网应用语言学旨在为不同的互联网用户在搜索、电子广告和网络安全方面遇到的语言管理问题提供解决方案。本研究遵循克里斯托尔（Crystal 2011：3）支持的研究方法，力求在描述网络语言形式属性与解释可能的交际目的和效果之间取得平衡。

克里斯托尔（Crystal 2001）认为，通过互联网进行的全球交流的重点已经慢慢从技术转移到人和交际目的。随着人们越来越多地从社会角度看待互联网，

① 该术语实际应该是指“语言规范”（Herring 2007）。然而，从翻译研究的角度看（Nord 1991a），规范具有约束力，违反规范通常会引起相关社区的某种反对。与规范不同，规约没有约束力，只体现偏好。为了与描述性翻译研究保持一致，目前的探索性研究使用了“语言规约”一词。

语言作为一种社会现象开始占据中心舞台。在这种背景下，本书采用语言学视角研究英文网站，希望推动对网站这一应用最广泛的互联网输出类型的实证探索（互联网输出被定义为形成互联网话语的一种实体，如网站、电子邮件和博客；参见 Crystal 2011：10）。本书的第二个研究课题对选定的网站文本进行了规约，调查分析了网页上常规性可能不及导航文本的内容文本，以便更好地把握本地化和非本地化英语网站中的文本规约情况。

三、解决商业、经济和社会问题：语言规划和管理

如果稍微改写一下克里斯托尔（2011：1）对语言学家工作的定义，我们可以说互联网语言学家的工作是在互联网上寻找、描述和分析语言的表现形式。与任何应用语言学家类似，互联网应用语言学家的一部分任务是识别、分类和分享互联网社区中的语言实践，希望观察到的特定现象数量足够多，可以发展为常规实例，进而体现出监管机构或组织对于网络媒介传播的必要性。可以根据与专业语言学家和翻译的沟通和咨询协议来改进本地化实践，以避免忽视基本的沟通原则，例如，遵守使用中的语言规则（Gâţă，Praisler 2015：150）。总体而言，在当今国际公司在地方层面开展商业活动的背景下，基于理论和实践的语言规划和管理都是有必要的（Neustupný，Nekvapil 2003；Nekvapil，Herman 2009）。

在所有的互联网用户中，组织应该是对网站语言规划和管理最感兴趣的，因为它们希望自己的网站可以有效地接触到包括利益相关者和/或潜在客户在内的公众，这符合组织最大的商业、经济或社会利益。大多数已发表的关于组织网站的研究都集中在以吸引商业兴趣为发展目标的商业组织。在当前的全球化时代，许多公司正在将业务扩展到新市场，其中大多数公司都有自己的网站，用于宣传和销售产品和服务。这意味着他们需要对网站进行本地化以吸引全球受众（Sierro Fernández 2016：84）。相关研究的文献综述（Bahri 2015：34）强调，本地化的网络内容提高了可用性、访问性和网站交互性，从而带来更多的网络流量和在线商业活动。

在商业实践中，组织网站往往先推出一个语言版本，最常见的是英语，然后进一步本地化为其他语言版本，“同时出货”（simshipping）是很少见的。同时出货被定义为同时发布产品的所有语言版本的企业活动（Ressin，Abdelnour-Nocera，Smith 2011：320）。这可能反映了在评估当前本地化工作和建议改进领域方面缺乏指导（Chao，Singh，Chen 2012）。除了首先推出哪种（或哪些）语言版本外，本地化行业还需要考虑本地化网站是否很好地达成了接触目标群体

的目的，从而对投资回报率（ROI）做出适当的衡量。因此，本书将对本地化网站的真实状况进行分析，为针对英语市场的网站本地化提供参考。

中国企业深知在线企业传播的重要性，已投入大量资源建设英文网站。如果这些网站只是简单地从中文翻译而来，而无法传达品牌的适当身份和个性，可能浪费英文网站方面的支出，甚至适得其反（Shan, Wang 2017：1178）。强劲而有利的品牌个性有助于建立积极的品牌联想，强化品牌认同，从而维持公司独特的竞争优势，提升客户满意度和忠诚度，影响他们的购买决策，进而提高公司的营业额、利润、市值和利益相关者价值。本研究通过比较选定的中国组织的本地化英文网站与美国同类组织的非本地化英文网站，提出最佳管理实践建议，以有效管理英文网站文本中体现的品牌个性维度，形成国际舞台上独特的组织身份。

本研究涉及的一个关于组织网站的重要主题是行业影响力。之前的一项比较中美电子和汽车公司网站的文化维度的研究（Singh, Zhao, Hu 2005：141）显示，主要行业效应似乎并不显著，但研究人员还建议，未来的研究将扩展到其他行业领域，应该会揭示出在文化价值描述方面的行业差异。遵循这一思路，当前的研究重点关注五个行业——语言服务、电子商务、高等教育、政府和旅游，以期更广泛地了解行业因素对本地化英语网站文本表达的影响（行业选择标准见第三章）。

四、教学启示

本地化和非本地化英语网站的研究结果（详见第四章）还可以助力本地化教学。将本地化定义为面向翻译和技术密集型的学科（Torres del Rey, Rodríguez 2017）意味着虽然翻译不一定涉及数字化资料，但本地化总是以数字方式进行，因此需要从业者具备更高的数字素养（Schäler 2008）。

在数字世界中，面对众包、同人翻译以及与大数据相关的自动翻译生成等民主化翻译活动的新兴趋势的挑战，我们比以往任何时候都更需要专业人员或专家来管理、处理和执行对大量数据的质量控制，并执行涉及跨语言和文化交流的转换过程（Pym 2000）。本地化从业者需要对企业网站进行文化和语言方面的本地化（Shan, Wang 2017：1170），并成为目标文本所处的行业和文化的专家（Bahri, Mahadi 2015：35），达成这两方面的目标都需要指导。因此，对选定网站文本进行文本和行业分析，可以为本地化培训提供真实场景的参考。

除了为本地化培训师和学员提供实证支持外，目前的研究还可以将本地化培训融入现实生活中。本地化实践对所有网站文本块往往“一视同仁”，因为电子工具根本的设计理念是将文本与环境完全分开，这使得翻译人员对总体交流动态一无所知（Pym 2010：6）。例如，在一款使用广泛的计算机辅助翻译（CAT）工具的编辑器窗口中，提取的原始文本及其译文以成对句子的形式一一对齐，以便翻译人员进行逐句处理。在大多数情况下，译者需要根据去除了语境的原文（左栏）生成译文（右栏）。由于版权问题或时间限制，译者一般无法获得原始网页作为参考。

一般来说，网站很少被视为翻译对象。翻译人员很少参与整个过程，只翻译去语境的文本材料。涉及文化背景知识的网页设计决策通常由广告公司完成（Nauert 2007：3）。

从这个意义上说，当前对本地化网站的描述性规约分析可以产生情境化的教学材料，帮助学生为去情境化的专业环境做好准备。皮姆（2003）建议，翻译培训应该与上下文相关，以示例为导向，需要帮助学生在真实的翻译情境中创建和使用他们自己的动态策略，这些情境应包含现实生活中语言调解任务的复杂性（Kiraly 2000）。因此，当前研究呈现的描述性文本语言分析所提供的实证证据对于本地化和翻译从业者更好地理解基于网络的文本规约至关重要。本书第六章将结合本研究的发现和结论，介绍为小学、中学和大学英语课程思政教学设计的相关教案。

如果将注意力从本地化实践和行业转向教学实践，我们会发现，由于缺乏关于本地化和本地化能力的实证研究（Jiménez-Crespo，Tercedor 2011：999），在本地化能力及其与翻译能力的关系方面缺乏界定标准，这意味着本地化培训往往集中于习得工具能力（PACTE 2005）。正是因为关注这种工具能力的习得，本地化行业培训方法更侧重于培养与技术相关的能力，与双语、文本外和翻译知识能力完全分离（Jiménez-Crespo，Tercedor 2011：1000）。工具能力的例子包括关于 CAT 和本地化工具、文档格式和解决编码问题的知识（Jiménez-Crespo，Tercedor 2011：1018）。

在本地化培训中过分强调工具能力还有一个原因：人们认为本地化文本的功能方面与语言或语用问题相比，可以得到更客观的评估和识别（Dunne 2006）。为了抵消目前本地化教学的上述发展趋势，本文主要侧重于分析需要解决的文本、语用话语和交际问题，人们通常认为翻译学生在接受本地化培训之前就已习得这些层面的知识（Jiménez-Crespo，Tercedor 2011：1001）。这些层面的问题主要与 PACTE（2005）模型中的双语能力、文本外能力和翻译知识能力有关。

第三节　本章小结

本章首先确定当前研究需要关注的重点，从而明确本研究的范围。同时，本章解释了解决每个相应研究问题的意义，涉及文本语言学、文体学、在线组织传播的话语分析和社会语言学等领域。从第三章开始，本书将主要对中国组织的本地化英语网站和可比美国组织的非本地化英语网站进行比较文本语言分析。分析将具体处理四方面：导航文本，不同交际部分的网站正文，行业特定影响对组织网站文本表达的影响的可能性，以及中文源语言对可能存在的本地化英语变体产生的影响。下一章将在第一章和第二章所描绘的总体情况的基础上，解释所采取的技术路线和研究方法，描述当前研究的文本采样和数据收集过程以及多维度比较分析框架。讨论了数据的可信度、有效性和可靠性，还将对从不同行业收集的网站数据进行交叉比较，以确保有效性。

第三章

中美组织英文网站比较研究的方法和框架设计

本章在前一章将当前研究置于网络媒介组织语篇分析学科范畴的基础上，介绍当前研究采用的技术路线和方法论框架。霍曼（Hohmann 2014）指出，技术路线（approach）和方法论（methodology）之间的概念区别在于，技术路线可以被视为处理情况或问题的一种集中方式，而适当的方法论通过提供方法和工具有助于将技术路线付诸实践。

在总体技术路线方面，目前的研究遵循源自语料库描述性翻译研究的概念框架，将定性和定量分析相结合。欧罗汉（Olohan 2004：17）指出，基于语料库的翻译研究的目的不应该仅仅是基于定量数据的模糊概括，而是定量和定性分析相结合，探索与语篇、体裁和文字设计相关的语用因素。定性研究具有归纳性，即从研究结果中提炼出理论，定性分析常用于初步研究，以评定研究范围。相比之下，定量研究具有演绎性，即从理论得出的假设在实证研究中得到证明或反驳。根据雷新尔（Rasinger 2013）的定义，语言学领域的定量分析通常指的是对文本、模式和质量的分析，最常见于语篇分析研究，这符合当前研究的情况。

就方法论而言，本章的一大特色是介绍了一个用于对英文网站文本进行统计分析的多维比较框架的实现过程。这可以看作是辩证思维的应用：定性分析为数据分类提供类别，有助于理解大量数据，而定量分析产生数学上合理的结果，这通常是在初始框架内进行进一步解释的起点。然后，该框架通常需要经历几次循环过程才能不断完善，定性和定量研究交替进行，直至透彻理解所研究的数据。在此过程中，定性分析要求分析师深入研究数据，而不仅仅像定量分析那样对数据进行量化描述。本研究使用的分析框架将在未来的研究中不断完善和发展。

在实际实践中，为了在定性和定量思维之间获得平衡，目前的研究分为两个阶段：具有归纳性的第一阶段和具有演绎性的第二阶段。第一阶段分两步实施，主要是行业内和跨行业的中国和美国组织网站的配对比较，对比较结果进行定性分析，并辅以描述性统计测量。接下来第一步配对比较中提出的假设在第二步得到检验，第二步的分组比较有助于确定第一步的结果是否可以应用于更多的本地化和非本地化网站样本。第一阶段完成后，第二阶段扩大数据集规模，继续研究第一阶段的案例研究中确定的一些可量化的文本特征。第二阶段对扩展后的本地化和非本地化网站数据集执行推论统计检验。这种兼容并蓄的文本分析方法应该（Cristafulli 2014：37）：

> 协调定量和定性的研究类型。基于语料库的定量研究是描述性经验主义技术路线的典型特征，会产生翻译行为的趋势或规律（无论是历史决定的还是普遍的）。另一方面，定性分析基于对文本证据的批判性解释方法，试图将译者的干预与同时代的历史背景联系起来，旨在揭示译者个人的政治意识形态观（笔者翻译）。

图 3-1 展示了第一阶段和第二阶段之间的逻辑关系。第一阶段首先对同一行业的中美领先组织进行配对比较，然后将第一步的配对比较结果与第二步的分组比较结果进行交叉验证，第二步分组比较的各组包含来自同一个行业部门的多个组织网站（有关所需样本量的计算，请参见第四章第三节）。第二阶段仅选择中美组织网站具有可比版块的行业板块进行统计分析。网站版块是引导访问者浏览网站的网站组成要件，例如，“关于我们”和“联系我们”（Bell 2012）。一个合理的假设是，并非所有选定的组织网站都一定有可比较的版块，因此可以预期，第二阶段涉及的网站版块和行业部门数量均少于第一阶段。

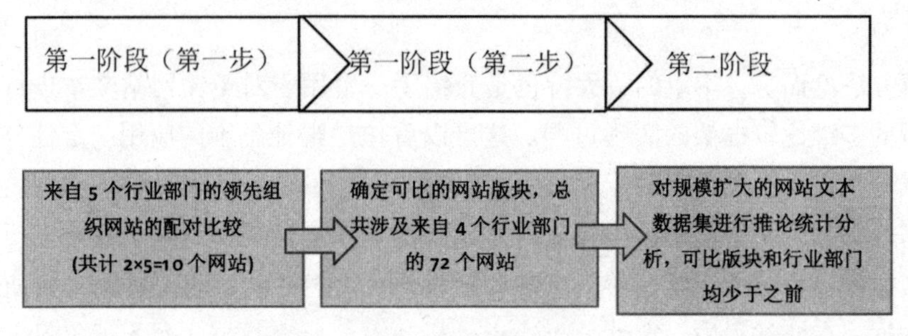

图 3-1　阶段示意图

本章的总体结构如下：第一节介绍了用于提取和处理网站文本并开展统计检验的软件工具，以及相应的描述和推论统计分析方法。接下来，第二节解释了相关统计分析涉及的网站文本的选择、抽样和预处理。然后，第三节介绍了针对本研究关注的文本特征的总体分析框架。最后，第四节对第三章进行了总结。

第一节　技术路线和软件工具

当前研究遵循的数据处理、管理和分析的总体流程如图 3-2 所示。

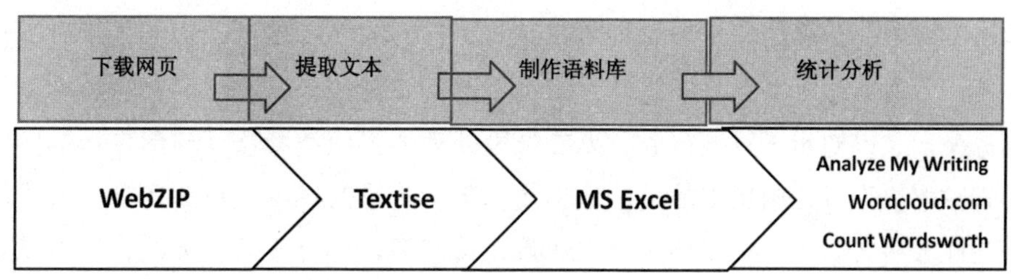

图 3-2　研究流程图

首先，研究人员使用 WebZIP 7.0 从选定的网站下载指定层级的网页。该工具可以指定网站文本的提取深度，基本无须人工干预检查提取结果的有效性。

接下来，选择在线工具 Textise 提取不同的网站版块的文本，然后完成词汇分析，对包括词频（Bowker 2002：75）在内的结果进行比较。为了从网站版块中提取符合研究条件的文本，所有提取的文本都经过人工检查，删除快捷链接和不需要的图像标题，以确保仅提取相关的版块文本。

然后，使用 Microsoft Office Excel 2016 管理和维护文本段。由于当前的研究对提取自同一网站版块的本地化和非本地化英文文本进行比较，据此制作的语料库需要区分导航文本和内容文本，区分不同的组织类型，并对从不同网站版块提取的文本进行分组。所有这些元数据信息都记录在 MS Excel 电子表格的不同列中。

数据分析的最后一项任务是进行统计分析。研究人员选择了在线工具 Analyze My Writing 在第一阶段进行描述统计分析，计算本研究涉及的两个词汇特征——高频实词和词汇密度。作为 Analyze My Writing 的补充，在线词云生成器 wordclouds. com 用于生成给定文本中词频的图形化呈现。在词云中，一个词的显示大小与其在文本中出现的频率成正比。至于句子层面的文本特征的测量，研究人员使用在线工具 Count Wordsworth 计算了本研究涉及的两个句子特征——平均句长及第一和第二人称句子所占的百分比。本研究使用 IBM SPSS 24 对具有可比性的组进行推论统计分析。

适用于第二阶段的推论统计分析的类型是通过运行在线向导工具 Statistical

Decision Tree（统计决策树）来确定的。该工具根据独立变量（预测变量）和因变量（结果变量）的基本概况，输出推荐的统计检验类型。换言之，只要指定自变量和因变量的数量，该工具就可以提示适用的统计检验类型。

目前的研究涉及两个预测变量，本地化概况（具有两个级别——本地化和非本地化）和组织类型。第二阶段的分析排除了电子商务网站，因为中国领先的电子商务公司现阶段主要针对本土市场，还没有英文网站。因此，本研究仅在第一阶段对电子商务公司这种组织类型进行了讨论，比较了两家领先的电子商务公司，以初步了解该行业。第二阶段处理的组织类型这一预测变量的实际级别数取决于可比版块中的可用数据集。第二阶段的样本量只能在第一阶段的描述性分析之后才能最终确定（关于确定第二阶段的样本量的方法，请参见第四章第三节）。接下来，结果变量个数的输入参数设置为 3，这意味着研究人员计划选择三个具有连续变量性质的文本语言特征作为结果变量，用于在第二阶段进行推论统计分析。图 3-3 显示了输入决策树的运行结果摘要页面，输入参数为 2 个分类预测变量和 3 个连续结果变量。可以看出，推论统计检验方法中的双向 MANOVA 适用于当前研究。

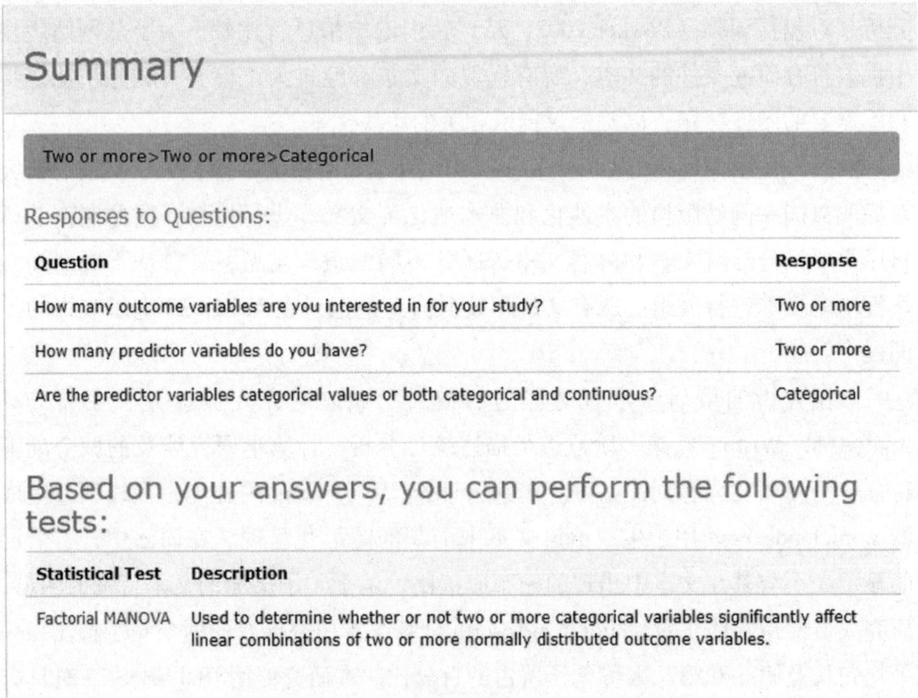

Summary

Two or more>Two or more>Categorical

Responses to Questions:

Question	Response
How many outcome variables are you interested in for your study?	Two or more
How many predictor variables do you have?	Two or more
Are the predictor variables categorical values or both categorical and continuous?	Categorical

Based on your answers, you can perform the following tests:

Statistical Test	Description
Factorial MANOVA	Used to determine whether or not two or more categorical variables significantly affect linear combinations of two or more normally distributed outcome variables.

图 3-3　统计决策树的运行结果摘要页面

根据 Field（2013）的定义，MANOVA 可以检验多个结果变量的组间差异以及预测变量和结果变量之间的相关性。由于本研究的主题是不同行业和国家网站的多个文本特征的比较，所以 MANOVA 分析结果可以解答与本地化和非本地化的网站文本比较有关的研究问题。

基于第一阶段的分组比较结果，第二阶段扩大数据集规模，进行了比较分析，对三个文本特征进行了推论统计分析。第三节还将进一步讨论这三个文本特征。

第二节 样本选择和数据验证

本研究采用目的性抽样策略，从代表五个行业部门的领先组织中收集了指定版块的网站文本。根据 2017 年北美行业分类系统（NAICS；行政管理和预算执行总裁办公室 2017）的规定，选定的组织类型对应五个行业部门：语言服务提供商或 LSP、电子商务公司（零售贸易）、大学（教育服务）、市政府（公共管理）和旅游目的地（休闲和娱乐服务）。第一种组织类型与翻译研究的职业研究分支领域的关联性最大，而其余四种是信息系统（IS）和市场营销文献中最常见的研究主题（Díaz，Rusu，Collazos 2017；Antonucci et al . 2017；Feeney，Brown 2017；Mele，Cantoni 2018）。此外，后四个行业部门和语言行业一样具有服务导向特性，这些相对成熟的行业构成了语言行业的横向比较基准。

为了收集具有归纳性的第一阶段第一步的数据，研究人员从每种组织类型中选出了一对可比较的中国和美国领先组织，研究其英语网站。基于以下标准，从五个组织类型中选择具有代表性的示例进行配对比较：对包括 LSP 和电子商务在内的商业公司进行了评估，以了解其在本国的总收入、市场份额和商业影响力；根据国家排名选出顶尖大学；选择中美两国首都开展旅游目的地城市和市政府的网站研究，以确保可比性。如此选出的组织都在各自的行业中发挥了示范作用，它们的网站可以被视为行业标准。第一阶段第一步选出的网站如表 3-1 所示。

表 3-1 第一阶段第一步选定的本地化和非本地化英文网站

组织类型	本地化	非本地化	备注
LSP	文思海辉（https：//en. pactera. com/）	创博翻译（http：//www. transperfect. com/）	中美领先的 LSP 私营企业（Common Sense Advisory 2017）
电子商务公司	阿里巴巴（http：//www. aliexpr ess. com/）	亚马逊（https：//www. amaz on. com/）	2021 年福布斯全球企业排行榜列出的中美顶尖电商网站（Forbes，2022）
大学	清华大学（http：//www. tsingh ua. edu. cn/publish/n ewthuen/）	加州大学伯克利分校（http：//berke-ley. edu/index. html）	中美领先的公立大学，均以工科和商学院闻名。美国大学排名采用 U. S. News（2018）提供的数据；中国大学排名采用 topuniversities. com（2018b）提供的数据
政府	中国北京市政府（http：//www. ebeijing. gov. cn/Gov-ernment/）	美国华盛顿市政府（https：//dc. gov/）	北京和华盛顿分别是中国和美国的首都
旅游目的地	“北京旅游”——北京市旅游发展局（http：//english. visit beijing. com. cn/）	Washington. org— 华盛顿市的官方旅游网站（washington. org）	北京和华盛顿分别是中国和美国的首都

本研究涉及的网站文本是从选定的网站中提取的导航文本和内容文本。两个阶段均指定了两个层级的网页提取深度，即从每个选定网站的首页和所有一级网页（比首页低一级）中提取需要研究的文本。第一阶段的后续比较都遵循第三章第一节介绍的分析框架，进而提出将在第二阶段检验的假设。

第一阶段第二步的网站选择标准见表 3-2（选出的网站详细列表见附录

A)。在 Common Sense Advisory 排行榜中，全球领先的中国 LSP 中只有 9 家拥有英文网站，因此将每组的样本数调整为 9 个以形成同等规模的可比组。因此，总共选择了 72 个（9×4×2）英文网站（或样本）开展第一阶段的分组比较。

表 3-2　第一阶段第二步的本地化和非本地化英文网站的选择标准

组织类型	本地化	非本地化	选择标准
LSP	全球领先的中国 LSP	全球领先的美国 LSP	依据 2017 年 LSP 的全球和亚洲排名（Common Sense Advisory 2017a；Common Sense Advisory 2017b）
大学	中国领先工科大学	美国领先工科大学	依据 2018 年 QS 世界大学排行榜（QS Top Universities 2018a）
政府	中国主要城市	美国主要城市	依据 2018 年城市人口统计数据（World Population Review 2018a 2018b）
旅游目的地	中国主要旅游城市	美国主要旅游城市	依据 Chinahighlights（2017）和 INSIDER（Schmalbruch 2017）发布的 2017 年接待游客人数最多城市排行

选定网站后，需要提取文本，再对文本进行分组比较。基于前人研究中介绍的网站原型超结构（Jiménez-Crespo 2009），对从每个网站提取的文本进行分组，如图 3-4 所示。希门尼斯-克雷斯波的研究仅关注企业网站，因此本研究对所有选定网站的分析，均参考相关版块和子版块的分析，无论企业网站与否，都进行了必要的修改和调整。当前研究采用的比较分析方法仅适用于从本地化和非本地化英文网站的等效版块中提取的文本数据集。

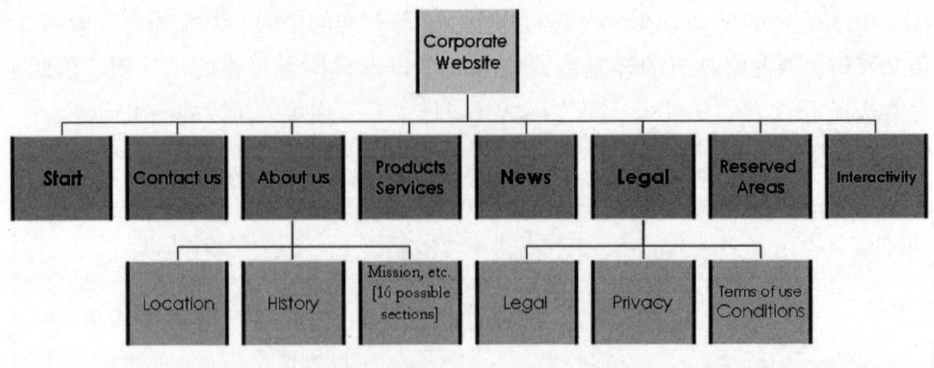

图 3-4 企业网站原型超结构（Jiménez-Crespo 2009）

第三节 多维度比较分析的框架设计

为确保一一对应的比较，本研究比较的对象确定为本地化网站上的导航文本和内容文本与其非本地化同业网站同一版块内的对应文本（导航文本和内容文本这两种文本类型的定义参见第二章第一节）。本节确定了本研究涉及的网站比较项目，研究了比较项的相对发生频率，并讨论了一些文本特征背后的原因或作用。此外，网站文本比较还探讨了按语境或语用对文本现象进行归类分组的可能性。

本研究采用基于频率统计的研究方法，在对比语言学研究中可以获得理论支持。对比语言学为评估翻译文本的典型特征（Zanettin 2012：25）受到源语言影响的程度提供了基本标准。目前的比较分析除了研究中文源语言对本地化组织网站文本的影响外，还评估了组织类型对本地化和非本地化组织网站文本的影响。

国外学术文献很少涉及对我国组织本地化英文网站的文本分析。因此，当前研究涉及的大部分文本特征都来自 2006 年以来国内发表的相关学术文章，2016 年发表了第一篇关于中英网站翻译的研究。回顾相关学术文章发现，中文源语言的组织本地化英文网站文本的最新实证研究大多是对翻译错误和不足进行了示例分析，或试图制定网站文本的通用翻译指南或策略。与以往研究不同，本研究在考虑本地化过程对网站场景下的组织话语产品的影响的基础上，开展了描述性对比分析。接下来的四个小节与本研究关注的四个问题一一对应。前两小节定义了前两个研究问题反映的特定文本语言特征，并引用相关研究来支持文本语言特征的选择。在缩小所研究的文本语言特征的范围后，第二阶段为回答关于行业和语言特定影响的第三个研究问题（第三章第三节）提供了统计证据。

比较分析均在等效的网站版块之间进行。图 3-4 列出了公司网站的一些版块（第二行）和子版块（第三行），以提供图示说明。

一、术语和词汇

首先，本研究分析了导航术语和短语的标准化程度（Jiménez Crespo 2009），特别是版块标题，例如，Home（主页）、About Us（关于我们）和 Contact Us（联系我们）。此外，还研究了高频内容词（李良博、李占喜 2015）、计算文本中实词或内容词所占百分比（Baker 1996）或词汇密度（汤君丽 2014），是词汇层面分析的第三项也是最后一项内容。实词或内容词包括名词、形容词、大多数动词和大多数副词。构成文本其余部分的语法词或功能词包括代词、介词、连词、助动词、一些副词、限定词和感叹词。有文献（Laviosa 2002：55）对于过去关于词汇密度的实证研究结果持保留态度，因为那些研究的翻译文本对象的源语言基本上都属于罗曼语系。因此，本研究分析源语言为中文的本地化网络文本，以期为词汇密度的实证研究提供新的启示。

综上所述，第一阶段的词汇分析涵盖了三个特征：（1）导航文本表达的标准化程度，（2）高频内容词以及（3）词汇密度。

二、句法、语法和语篇

词汇分析之后，在句子层面对网站文本进行分析。人们一般的直觉感受是，与传统印刷文本相比，网站文本的句子较简单，语法结构较简单，且段落较短。为了对网站文本进行实证分析，第一阶段通过具体分析，研究了本地化和非本地化组织网站的句法模式：（1）平均句长（杨进 2013；周红 2015；马会峰 2014；李洁 2014；蒋文莎 2013；李良博，李占喜 2015；张佩 2013；何森梅 2008）和（2）第一和第二人称句子的相对频率（杨进 2013；周红 2015；李良博，李占喜 2015；卢小军 2012；何森梅 2008；彭金玲 2013；蒋文莎 2013；杨晓侠 2016；王文 2013）①。

① 第一和第二人称句子是指使用 I、we、you、me、us、my、mine、your、yours、our 和 ours 的句子，第三人称句子是指使用第三人称代词 he、she、it、they、his、her、its、hers 和 theirs 的句子。

第一阶段本地化和非本地化网站基于上述文本特征的比较可以被视为当前网络生态系统的局部快照，为本地化培训师、学员和从业者提供来自真实场景的参考信息。不同网站版块的多层面研究结果也可以给面向用户的研究提供反馈信息，以提升网站的可用性。未来的用户实验可以建立在本次研究分析结果的基础上，针对本地化和非本地化英语网站的特定版块，收集关于用户体验的数据。

在第一阶段完成小规模文本分析之后，第二阶段扩大文本数据集规模，进行了推论统计分析，涉及更多的组织网站。第二阶段的目的是对第一阶段的配对和分组比较中得出的假设进行定量检验。综上所述，两个阶段研究的特征标有星号（“ * ”），如表 3-3 所示。其中一个特征——高频内容词——仅在第一阶段的第二步进行了研究，因为对频率统计而言，可供配对比较的样本量过小。

表 3-3　第一阶段和第二阶段涉及的比较项

比较项			第一阶段：定性分析和描述统计分析		第二阶段：推论统计分析
			第一步：配对比较	第二步：配对比较	
词汇分析	L1	导航文本的标准化程度	*	*	
	L2	高频内容词	注：样本量过小，不适合统计频率	*	
	L3	词汇密度	*	*	*
句子分析	S1	平均句长	*	*	*
	S2	第一和第二人称句子的相对频率	*	*	*

三、特定行业和特定语言的影响

在第一阶段进行的定性分析和描述统计分析有助于对具有代表性的组织网站进行行业内和跨行业的比较。此外，第二阶段将组织类型视为具有分类属性的预测变量，可以提供统计证据，用于评估特定行业对所研究的三个词汇和句子特征的影响。

MANOVA 统计检验可以解答以下问题：多个结果变量的组合，特别是在本研究第二阶段涉及的三个文本语言变量在不同预测变量（本地化概况和组织类型）之间是否存在显著差异。MANOVA 还可以从统计学上确定预测变量和结果变量之间是否存在相互作用。

第四节　本章小结

首先，本章讨论了将定性和定量分析相结合来实现基于文本比较的描述性研究的理论依据。在解释了指导研究的技术路径之后，研究人员简要解释了作为当前研究基础的双阶段数据分析的总体流程。第一节阐明了总体研究程序，并解释了完成数据处理各个步骤使用的不同软件工具。第二节介绍了数据选择和预处理的过程，阐明了执行统计检验的抽样标准和注意事项。第三节对完成预处理的文本数据进行统计分析，引入了本研究遵循的多维分析框架，并用数据分析的两个阶段涉及的词汇和句子特征对其进行了充实。

采用第三章设计的方法，下一章将从不同维度介绍和讨论相关网站版块的分析结果，不仅描述观察结果，还将对结果进行解释。当前研究所采用的描述性研究途径正如克里斯托尔（2006）所指出的那样，描述了在一种语言中发现的用法变化，并解释了出现某些变化的原因。

第四章

中美组织英文网站比较研究结果与分析

本章通过介绍和解释两个比较阶段产生的结果，将第三章聚焦的方法框架和文本分析工具付诸实践。第一节和第二节分别解释了第一阶段中网站配对和分组比较的所有分析结果。除了跨行业比较外，这两节以下的小节与本研究涉及的行业一一对应。第三节介绍了在第二阶段执行 MANOVA 统计分析的过程，对统计数据进行了分析，对研究发现进行了概括，从而探索经过英文本地化中国组织网站文本是否存在英文变体。最后，第四节对本章进行了总结。

本章涉及的所有网站文本的检索时间均为 2018 年 1 月 27 日。目前的研究主要关注可供比较和可用的网站版块，这些版块通常更新频率较低，特别是 About Us（企业简介）版块。如此选择可以尽量减少时间敏感性对网站实证研究的影响。

确定可供比较的网站版块是在各个行业内部进行配对或分组比较的第一步。这也是比较本地化和非本地化网站文本的前提条件，即比较的同行业不同组织机构网站文本应该来自同一个网站版块。在确定了本地化和非本地化网站共有的版块后，研究人员将更新频率高的版块与更新频率低的版块区分开来。出于时间敏感性的考虑，本研究仅关注后者。每次开始行业内和跨行业比较时，都会重复这个版块识别过程。

第一节　配对比较

本节介绍并讨论了代表五个行业的 10 个组织网站的比较结果，每个行业比较一个本地化网站和一个非本地化网站。配对比较所涉及的 10 个网站的列表见表 3-1。

一、语言服务提供商（LSP）：文思海辉与 TransPerfect 比较

两家语言服务提供商网站的站点地图显示的共有版块如下：（1）“公司简介”，内容包括企业概况、发展历史和使命宣言；（2）“服务内容”，列出企业提

供的服务类型；(3)“服务的行业”，列举企业所服务的行业；(4)“技术实力”，展示企业的技术专长；(5)“特色客户解决方案”，重点介绍成功案例和案例分析；(6)“联系我们”，展示企业的直接联系方式；(7)“加入我们”，发布职位空缺；(8)“新闻与活动”，发布过去、现在和未来的企业新闻和活动；(9)“隐私政策”，解释企业如何收集、使用、披露和管理客户数据；(10)“行业博客和资源”，为利益相关者提供教育资源；(11)“查找当地办事处”，显示企业当地办事处的联系信息；以及(12)“站点地图”，显示该网站所有网页的目录结构。本研究对上述所有版块的导航文本进行了分析。此外，由于(1)、(3)、(4)、(6)、(7)和(9)包含可比较的内容文本更新频率较低，故选择这几个版块进行内容文本的比较。

表 4-1 为交叉表模板，列出了所选网站版块（L：本地化文思海辉网站；NL：非本地化 TransPerfect 网站）的所有文本特征，列出了两个语言服务提供商网站的所有比较项目。

表 4-1　语言服务提供商网站选定版块所有待分析的文本特征的交叉表模板

网站版块			公司简介		服务的行业		技术实力		联系我们		加入我们		隐私政策	
企业			L	NL	L	NL	L	NL	L	NL	L	NL	L	NL
词汇分析	L1	导航文本的标准化												
	L2	词汇密度												
句子分析	S1	平均句长												
	S2	第一和第二人称句的相对频率												

如表 4-1 所示，对于两个语言服务提供商网站中可配对比较的版块，共分析四个文本特征，包括两个词汇特征和两个句子特征。该模板还将用于本研究涉及的其他四个行业部门，以便于后续进行跨行业比较。不过，可比较的网站版块存在一些差异，因为不同行业的组织网站的可比版块不一定完全相同，这是可以理解的。

表 4-2 列出了在本地化和非本地化语言服务提供商网站（L：本地化文思海

辉网站；NL：非本地化 TransPerfect 网站）中实现相近导航目的的词汇。从表4-2 中可以得出与导航文本共性相关的三点发现。第一点发现是，链接到位于不同网页上的版块或同一网页上的位置的所有导航文本长度都不超过三个单词。导航文本较长的例外情形只出现在网页底部，通常是重复显示链接到页面顶部列出的重要版块的链接。其次，词汇表述相同的两个版块是“服务的行业”和“技术实力”，这表明两个 LSP 网站的这两个版块的导航文本标准化程度较高。第三个发现是两个网站主页都没有“home”（主页）字样的导航文本，不过在本地化文思海辉网站上，仍然可以在每个子页面顶部的面包屑导航①路径中找到作为文本链接的“主页”，可引导访客返回主页。无论如何，对语言服务提供商网站而言，“主页”图标或文本链接似乎是可有可无的，因为点击页面左上角的公司徽标通常会将访客引导回主页，但还需要更多的实证证据才能作出进一步结论。随后的行业内和跨行业比较还将再次探讨导航文本的这些特征。

表 4-2　文思海辉与 TransPerfect 网站各版块的词汇

网站版块	L	NL
企业简介	Company	Who We Are
服务内容	（分成了多个版块）	What We Do
服务的行业	Industries	
技术实力	Technology	
用户解决方案	Our Work	Client Solutions
联系我们	Contact Us/Work with Us/ Connect with Us	Get in Touch
加入我们	Careers，Culture	Join Our Team
新闻与活动	News，Press	Press Center
隐私政策	Privacy Policy	Privacy
行业博客与资源	Insights，Trends	Thought Leadership
当地办事处信息	Find Locations	Find Your Local Office
站点地图	Site Index	Sitemap

① 设计网站时，面包屑导航提供可点击的页面路径，引导用户确定在网站系统中的当前位置。

在导航文本的差异方面，第一和第二人称句子在非本地化 TransPerfect 网站的导航文本中出现的频率高于本地化文思海辉网站。这可以归因于源语言中文的影响；正式中文写作倾向于避免口语化风格，特别是针对特定组织的描述。其次，研究发现“联系我们”版块是一个有趣的测试区，可用于确定两个语言服务提供商网站所针对的目标受众。例如，本地化文思海辉网站为不同的受众设置了不同的“联系我们”链接，目标受众包括感兴趣的求职者、潜在客户和对行业更新感兴趣的访客。尽管这些单独的链接都指向同一个网页，显示用于填写联系方式的表格，但该方法显示了该网站希望满足不同利益相关者需要的意图。与此相比，非本地化 TransPerfect 网站的理念相似，但实现方式略有不同，它的主页为潜在客户提供了一个显眼的直接链接“Get in Touch（取得联系）”，并设有专门针对求职者［Join Our Team（加入我们的团队）］和其他感兴趣的访客［Connect with Us（与我们联系）］的单独子页面。

至于两个语言服务提供商网站在导航文本方面的差异，表 4-3 列出了语言服务提供商网站各自独有的版块（L：本地化文思海辉网站；NL：非本地化 TransPerfect 网站）。仔细观察这些网站版块可以发现，这两个网站体现了两家企业不同的商业战略重点。本地化文思海辉网站致力于为投资者和客户打造值得信赖的企业形象，在线发布公司及其供应商的商业道德准则，而非本地化 TransPerfect 网站更关注其技术优势和行业专业知识，其主页突出显示与技术相关的版块。这种差异可以通过两家语言服务提供商在网站上展示的不同的服务组合来解释。本地化文思海辉网站提供了多种技术解决方案，其中语言服务被称为“全球化解决方案”，即语言服务只是其旗下的一项业务。本地化文思海辉网站上的口号“more than a technology company（不仅仅是一家技术公司）”进一步说明了这一点。另一方面，非本地化 TransPerfect 网站的业务发展对语言服务的依赖程度更高，因此企业希望通过提升技术专长来吸引潜在客户和合作者。

表 4-3　两个语言服务提供商网站各自独有的版块

L	NL
商业道德准则（Code of Ethics） 订阅企业通信［Subscribe（Newsletters）］ 活动（Events）	The TransPerfect Advantage GlobalLink（一项系统集成的特色技术）

下文的所有行业内和跨行业的导航文本比较也将涉及上述主题：（1）导航

文本的字数，(2) 标准化程度最高的网站版块，(3) 主页“Home”字样导航文本的存在与否，(4) 第一、第二和第三人称视角的使用，(5) 导航文本指向的网站目标用户，(6) 组织机构独有的网站版块。

语言服务提供商配对比较分析的下一个研究主题是内容文本的词汇密度。表 4-4 列出了可用于内容文本比较的语言服务提供商网站版块的词汇密度（L：本地化文思海辉网站；NL：非本地化 Transperfect 网站）。一般而言，非本地化 TransPerfect 网站的词汇密度高于本地化文思海辉网站的词汇密度，但如果将此发现应用于所有本地化和非本地化网站，可能失于轻率，因为有些网站版块的网页层级多于其他版块。一个例子是“Technology”（技术实力）。作为非本地化 TransPerfect 网站上的第一级网页（比主页低一级），“技术实力”版块的文本是一些短语，导致词汇密度达到 100%。本地化文思海辉网站词汇密度高于非本地化 TransPerfect 网站的唯一版块是“Join Us”（加入我们），这在很大程度上与以下事实有关：非本地化 TransPerfect 网站的该版块包含多个短句，而本地化文思海辉网站的对应版块只有一个长句。这表明词汇密度在一定程度上与平均句长相关。后续比较还将再次考查词汇密度这一主题，探讨其作为网站内容文本的一个特征指标，如何体现词汇多样性和创造力。

表 4-4　语言服务提供商网站可用于内容文本比较的版块的词汇密度

网站版块	L（%）	NL（%）
公司简介	63.3	64.5
服务的行业	68.6	77.0
技术实力	69.1	100.0
联系我们	59.4	77.0
加入我们	76.0	64.0
隐私政策	51.4	59.1

关于句子层面的分析，表 4-5 列出了语言服务提供商网站可用于内容文本比较的版块的平均句长（L：本地化文思海辉网站；NL：非本地化 TransPerfect 网站）。非本地化 TransPerfect 网站的两个版块都标有“N/A”，这是因为大部分网站版块文本均采用单词名词或双词名词短语的形式，不适合计算句子长度。这表明非本地化网站可能享有更大的文本架构自由度，可以尝试更多种类的表达形式。在参与比较的大多数网站版块中，非本地化 TransPerfect 网站文本的句

子比本地化文思海辉网站长。对具体文本进行深入审读，发现了一种可能的解释：非本地化 TransPerfect 网站的所有版块均使用平行句子结构，以满足不同受众的需要，例如“If you are …，… If you are…”，故该版块句式相对较长。

表 4-5　语言服务提供商网站可用于内容文本比较的版块的平均句长

网站版块	L	NL
公司简介	18. 3	19. 0
服务的行业	24. 5	N/A
技术实力	15. 7	N/A
联系我们	12. 5	15. 7
加入我们	16. 0	15. 3
隐私政策	19. 8	23. 5

表 4-6 列出了用于内容文本比较的语言服务提供商网站版块中第一和第二人称句子的相对频率（L：本地化文思海辉网站；NL：非本地化 TransPerfect 网站）。与表 4-5 的分析类似，非本地化 TransPerfect 网站有的版块标有“N/A”，因为这些版块不适合开展句子层面的分析。一般而言，非本地化 TransPerfect 网站的第一和第二人称句子的相对频率高于本地化文思海辉网站，与之前预料的相同。并且，非本地化网站的大部分版块以第一和第二人称句子为主。这表明非本地化网站通常比本地化网站的口语化程度更高。唯一的例外是“Privacy Policy（隐私政策）”：非本地化 TransPerfect 网站在进行自我陈述时，并未用“We（我们）”代替公司名称。

表 4-6　语言服务提供商网站可用于内容文本比较的版块中第一和第二人称句子的相对频率

网站版块	L（%）	NL（%）
公司简介	57. 0	100. 0
服务的行业	45. 0	N/A
技术实力	79. 0	N/A
联系我们	66. 0	100. 0
加入我们	100. 0	100. 0
隐私政策	94. 0	68. 0

综上所述，研究人员在语言服务提供商网站的配对比较中研究了导航文本和内容文本的以下特征：（1）导航文本的字数；（2）标准化程度最高的网站版块；（3）“Home”（主页）存在与否；（4）导航文本中第一人称、第二人称和第三人称视角的使用；（5）导航文本提示的网站目标受众；（6）网站独有的版块；（7）内容文本的词汇密度；（8）内容文本的平均句长；（9）内容文本中第一和第二人称句子的相对频率。在随后其他行业的配对比较以及本章第二节的分组比较中，还将继续讨论这些特征。

二、电子商务：阿里巴巴旗下的“全球速卖通”（AliExpress）与亚马逊（Amazon）比较

本研究分析的两个电子商务网站相同的版块如下：（1）产品分类，列出在线销售的产品类型，以便客户快速找到感兴趣的商品；（2）自由参观，列出热门产品类别以引起潜在客户的兴趣；（3）特色商店，突出某些商店以促进全店销售；（4）交易，促进某些产品项目以实现快速销售；（5）推荐，根据客户的搜索、浏览历史推荐产品项目；（6）召集合作伙伴，邀请业务伙伴推广产品链接以换取商业奖励；（7）帮助，在线客服中心解答在线交易过程中的问题；（8）使用条款与条件，列出访问者使用网站服务必须遵守的规则；（9）隐私政策，解释网站如何使用的法律文件，使用、披露和管理用户数据。本研究分析了（1）至（9）所有版块的导航文本。此外，选择（1）、（8）和（9）三个版块用于内容文本的配对比较，因为这些版块包含的可供比较的内容文本的更新频率较低。

表4-7是一个交叉表模板，列出了所选网站版块（L：本地化全球速卖通网站；NL：非本地化亚马逊网站）的所有文本特征，概括了比较两个电子商务网站的所有项目。值得注意的是，只对“产品分类”版块的导航文本进行了定性分析，因为其内容文本由单词和短语组成，而不是完整的句子，所以不适合进行词汇密度计算或句子层面的分析。

表 4-7　列出所选电子商务网站版块待分析的所有文本特征的交叉表模板

网站版块			产品分类		使用条款与条件		隐私政策	
公司			L	NL	L	NL	L	NL
词汇分析	L1	导航文本的标准化程度						
	L3	词汇密度	N/A	N/A				
句子分析	S1	平均句长	N/A	N/A				
	S2	第一和第二人称句子的相对频率	N/A	N/A				

表 4-8 展示了本地化和非本地化电子商务网站（L：本地化全球化速卖通网站；NL：非本地化亚马逊网站）中导航文本的词汇项。首先，非本地化亚马逊网站的导航文本字数总体而言略多于本地化全球速卖通网站，这是因为非本地化的亚马逊网站的某些版块有四个和五个单词组成的词汇。此外，非本地化亚马逊网站使用第一人称和第二人称视角的情况更多，导致词汇较长，例如，“We Have Recommendations for You”（我们为您推荐好货）、“Get to Know Us”（了解我们）和“Let Us Help You”（让我们帮助你）。其次，标准化程度最高的网站版块是提供客户服务的“Help”（帮助）。再次，除了位于网页左上角的公司徽标暗示主页外，这两个网站都没有包含用于导航回主页的明确文本。复次，非本地化的亚马逊网站与本地化的全球速卖通网站相比，第一人称和第二人称视角的比重更大。最后，这两个网站的大部分内容都直接针对当前和潜在客户，只有一两个不太突出的版块针对潜在的业务合作伙伴，非本地化亚马逊网站上只有一个版块针对求职者。

表 4-8　全球速卖通和亚马逊网站不同版块标题的用词

网站版块	L	NL
产品分类	Categories	Departments
自由浏览	Inspiration	New and Interesting Finds
特色商店	Spotlight Stores	(…) Bestsellers
特别优惠	Flash Deals/ $5 Deals	Today's Deals

续表

网站版块	L	NL
推荐好物	More to Love	We Have Recommendations for You
招募合作伙伴	Partner Promotion	Get to Know Us
帮助	Help	Help（位于 Let Us Help You 之下）
使用条款与条件	Terms of Use	Conditions of Use
隐私政策	Privacy Policy	Privacy Notice

表 4-9 显示了单个网站独有的版块。总体而言，该表指出本地化和非本地化电子商务网站由于企业运营面向的文化和商业环境不同，实施了不同的推广策略。我们可以看到，本地化全球速卖通网站向网站访问者推介其手机端应用程序，以通过“移动”订购和支付来促进销售［“Save big on our app!”（使用我们的手机端应用程序，节省大笔费用!）］，强调享受优惠有时间期限（在“LIVE”这一网站版块上，卖家以直播演示的形式展示其产品，带有倒计时时钟，表明需要在优惠结束前下单的紧迫性）。本地化全球速卖通网站还对潜在买家担忧国际电子商务渠道可能销售假冒产品的问题予以积极回应［“How to Buy”（购买指南）、“Intellectual Property Protection”（知识产权保护）和“Law Enforcement Compliance Guide”（执法合规指南）］，并通过展示其自身的竞争优势［“Why us”（为什么选择我们）］来建立客户信任。相比之下，非本地化的亚马逊网站从文化流行趋势和文化活动中挖掘商业可能性［“Gift Cards”（礼品卡）和“Registry”（婚礼礼物）这两个版块针对那些有意为婚礼或迎婴聚会选购礼物的客户］，并努力加强与卖家的合作［“Sell”（销售）］。在本书成稿时，本地化的全球速卖通网站尚未向国际卖家开放其 B2C 网站，不过阿里巴巴的中文网站显示，企业正在开展更广泛的海外合作。①

① 全球速卖通服务平台. 全球速卖通免费会员协议［EB/OL］.［2023-07-21］.

表 4-9 配对比较的电子商务网站各自独有的版块

L	NL
Save big on our app! Brand Zone Why Us LIVE How toBuy (Buyer Protection) Intellectual Property Protection Law Enforcement Compliance Guide	Gift Cards Registry Sell

表 4-10 显示了可用于内容文本比较的电子商务网站版块的词汇密度（L：本地化全球速卖通网站；NL：非本地化亚马逊网站）。总体而言，非本地化亚马逊网站在“Terms and Conditions of Use”（使用条款与条件）和“Privacy Policy”（隐私政策）这两个可配对比较的版块中的词汇密度高于本地化速卖通网站。在研究目前关注的所有顶级和一级网页中，只有“使用条款与条件”和“隐私政策”两个版块包含可比较的文本，因为这两个电子商务网站都突出显示了首页和一级网页上的优惠商品和产品的缩略图。

表 4-10 内容文本可比较的电子商务网站版块的词汇密度

网站版块	L (%)	NL (%)
使用条款与条件	54.7	55.8
隐私政策	52.7	58.9

表 4-11 列出了配对可比的电子商务网站版块的平均句长（L：本地化全球速卖通网站；NL：非本地化亚马逊网站）。从表中可以看出，本地化的全球速卖通网站的平均句长高于非本地化的亚马逊网站，而研究涉及的其他版块的对比结果则与此相反。

表 4-11 内容文本可比较的电子商务网站版块的平均句长

网站版块	L	NL
使用条款与条件	20.3	21.1
隐私政策	21.0	17.7

表4-12显示了内容文本可比的电子商务网站版块中第一和第二人称句子的相对频率（L：本地化全球速卖通网站；NL：非本地化亚马逊网站）。可以看出，第一人称和第二人称在两个电子商务网站的这两个版块中均占据主导地位。

表4-12　内容文本可比较的电子商务网站版块中第一和第二人称句子的相对频率

网站版块	L	NL
使用条款与条件	85.0	87.0
隐私政策	94.0	92.0

三、大学：清华大学与加州大学伯克利分校网站比较

比较网站总体结构可以发现，两个大学网站的共有版块如下：（1）大学简介，简要概述大学，包括历史、重要人物和事实；（2）面向有意就读该校的准学生的招生、政策和申请表格；（3）教学，介绍学校和院系提供的学位和非学位课程；（4）研究，展示教职员工和研究实验室支持的研究项目的概况；（5）校园生活，介绍校园服务和欢迎学生参加的活动；（6）新闻，定期更新校园新闻以及关于本校的媒体报道；（7）加入我们，发布职位空缺；（8）联系我们，向公众公布校方的联系方式以及（9）募捐。本研究分析了所有版块的导航文本。此外，为开展内容文本的配对比较，选定的版块是（1）、（2）和（5），因为这些版块包含可比较的内容文本，且更新频率较低。

表4-13是一个交叉表模板，列出了所选网站版块（L：本地化清华大学网站；NL：非本地化加州大学伯克利分校网站）的所有文本特征，列出了本研究比较的两个大学网站所有项目。

表4-13　列出所选大学网站版块待比较的所有文本特征的交叉表模板

<table>
<tr><td colspan="3">网站版块</td><td colspan="2">关于我们
（大学简介）</td><td colspan="2">校园生活
（学生组织概览）</td><td colspan="2">招生（本科生）</td></tr>
<tr><td colspan="3">大学</td><td>L</td><td>NL</td><td>L</td><td>NL</td><td>L</td><td>NL</td></tr>
<tr><td rowspan="2">词汇分析</td><td>L1</td><td>导航文本标准化程度</td><td></td><td></td><td></td><td></td><td></td><td></td></tr>
<tr><td>L3</td><td>词汇密度</td><td></td><td></td><td></td><td></td><td></td><td></td></tr>
</table>

续表

<table>
<tr><td colspan="3">网站版块</td><td colspan="2">关于我们
（大学简介）</td><td colspan="2">校园生活
（学生组织概览）</td><td colspan="2">招生（本科生）</td></tr>
<tr><td rowspan="2">句子分析</td><td>S1</td><td>平均句长</td><td></td><td></td><td></td><td></td><td></td><td></td></tr>
<tr><td>S2</td><td>第一和第二人称句子的相对密度</td><td></td><td></td><td></td><td></td><td></td><td></td></tr>
</table>

表 4-14 显示了本地化和非本地化大学网站中导航文本的词汇项目（L：本地化清华大学网站；NL：非本地化加州大学伯克利分校网站）。第一，所有导航文本的长度都是一两个单词，唯一的例外是在本地化清华大学网站首页的下半部分发现了一处三词文本。第二，大学网站的配对比较看到了目前比较的所有三个网站对中标准化程度最高的版块标题，包括“About Us”（关于我们）、“Admissions”（招生）、“Research”（研究）、“News”（新闻）和“Join Us”（加入我们）。在本地化的清华大学网站中，“Academics”（教学）被“International”（国际）版块所取代，表明本地化网站专门面向国际学生和学者，而非本地化加州大学伯克利分校则采用更笼统的语气。第三，两个大学网站都没有为主页提供基于图标或按钮的导航提示。第四，值得注意的是，从这种配对比较中可以看出，无论是本地化的还是非本地化的大学网站，都是最超然的组织网站类型，导航文本中的第一人称和第二人称不存在或存在感很弱，可以为这一点提供论据。第五，非本地化的加州大学伯克利分校网站为学生、教职员工、家长和校友设计了单独的网站入口，而本地化的清华大学网站则没有这样明确的设计，“教职员工”和“校友”两个版块和无明确受众群体的其他版块一并在导航栏内列出。

表 4-14　清华大学和加州大学伯克利分校网站不同版块标题的用词

<table>
<tr><td>网站版块</td><td>L</td><td>NL</td></tr>
<tr><td>关于我们</td><td colspan="2">About Us</td></tr>
<tr><td>招生</td><td colspan="2">Admissions</td></tr>
<tr><td>教学</td><td>International</td><td>Academics</td></tr>
<tr><td>研究</td><td colspan="2">Research</td></tr>
<tr><td>校园生活</td><td>Campus</td><td>Campus Life</td></tr>
</table>

续表

网站版块	L	NL
新闻	News	
加入我们	Join Us	
联系我们	Contacts	Contact us
募捐	Giving to TH	Give

表4-15显示了单个网站独有的版块（L：本地化清华大学网站；NL：非本地化加州大学伯克利分校网站），这是关于中美大学网站配对比较的导航文本分析的最后一部分。首先，如前所述，非本地化的加州大学伯克利分校网站的一大特点是为网站版块进行有针对性的分组，以面向不同受众（包括学生、教职员工、家长和校友）。其次，加州大学伯克利分校网站的主页上突出显示校园参观活动的信息，为其安排了一块单独的版面，清华大学网站主页则没有这样设计，这在一定程度上表达了加州大学伯克利分校希望与未来学生和社区加强交流的意愿。此外，非本地化加州大学伯克利分校网站发布了通信录，用于对外公布教职员工和学生同意共享的联系信息，而本地化清华大学网站并未发布通信录，这表明维护大学人员联系信息的公共集体数据库可能并不是清华等中国大学网站的常规做法。与人员通信录的情况类似，加州大学伯克利分校网站在主站点下提供了子站点的A-Z目录，清华大学网站也没有此设计。此外，本地化清华大学网站没有包含“课业问题咨询和辅导”版块，而在非本地化加州大学伯克利分校网站上，该版块被视为向学生提供的一项重要服务。最后，在研究版块，本地化清华大学网站强调知识产权（IP）保护和国际合作，而非本地化的加州大学伯克利分校网站则宣传本科生研究动议。对这种差异的一种可能解释是，本地化清华大学网站打算通过其英文网站展示其学术开放性，以吸引全球研究人员的注意力；而非本地化加州大学伯克利分校网站则希望通过具有竞争力的研究项目吸引潜在学生，从而为学生在未来的就业市场上提供优势。

表 4-15　配对比较的大学网站的独有版块

L	NL
Research - Intellectual Property, Research Cooperation, International Communication	Student | Faculty&Staff | Parents Visit Directory Academics - Advising and Tutoring Websites A - Z Research - Undergraduate Research

表 4-16 显示了可用于内容文本比较的大学网站版块的词汇密度（L：本地化清华大学网站；NL：非本地化加州大学伯克利分校网站）。本地化清华大学网站的“本科”和“学生组织概况”两个子版块的词汇密度高于非本地化加州大学伯克利分校网站，前者的大学简介版块的词汇密度则低于后者。

表 4-16　可用于内容文本比较的大学网站版块的词汇密度

网站版块	L（%）	NL（%）
关于我们（大学简介）	56.7	58.9
招生（本科）	64.1	62.7
校园生活（学生组织概况）	77.8	67.6

表 4-17 显示了可用于内容文本比较的大学网站版块的平均句长（L：本地化清华大学网站；NL：非本地化加州大学伯克利分校网站）。总体而言，本地化清华大学网站的三个可比版块的平均句长值高于非本地化加州大学伯克利分校网站。

表 4-17　可用于内容文本比较的大学网站版块的平均句长

网站版块	L	NL
关于我们（大学简介）	19.8	14.3
招生（本科）	30.6	13.7
校园生活（学生组织概况）	24.5	16.6

表 4-18 显示了可用于内容文本比较的大学网站版块中第一和第二人称句子的相对频率（L：本地化清华大学网站；NL：非本地化加州大学伯克利分校网站）。研究目前涉及的本地化清华大学网站版块没有第一人称或第二人称句子，与以第一人称或第二人称句子为主的加州大学伯克利分校网站对应版块形成了鲜明对比。

表 4-18　可用于内容文本比较的大学网站版块中第一和第二人称句子的相对频率

网站版块	L（%）	NL（%）
关于我们（大学简介）	0	71
招生（本科）	0	85
校园生活（学生组织概况）	0	100

四、市政府：北京市与华盛顿市网站对比

比较两个市政府网站的总体结构可以发现，二者相同的版块如下：（1）关于我们，网站简介；（2）教育，本市居民可享受的教育资源介绍；（3）新闻与活动；（4）反馈；（5）FAQ（常见问题）；（6）隐私政策以及（7）使用条款与条件。所有这些部分都针对导航文本进行了分析。此外，为内容文本的配对比较选择的部分是（1）、（6）和（7），因为发现这些部分包含可比较的内容文本，且更新频率较低。

表 4-19 是一个交叉表模板，列出了所选网站版块（L：本地化的北京政府网站；NL：非本地化的华盛顿市政府网站）的所有文本特征，概述了两个政府网站的所有比较项目。

表 4-19　列出所选政府网站版块待分析的所有文本特征的交叉表模板

<table>
<tr><th colspan="3">网站版块</th><th colspan="2">关于我们</th><th colspan="2">使用条款与条件</th><th colspan="2">隐私政策</th></tr>
<tr><td colspan="3">市政府</td><td>L</td><td>NL</td><td>L</td><td>NL</td><td>L</td><td>NL</td></tr>
<tr><td rowspan="2">词汇分析</td><td>L1</td><td>导航文本的标准化程度</td><td></td><td></td><td></td><td></td><td></td><td></td></tr>
<tr><td>L3</td><td>词汇密度</td><td></td><td></td><td></td><td></td><td></td><td></td></tr>
<tr><td rowspan="2">句子分析</td><td>S1</td><td>平均句长</td><td></td><td></td><td></td><td></td><td></td><td></td></tr>
<tr><td>S2</td><td>第一和第二人称句子的相对频率</td><td></td><td></td><td></td><td></td><td></td><td></td></tr>
</table>

表4-20显示了本地化和非本地化政府网站中导航文本使用的词汇（L：本地化的北京市政府网站；NL：非本地化的华盛顿市政府网站）。第一，非本地化的华盛顿市政府网站的字数略多于本地化的北京市政府网站，这在很大程度上是因为前者文本使用了较多的三词和四词词组。第二，在比较的所有网站版块中，实现相似交际目的的可比版块使用了不同措辞。第三，本地化的北京市政府网站提供了明确的主页导航功能——点击“Home”（主页）按钮可以打开一个显示网站主页的新窗口，而非本地化的华盛顿市政府网站则没有这样的设计。第四，和上节分析的两个大学网站一样，两个市政府网站的导航文本也都以第三人称视角为主。关于市政府网站导航文本的配对比较，值得注意的最后一点是教育版块：本地化北京市政府网站上的“Study”（学习）重点介绍了本市大学课程或高等教育服务，以鼓励适龄的国际学生来北京学习，在北京读书；而非本地化华盛顿市政府网站的“Education”（教育）则主要针对当地居民，全方位展示了本市可提供的各学段教育资源（包括幼儿园至高三即K-12和中学后的成人教育）。在目标受众方面，本地化北京市政府网站针对的是临时居民、旅客、学生和潜在的商业伙伴，而非本地化华盛顿市政府网站针对的是当地居民、旅客和求职者。

表4-20 本地化和非本地化政府网站不同版块的用词

网站版块	L	NL
关于我们	About Us	About DC. Gov
教育	Study	Education
新闻与活动	Official Activities | Mayor's Bulletin	News, Events | Featured News
反馈	Feedback	Feedback, Complaints, and Appeals
常见问题解答	Q&A	Popular Searches
隐私政策	Services and Privacy	Privacy and Security
使用条款与条件	Copyright	Terms and Conditions

表4-21显示了单个网站独有的版块（L：本地化的北京政府网站；NL：非本地化的华盛顿市政府网站），可作为市政府网站导航文本配对比较的收尾。显然，本地化北京市政府网站主要面向外国访客，突出展示了外国访客可能感兴

趣的版块，包括“Visa”（签证）、“Cooperation”（合作）、“Recruitment of Experts”（专家招聘）以及介绍领导人来访和表彰荣誉市民的聚焦式版块。在随后对市政府网站开展的分组比较中可以看出，大多数市政府网站都突出展示“Sister Cities”（姐妹城市）这一版块，因为它旨在反映市政府在促进国际交流方面发挥的积极作用。此外，本地化北京市政府网站将“Survey”（调查）视为一种收集反馈的方式，让网站可以与使用英语的网站访客进行互动。另一方面，非本地化华盛顿市政府网站设有单独的网站入口，将不同访客引导到最相关的网站版块。

表 4-21　市政府网站配对比较时发现的网站独有版块

L	NL
Visa Sister Cities Cooperation Recruitmentof Experts Visiting Leader ǀ Honorary CitizenVSitemap Surveys	Residents ǀ Government ǀ Visitors ǀ Jobs ǀ Online Services ǀ Media, Communication District Initiatives

表 4-22 显示了用于内容文本比较的政府网站版块的词汇密度（L：本地化的北京市政府网站；NL：非本地化的华盛顿市政府网站）。从总体上看，本地化北京市政府网站参与配对比较的三个版块的词汇密度均高于非本地化华盛顿市政府网站。

表 4-22　可用于内容文本比较的政府网站版块的词汇密度

网站版块	L（%）	NL（%）
关于我们	64.5	58.1
隐私政策	59.4	58.1
使用条款与条件	82.5	51.0

表 4-23 显示了用于内容文本比较的政府网站版块的平均句长（L：本地化的北京市政府网站；NL：非本地化的华盛顿市政府网站）。在参与配对比较的三个网站版块中，本地化北京市政府网站的平均句长小于非本地化华盛顿市政府网站。

表 4-23 用于内容文本比较的政府网站版块的平均句长

网站版块	L	NL
关于我们	13.7	14.0
隐私政策	15.6	16.0
使用条款与条件	8.4	22.6

表 4-24 显示了用于内容文本比较的市政府网站版块中第一和第二人称句子的相对频率（L：本地化的北京市政府网站；NL：非本地化的华盛顿市政府网站）。两个网站的第一和第二人称句子比例都较高，除了本地化北京市政府网站的“使用条款与条件”版块。该版块只用了几个句段介绍了参与网站设计和开发的相关组织和机构，以此声明网站版权。总体而言，非本地化华盛顿市政府网站的第一人称和第二人称视角所占比重高于本地化的北京市政府网站。

表 4-24 用于内容文本比较的政府网站版块中第一和第二人称句子的相对频率

网站版块	L（%）	NL（%）
关于我们	80	82
隐私政策	74	85
使用条款与条件	0	78

五、旅游目的地城市：北京市与华盛顿市网站比较

从整体结构上看，两个旅游目的地城市网站的共有版块如下：（1）推荐活动，旅游目的地的热门活动介绍；（2）住宿，推荐不同标准的住宿地点；（3）路线与跟团游，推荐旅行路线以满足不同旅客的需求；（4）周边旅游，介绍附近的旅游景点；（5）交通，提供有关如何前往旅游目的地及其周边地区的信息；（6）事件，介绍旅游目的地举办的季节性活动；（7）新闻，定期更新的当地旅游新闻；（8）关于我们，赞助网站建设的旅游促进机构的简介以及（9）联系我们，提供赞助机构的联系信息。下文将对所有共有版块的导航文本进行分析。此外，内容文本的配对比较选择的版块是“关于我们”和“城市概况”（二者分别是北京旅游网站的“关于北京”和华盛顿市旅游网站“新闻”下的一个子版块），因为这两个版块包含可比较的内容文本，且更新频率较低。

表 4-25 是一个交叉表模板，列出了所选网站版块（L：本地化北京市旅游网站；NL：非本地化华盛顿市旅游网站）的所有文本特征，概述了两个旅游目

的地城市网站的所有比较项目。

表 4-25　列出所选旅游目的地城市网站版块待分析的所有文本特征的交叉表模板

网站版块			关于我们		城市概况	
旅游目的地			L	NL	L	NL
词汇分析	L1	导航文本标准化程度				
	L3	词汇密度				
句子分析	S1	平均句长				
	S2	第一和第二人称句子的相对频率				

表 4-26 展示了本地化和非本地化旅游网站导航文本的用词（L：本地化北京市旅游网站；NL：非本地化华盛顿市网站）。首先，非本地化华盛顿市旅游网站导航文本的平均单词数略高于本地化北京市旅游网站，主要是因为前者使用三词词组较多。其次，两个网站的“推荐活动”和“事件”两个版块的导航文本均呈现出标准化。再次，在首页导航方面，本地化北京市旅游网站具有显示导航的功能——点击“Home”（首页）按钮打开一个显示网站首页的新窗口，而非本地化华盛顿市旅游网站则没有这样的设计。最后，两个网站的第一和第二人称句子的比重没有太大差异，因为两个网站的主要版块都以第三人称视角为主。

表 4-26　北京市和华盛顿市旅游网站不同版块的用词

网站版块	L	NL
推荐活动	Thingsto Do	
住宿	Accommodation	Places to Stay
路线与跟团游	Routes，Strategy	Tours，Sightseeing
周边旅游	Around Beijing	Neighborhoods
交通	Transportation	Getting Around DC
事件	Events	
新闻	News	DC Insider Newsletter (for email subscription)
关于我们	About Us	About Destination DC

续表

网站版块	L	NL
联系我们	Contact Us （点击链接可发送电邮）	Contact Destination DC

表4-27展示了单个网站独有的版块（L：本地化北京市旅游网站；NL：非本地化华盛顿市旅游网站），作为旅游目的地城市网站的导航文本配对比较的收尾。本地化北京市旅游网站以游客教育为重点，宣传旅游品牌大使倡议，介绍中国旅游和学习汉语的小贴士。此外，网站还展示了国际旅行者撰写的博客文章，讲述他们在中国有趣的经历，希望通过个人故事与网站访客建立起情感上的联系。本地化北京市旅游网站面向对中国旅游感兴趣的国际旅行者，而非本地化华盛顿市旅游网站则针对不同的受众群体，包括访客、会议组织者、旅行社和媒体，将不同版块有目的性地分组。此外，非本地化华盛顿市旅游网站突出显示了吸引潜在游客的旅游优惠和免费景点，“Careers”（职业）版块专门针对求职者。

表4-27 配对比较的旅游网站的独有版块

L	NL
GDP Programs Learn Chinese Tips（travel essentials） Blog（Travelogue）	Visit DC ｜ Meetings ｜ Travel Trade ｜ Members ｜ Press ｜ Book（button） Deals Free Attractions Careers

表4-28展示了用于内容文本比较的旅游网站版块的词汇密度（L：本地化北京市旅游网站；NL：非本地化华盛顿市旅游网站）。可以看出，有两个网站版块参与配对比较，非本地化华盛顿市旅游网站的词汇密度均高于本地化北京市旅游网站。

表4-28 用于内容文本比较的旅游网站版块的词汇密度

网站版块	L（%）	NL（%）
关于我们	56.6	62.1
城市概况	63.4	64.2

表4-29展示了用于内容文本比较的旅游网站版块的平均句长（L：本地化

北京市旅游网站；NL：非本地化华盛顿市旅游网站）。通过配对比较这两个版块发现，本地化北京市旅游网站的平均句长大于非本地化华盛顿市旅游网站。值得注意的是，两个网站的“城市概况”版块的句子都短得多，细察后发现，“城市概况”版块文本由包含引人注目的数字的词组和短句组成。

表 4-29 用于内容文本比较的旅游网站版块的平均句长

网站版块	L	NL
关于我们	25.2	21.5
城市概况	10.4	8.7

表 4-30 展示了用于内容文本比较的旅游网站版块中第一和第二人称句子的相对频率（L：本地化北京市旅游网站；NL：非本地化华盛顿市旅游网站）。两个网站配对比较的两个版块都由不同类型的人称视角主导。

表 4-30 用于内容文本比较的旅游网站版块的第一和第二人称句子的相对频率

网站版块	L（%）	NL（%）
关于我们	85	0
城市概况	0	76

六、跨行业比较

作为五个行业部门的本地化和非本地化网站配对比较的总结，表 4-31 列出了对 10 个网站进行配对分析得出的所有结论，为跨行业比较提供参考。每个行业内的配对比较需要处理不同的网站版块集合，且本研究分析的五个行业部门网站并未共有任何一个网站版块，考虑到这一实际限制，本研究提出以下假设，将在第一阶段第二步的分组比较中进行检验：

H1：在内容文本可比较的版块的可量化文本特征方面，非本地化网站与本地化网站的比较结果普遍一致，但配对比较结果尚无定论的平均句长除外。

H2：一个网站版块的导航文本的单词数介于 1 和 5 之间，在大多数情况下介于 1 和 3 之间。

H3：不论本地化或非本地化，大学网站的导航文本是五个行业部门最简短和最标准化的，因此呈现出最超然的语气，具体表现为没有第一人称和第二人称的视角或存在感很弱。

H4：与非本地化网站相比，更多的本地化网站具有独立的“Home”（主页）导航功能，不拘泥于行业部门。

H5：大学、市政府和旅游目的地这三类非本地化组织网站对不同受众可能感兴趣的板块进行分组，而本研究涉及的其他两类非本地化组织网站（语言服务提供商和电子商务）和大多数本地化网站均未发现类似的定向传播策略。

第一阶段第二步将扩大数据集规模，进一步检验这些假设。

表 4-31　网站配对比较总结

文本特征＼行业		语言服务提供商	电商	大学	市政府	旅游目的地
导航文本	平均单词数	L<NL	L<NL	（五个行业中最短）	L<NL	L<NL
	标题标准化的版块	服务行业和技术实力	帮助	（共有 5 个版块标题标准化）	N/A	推荐活动和事件
	有无“Home”设计（主页）	面包屑路径设计（L）vs. N/A（NL）	N/A（不拘本地化与否）	N/A（不拘本地化与否）	是（L）vs. N/A（NL）	是（L）vs. N/A（NL）
	目标受众	目前和潜在客户、求职者、对行业新闻感兴趣的访客和媒体（不拘本地化与否）	当前和潜在买家（L）vs. 买家、卖家和求职者（NL）	国际学生和学者、教职工和校友（L）vs. 学生、家长和教职工（NL）	国际旅客和临时居民（L）vs. 本地居民、游客和求职者（NL）	国际旅客（L）vs. 旅客、会务人员、旅游公司、媒体和求职者（NL）
	独有版块	商业道德规范（L）vs. 技术（NL）	科技类版块和国际知识产权（L）vs. 企业文化类版块与卖家（NL）	与国际研究合作和国际知识产权有关的版块（L）vs. 课业辅导服务与本科生研究（NL）	本市向国际游客提供服务的相关版块（L）vs. 本地居民、游客、教育工作者、求职者和对城市公共管理新闻感兴趣的访客（NL）	旅行指南及个人游记（L）vs. 职业机会与旅游优惠（NL）

续表

文本特征 \ 行业		语言服务提供商	电商	大学	市政府	旅游目的地
内容文本	词汇密度	L<NL	L<NL	（无明确结论）	L>NL	L<NL
	平均句长	L<NL	（无明确结论）	L>NL	L<NL	L>NL
	第一和第二人称句子所占比重	L<NL	（不拘本地化与否，比重很高，但二者比较无明确结论）	L<NL	L<NL	（无明确结论）

第二节　第一阶段第二步：分组比较

在这步分析中，来自语言服务提供商、大学、政府和旅游目的地四个行业部门的本地化和非本地化网站被分为 8 组，每组包含各个行业部门选出的 9 个网站（分析的所有网站名单参见附录 A 的网站列表）。由于本地化的英文电子商务网站难觅，此次的分组比较排除了电子商务这一行业。首先，将每组本地化网站与同一行业的非本地化网站就表 3-3 确定的 5 个文本特征进行比较，行业内比较之后再进行跨行业比较。所有本地化组和非本地化组的比较内容都是在第一阶段第一步的行业内配对比较中确定的共有版块。

一、语言服务提供商（LSP）

本节总共研究了语言服务提供商网站配对比较时确定的可比网站版块的五个不同的文本特征（有关本地化和非本地化语言服务提供商网站共有的版块，请参见本章第一节）。所有版块都针对与导航文本相关的一个特征进行了比较，而与内容文本相关的其他四个特征只对“公司（组织）简介”一个版块进行了研究，因为“公司（组织）简介”是本研究涉及的所有网站样本共有的唯一一个版块。其他共有版块涉及两个以上层级的网页，超出了当前研究的范围。

为便于随后开展跨行业比较，同时考虑到不同行业部门并不共有相同的可比版块这一事实，对分组比较涉及的其他三个行业部门应用与语言服务提供商相同的比较模型。

附录B列出了本地化和非本地化语言服务提供商网站实现类似导航目的词汇项（L：本地化组；NL：非本地化组）。首先，将结果与表4-2的分析进行比较发现，大多数导航文本长度不超过三个单词，非可点击文本链接的页面标题是唯一较长的例外。其次，在语言服务提供商网站的分组比较中，“所服务的行业”版块的标准化程度仍然很高，而相当多的非本地化语言服务提供商网站并未突出显示“技术”版块。然而，此次比较发现，尽管“联系我们”这一版块旨在达成的目标因公司而异，但大多数本地化和非本地化语言服务提供商网站已呈现标准化。有些网站的“联系我们”版块旨在邀请潜在客户咨询报价，有的解答感兴趣人士的询问，还有的用于接收工作申请，还有些可提供部分或全部上述功能。再次，关于“Home”（主页）的存在与否，本地化和非本地化的语言服务提供商网站形成鲜明对比。在9个本地化语言服务提供商网站中，有8个在首页顶部有“Home”按钮，而在9个非本地化同行业网站中，只有3个提供主页导航功能。此外，在3个提供首页导航功能的非本地化网站中，有两个在首页上没有“Home”按钮。这两个网站的“Home”是位于子页面顶部的面包屑路径中的文本链接。至于导航文本中第一人称和第二人称视角所占的比重，本地化组和非本地化组之间没有太大差异；两组有些版块的第一人称和第二人称视角比重相对较大，例如“公司简介”和“联系我们”等。最后，导航文本显示，两个语言服务提供商网站组面向的主要受众类型相同，即客户和求职者两类目标受众。

表4-32列出了两组网站的内容文本的其他四个特征（L：本地化组；NL：非本地化组），图4-1显示了两组网站内容文本生成的词云（左：本地化组；右：非本地化组）。

两组网站内容文本出现频率最高的内容词是Language（语言）、Quality（质量）、Service（服务）、Solution（解决方案）、Company（公司）和Translation（翻译）。这些词代表了语言服务提供商的行业使命——提供优质的语言服务和解决方案，其中的一种典型形式就是翻译。另一方面，一个显著的区别是，本地化的语言服务提供商网站主要针对中国市场，强调技术专长，而非本地化的语言服务提供商网站则具有全球视野，强调团队合作对业务发展的重要性。

至于内容文本，与配对比较不同，非本地化组的词汇密度低于本地化组，平均句长也更短。然而，在非本地化组中，第一人称和第二人称视角所占的比重较大，这与配对比较一致。

表 4-32 与分组比较的语言服务提供商网站的内容文本相关的四个特征

LSP			L	NL
词汇分析	L2	出现频率最高的内容词（占单词总数百分比> 0.5%）	Localization	
			Translation	Language
			Service	Global
			China	Business
			Client	Company
			Language	Solution
			Quality	Service
			Technology	Quality
			Company	Team
			Solution	Translation
	L3	词汇密度	63.20%	62.00%
句子分析	S1	平均句长	17.05	12.08
	S2	第一和第二人称句子的相对频率	82%	88%

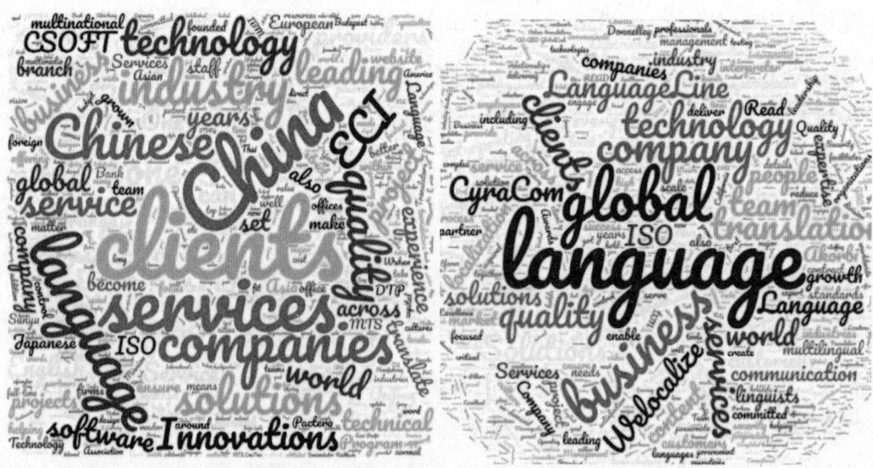

图 4-1 两个语言服务提供商网站组内容文本生成的词云

二、大学

附录 C 列出了在本地化和非本地化大学网站中实现类似导航目的的词项（L：本地化组；NL：非本地化组）。首先，将结果与表 4-14 的分析进行比较，可以看到，与语言服务提供商网站的分组比较一样，两个大学网站组的导航文本也普遍使用一词和双词词组。其次，本地化组与非本地化组的导航文本标准化程度都极高。在比较的所有版块的导航文本中，大学网站之间存在的唯一差异是是否包含大学名称，如 Life@ MIT（麻省理工大学生活）、Career at BNU（北京师范大学职业机会）等。再次，与配对比较一样，大学网站的分组比较也可以体现出整体语气的超然，导航文本中第一人称和第二人称视角比重很小就是例证，"Contact Us"（联系我们）和少数网站的"About Us"（关于我们）这两类版块除外。最后，9 个本地化大学网站中有 5 个具有主页导航功能，其中两个网站的"Home"（主页）显示为面包屑路径中的可点击文本链接，而非本地化大学网站中只有 3 个具有主页导航功能，均体现为面包屑路径中显示的"Home"（主页）。

表 4-33 显示了两个大学网站组的内容文本的其他四个特征（L：本地化组；NL：非本地化组）。两组出现频率最高的共有内容词是"University"（大学）和"Research"（研究），这表明大学网站都倾向于宣传学术研究实力。图 4-2 是两组内容文本生成的词云（左：本地化组；右：非本地化组）。两组在其他高频词方面的差异表明，本研究涉及的本地化大学网站反映了集体主义观点，强调科学相关活动和国家支持，而非本地化大学网站与非本地化语言服务提供商网站类似，具有全球视野，采取以人为本的团队管理方式支持学生和教师。

至于内容文本，词汇密度的结果与配对比较一样，没有确定性结论。此外，与配对比较一样，本地化大学网站组的平均句长更长，第一人称和第二人称视角所占比重比非本地化组小得多。

表 4-33 大学网站分组比较中与内容文本相关的四个特征

University			L	NL
词汇分析	L2	出现频率最高的内容词（占单词总数的百分比 > 0.5%）	University National Research China Education Science	Students University World Research Faculty
	L3	词汇密度	60.77%	60.27%
句子分析	S1	平均句长	25.66	11.43
	S2	第一和第二人称句子的相对频率	7%	64%

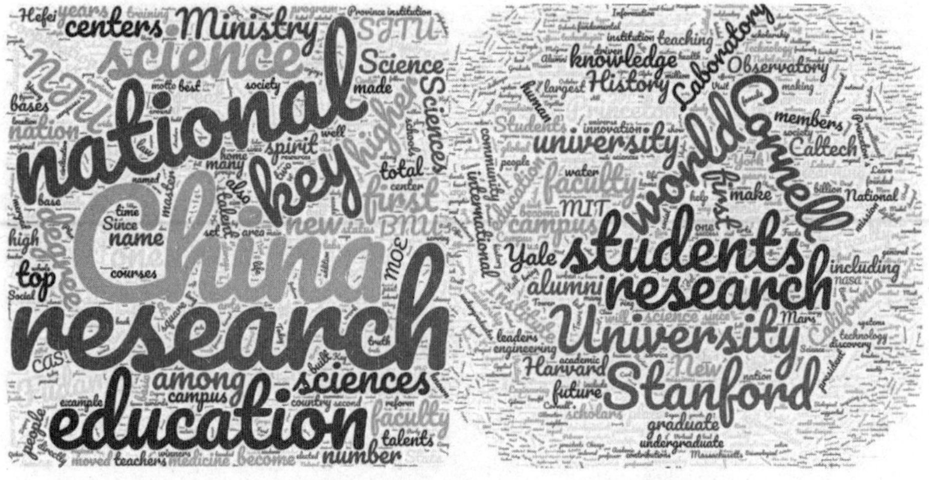

图 4-2 两个大学网站组内容文本生成的词云

三、市政府

附录 D 列出了在本地化和非本地化市政府网站中实现类似导航目的的词项（L：本地化组；NL：非本地化组）。将结果与表 4-20 的分析进行比较，可以看出两组导航文本的单词数也在 1 到 3 之间。与大学网站的分组比较类似，市政府网站的第一人称和第二人称视角比重较小，有些网站的“About Us”（关于我们）和“Contact Us”（联系我们）这两类版块除外。最后，所有本地化的市政府网站都以网页顶部导航栏中的“Home”（主页）按钮的形式提供了明确的主页导航功能。另一方面，9 个非本地化网站中有 6 个具有主页导航功能，其中两个网站将“Home”设计为位于面包屑路径中的可点击文本链接。

由附录 D 可见，两组市政府网站共有版块均无法提供可比文本。这可能是因为大部分非本地化市政府网站是为在线服务设计的，这样的互动服务平台与大多数非本地化市政府网站作为提供参考和咨询服务的信息平台所扮演的角色有很大不同。由于缺乏可比数据，本研究未对两个市政府网站组的内容文本进行比较。

四、旅游目的地城市

附录 E 列出了本地化和非本地化旅游目的地城市网站实现类似导航目的的词汇项目（L：本地化组；NL：非本地化组）。首先，将结果与表 4-26 的分析结果进行比较，我们可以看到，与配对比较类似，两组网站的导航文本长度均在 1 到 3 个单词之间，非本地化网站的导航文本平均单词数略长于本地化网站。其次，两组网站有三个版块呈现出导航文本用词标准化，分别是“Recommended Activities”（推荐活动）、“About Us”（关于我们）和“Events”（事件）。再次，两组网站的主要版块均以第三人称视角为主。最后，所有本地化市政府网站都提供显示主页导航的功能，非本地化网站则没有。

至于内容文本的比较，值得注意的是，本研究分析的旅游目的地城市网站只有几个有一个功能相同的可比版块。大多数网站共有的唯一版块是“About Us”（关于我们）。然而，这一版块的主题因具体网站而异。在本研究涉及的这两组旅游目的地城市网站中，总共可以确定三个主题。一是赞助网站建设的组织的简介（L1、L3、L4、L7、L8、NL1、NL2、NL3、NL6、NL7 和 NL8），二是网站简介（L3、L6），三是网站宣传的城市概况（L2）。考虑到主题的这种变化，表 4-34 列出了两组旅游目的地城市网站（L：本地化组；NL：非本地化组）的内容文本的其他四个特征，仅关注第一个主题所对应的“About Us”（关于我们）版块。两组出现频率最高的共有内容词是“Tourism”（旅游）、“City”（城市）和“Travel”（旅行），指明了网站所属的行业部门。图 4-3 是两组内容文本生成的词云（左：本地化组；右：非本地化组）。两组网站在高频词方面的差异表明，本地化组推广当地旅游套餐，非本地化组则致力于发掘本市作为会议目的地和旅游景点的双重潜力。

接下来比较内容文本的其他三个特征。首先，与配对比较类似，非本地化组唯一一个共有版块的词汇密度高于本地化组。其次，与配对比较一致，本地化组平均句长大于非本地化组。最后，与非本地化组相比，本地化组的第一人称和第二人称视角所占比重更大，这一结果再次与配对比较保持一致。

表 4-34　旅游目的地城市网站分组比较的与内容文本相关的四个特征

<table>
<tr><th colspan="3">旅游目的地</th><th>L</th><th>NL</th></tr>
<tr><td rowspan="2">词汇分析</td><td>L2</td><td>出现频率最高的内容词（占单词总数百分比 > 0.5%）</td><td>Tourism
Industry
Tibet
Beijing
City
Shanghai
Municipal
Travel
International
Service
Tour
Guilin
Local</td><td>San Francisco
Tourism
Destination
Travel
City
Marketing
Visitor
Convention
Orlando
NY
Business
Company
Organization</td></tr>
<tr><td>L3</td><td>词汇密度</td><td>58. 82%</td><td>62. 94%</td></tr>
<tr><td rowspan="2">句子分析</td><td>S1</td><td>平均句长</td><td>17. 14</td><td>13. 81</td></tr>
<tr><td>S2</td><td>第一和第二人称句子的相对频率</td><td>77%</td><td>72%</td></tr>
</table>

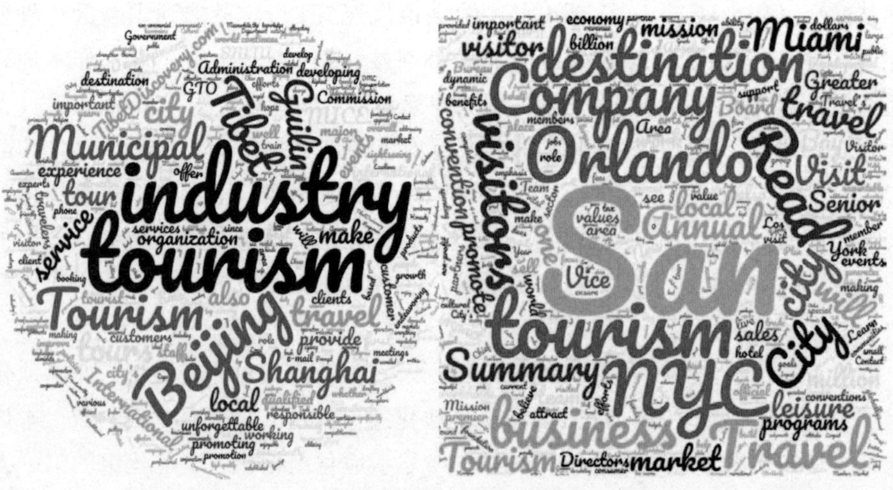

图 4-3　两组旅游目的地城市网站内容文本生成的词云

五、跨行业比较

作为对四个行业的本地化和非本地化网站的分组比较的总结，表 4–35 列出了对 72 个网站进行分组分析得出的结论，以便为跨行业比较提供参考（L：本地化组；NL：非本地化组）。

表 4–35　分组比较总结

		语言服务提供商	大学	市政府	旅游目的地
导航文本	显示主页导航功能	L（8）>NL（4）	L（5）>NL（3）	L（9）>NL（6）	L（9）>NL（0）
内容文本	词汇密度	L>NL	L>NL	N/A	L>NL
	平均句长	L>NL	L>NL		L>NL
	第一与第二人称视角	L<NL	L<NL		L>NL

基于分组比较的结果，第四章第一节提出的所有假设是否得到支持的结论如下：

（1）对于可比版块“关于我们”，非本地化网站的所有文本特征数值一般小于本地化网站，第一人称和第二人称视角所占比重除外。非本地化组的第一人称和第二人称视角所占比重大于本地化组。因此，研究结果不支持假设 H1。

（2）“关于我们”版块的导航文本单词数介于 1 至 5 之间，在大多数情况下介于 1 至 3 之间，不拘组别和行业。因此，假设 H2 得到支持。

（3）与大学网站一样，政府网站一般第一人称和第二人称的存在感较弱。因此，假设 H3 被拒绝。

（4）具有显示主页导航功能的本地化网站多于非本地化网站，特别是语言服务提供商和旅游目的地城市网站。因此，研究结果不支持假设 H4。

（5）表 4–36 显示了两个网站组（L：本地化组；NL：非本地化组）存在网站入口功能的比较结果。可以看出，在四个行业中有三个行业的为不同受众类型提供了单独的入口的非本地化网站多于本地化网站，而语言服务提供商网站则没有这样的设计，不论本地化与否。因此，假设 H5 在三个行业的网站分组比较中都得到支持。

表 4–36　网站多入口功能存在与否的统计

语言服务提供商	大学	市政府	旅游目的地
N/A	L（0）< NL（9）	L（3）< NL（6）	L（2）< NL（7）

至此，第二节完成了描述性统计分析，第三节将测试在本地化和非本地化网站组比较中发现的文本特征差异的统计显著性。此外，第三节还将运用统计学方法，探讨网站文本呈现的特征是否受到源语言和行业这两个独立因素的影响。

第三节　第二阶段：行业影响及语言影响的统计检验

目前的研究仅对可比网站版块的文本进行比较，基于这一前提，当前阶段的推论统计分析只涉及语言服务提供商和大学这两类组织网站，因为只有这两类组织网站具有可比的版块——“关于我们”可用于文本分析。此前研究涉及的其他组织网站要么缺少任何可比较的网站版块，要么“关于我们”版块以组织简介以外的主题作为特色。因此，第二阶段研究的自变量是行业（有两个层级——语言服务提供商和大学）和本地化概况（也有两个层级——本地化和非本地化）。推论统计分析的因变量是在配对和分组比较中研究的三个内容文本特征：（1）词汇密度；（2）平均句长以及（3）第一和第二人称句子所占百分比。

第二阶段执行多变量方差分析（MANOVA）所需的样本量由专门的样本量计算器 G＊Power 3.1 计算得出。计算器的输入和输出参数如图 4-4 所示，中等效应量设置为 0.0625，α 设置为 0.05，幂设为 0.8（Faul，Erdfelder，Lang，Buchner 2007）。第二阶段的预测变量“行业”的层级数是 2（语言服务提供商和大学）而不是 5，另一个预测变量“本地化概况”也有两个层级——本地化（源语言为中文）和非本地化（美式英语），因此分组规模的输入参数为 2×2=4。结果变量的个数设置为 3，对应于与本研究分析的内容文本相关的三个特征。为了执行具有统计意义的检验，第二阶段需要的样本量比第一阶段大。如 G＊Power 计算器所示，当前研究所需的样本量为 88，这意味着需要为每组选择 22 个网站样本。

先从全球领先的翻译服务求职网站 translationdirectory. com（2012a）上的中国翻译机构名单中随机选出 22 个中国语言服务提供商网站，再从 translationdirectory. com（2012b）的美国翻译机构列表中随机选出 22 个美国语言服务提供商网站。至于大学网站的选择，从 webometrics. info 的中国大学前 100 名名单中随机选出 22 个中国大学网站，再从同一网站上的美国大学前 100 名名单中随机选出 22 个美国大学网站。附录 F 列出了第二阶段选定的 88 个网站。从这些网站的“关于我们”板块中提取的文本数据即为本阶段的研究对象。

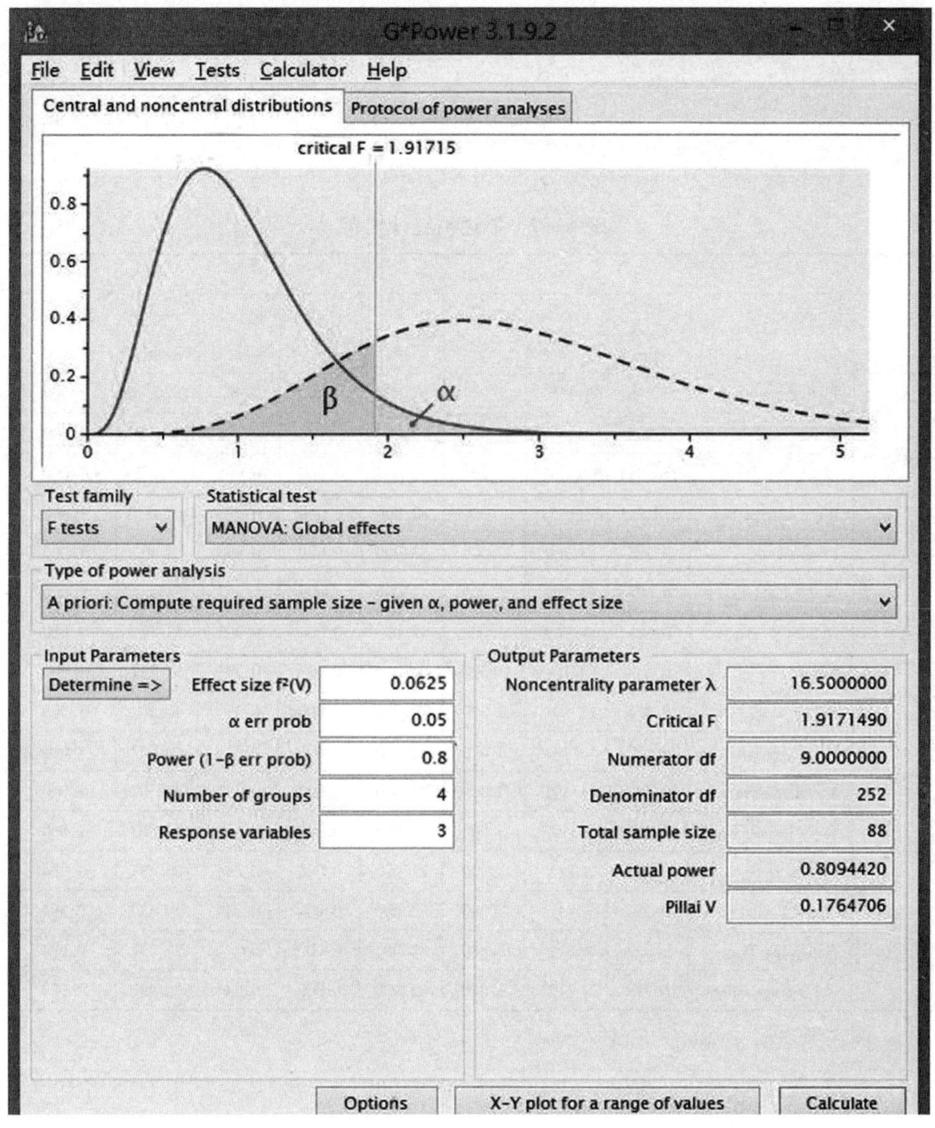

图 4-4　G * Power 计算器的输入和输出参数计算结果

然后，将每个网站的“关于我们”板块的内容文本上传至 analyzemywriting. com 和 countwordsworth. com 两个在线统计网站以计算三个内容文本特征，analyzemywriting. com 计算词汇密度，countwordsworth. com 计算平均句长及第一和第二人称句子所占的百分比。接着，将计算结果载入 SPSS 进行多元数据分析。

表 4-37 显示了四组的描述性统计结果（LocProfile：本地化概况；AveSent-

Leng：平均句长；PercentPerson：第一和第二人称句子所占的百分比）。可以看出，不拘行业，本地化组的平均句长均高于非本地化组，而第一人称和第二人称的比重则与之相反，未发现本地化组和非本地化组之间存在词汇密度的显著差异。

表 4-37　描述性统计结果

Multivariate Test[a]									
Effect		Value	F	Hypothesis df	Error df	Sig.	Partial Eta Squared	Noncent. Parameter	Observed Power[c]
Intercept	Pillai's Trace	0.996	6311.57[b]	3.000	82.000	0.000	0.996	18934.700	1.000
	Wilks' Lambda	0.004	6311.57[b]	3.000	82.000	0.000	0.996	18934.700	1.000
	Hotelling's Trace	230.911	6311.57[b]	3.000	82.000	0.000	0.996	18934.700	1.000
	Roy's Largest Root	230.911	6311.57[b]	3.000	82.000	0.000	0.996	18934.700	1.000
Industry	Pillai's Trace	0.393	17.709[b]	3.000	82.000	0.000	0.393	53.127	1.000
	Wilks' Lambda	0.607	17.709[b]	3.000	82.000	0.000	0.393	53.127	1.000
	Hotelling's Trace	0.648	17.709[b]	3.000	82.000	0.000	0.393	53.127	1.000
	Roy's Largest Root	0.648	17.709[b]	3.000	82.000	0.000	0.393	53.127	1.000
LocProfile	Pillai's Trace	0.331	13.501[b]	3.000	82.000	0.000	0.331	40.502	1.000
	Wilks' Lambda	0.669	13.501[b]	3.000	82.000	0.000	0.331	40.502	1.000
	Hotelling's Trace	0.494	13.501[b]	3.000	82.000	0.000	0.331	40.502	1.000
	Roy's Largest Root	0.494	13.501[b]	3.000	82.000	0.000	0.331	40.502	1.000
Industry * LocProfile	Pillai's Trace	0.244	8.812[b]	3.000	82.000	0.000	0.244	26.437	0.994
	Wilks' Lambda	0.756	8.812[b]	3.000	82.000	0.000	0.244	26.437	0.994
	Hotelling's Trace	0.322	8.812[b]	3.000	82.000	0.000	0.244	26.437	0.994
	Roy's Largest Root	0.322	8.812[b]	3.000	82.000	0.000	0.244	26.437	0.994

a. Design：Intercept + Industry+ LocProfile + Industry * LocProfile

b. Exact statistic

c. Computed using alpha = .05

表4-38展示了主体间效应检验结果，以探索源语言和行业对内容文本的每个特征的影响（LocProfile：本地化概况；AveSentLeng：平均句长；PercentPerson：第一和第二人称句子所占的百分比）。可以看出，词汇密度没有受到源语言或行业甚至二者交互作用的显著影响（*sig.* > 0.05），而其他两个特征——平均句长及第一和第二人称句子所占的百分比——受到源语言和行业这两个自变量以及二者之间相互作用的显著影响（*sig.* = 0.00 < 0.05）。

表 4-38 主体间效应检验

Tests of Between-Subjects Effects									
Source	Dependent Variable	Type III Sum of Squares	df	Mean Square	F	Sig.	Partial Eta Squared	Noncent. Parameter	Observed Power[d]
Corrected Model	AveSentLeng	1486.8[a]	3	495.601	16.409	0.000	0.369	49.227	1.000
	LexicalDensity	0.002[b]	3	0.001	0.365	0.779	0.013	1.094	0.119
	PercentPerson	5.739[c]	3	1.913	34.421	0.000	0.551	103.264	1.000
Intercept	AveSentLeng	34637.86	1	34637.860	1146.825	0.000	0.932	1146.825	1.000
	LexicalDensity	33.397	1	33.397	18215.320	0.000	0.995	18215.320	1.000
	PercentPerson	29.118	1	29.118	523.929	0.000	0.862	523.929	1.000
Industry	AveSentLeng	728.238	1	728.238	24.111	0.000	0.223	24.111	0.998
	LexicalDensity	0.001	1	0.001	0.660	0.419	0.008	0.660	0.127
	PercentPerson	2.442	1	2.442	43.944	0.000	0.343	43.944	1.000
LocProfile	AveSentLeng	575.540	1	575.540	19.056	0.000	0.185	19.056	0.991
	LexicalDensity	0.000	1	0.000	0.256	0.614	0.003	0.256	0.079
	PercentPerson	1.856	1	1.856	33.396	0.000	0.284	33.396	1.000
Industry * LocProfile	AveSentLeng	183.024	1	183.024	6.060	0.016	0.067	6.060	0.682
	LexicalDensity	0.000	1	0.000	0.178	0.674	0.002	0.178	0.070
	PercentPerson	1.441	1	1.441	25.924	0.000	0.236	25.924	0.999
Error	AveSentLeng	2537.075	84	30.203					
	LexicalDensity	0.154	84	0.002					
	PercentPerson	4.668	84	0.056					
Total	AveSentLeng	38661.74	88						
	LexicalDensity	33.553	88						
	PercentPerson	39.525	88						
Corrected Total	AveSentLeng	4023.877	87						
	LexicalDensity	0.156	87						
	PercentPerson	10.407	87						

a. R Squared = .069 (Adjusted R Squared = .347)

b. R Squared = .013 (Adjusted R Squared = -.022)

c. R Squared = .551 (Adjusted R Squared = .535)

d. Computed using alpha = .05

为直观展示自变量和因变量之间的相关性，图 4-5 是本地化组和非本地化组与行业相关的三个文本特征的估计边际均值的轮廓图（从左至右依次为：平均句长、词汇密度和第一和第二人称句子所占的百分比）。图上的相交线表示相关性，可以看出，词汇密度的相关性强度不及其他两个特征。

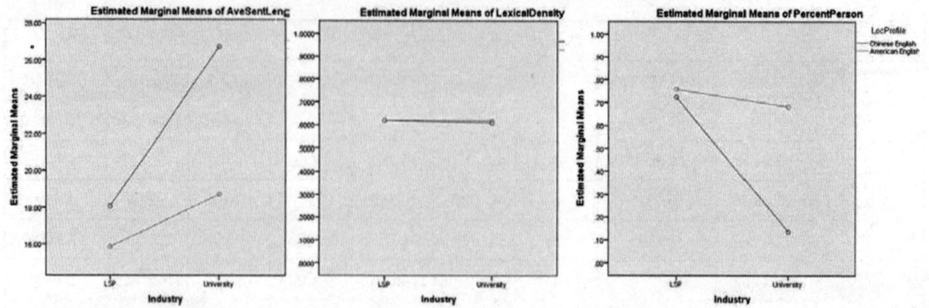

图 4-5　本地化组和非本地化组与行业相关的三个文本特征的估计边际均值的轮廓图

综上所述，行业和源语言对作为因变量的内容文本特征组合存在具有统计学显著意义的交互效应，F（3，82）= 8.812，p = .000；Wilks' Λ = .756。至于“关于我们”版块的内容文本，不论是语言服务提供商还是大学网站，本地化组和非本地化组在平均句长和第一和第二人称句子所占比重方面存在显著差异，但在词汇密度方面，未发现本地化和非本地化组之间存在显著差异。

考虑到样本量有限和研究涉及的可比行业部门数量较少，现阶段判定本地化中国组织英文网站是否存在英语变体为时尚早。目前可以明确的是，一些中国组织的英文网站已经表现出不同于同业美国组织的非本地化网站的文本语言特征。目前研究中发现的偏差是否会在网络媒体传播未来的发展过程中进一步彰显，还有待观察。

第四节　本章小结

本章展示并分析了可比网站版块，特别是用于统计分析的“关于我们”版块的定性和定量结果。本研究对本地化和非本地化网站的导航和内容文本的具体特征进行了比较。第一节介绍了对五个行业部门的本地化和非本地化网站进行配对比较的情况。基于由此产生的初步比较结果，第二节对四个行业部门的本地化和非本地化网站进行了分组比较，以证实或反驳第一节的研究结果。最后，第三节对其中两个行业部门——语言服务提供商和大学——的本地化和非本地化网站的文本特征进行了推论统计分析。推论统计分析表明，行业和本地化概况对两个文本特征——平均句子长度及第一人称和第二人称视角所占比重——均具有主效应和交互效应，不论这两个文本特征组合或分开皆是如此。下一章将讨论本研究的独创性，探讨其局限性，并为未来研究进一步深入指明可能的方向。

第五章

研究反思与结论

本章的总体结构与第三章相呼应，从三个角度对当前研究进行了反思：工具（第一节）、数据（第二节）和分析框架（第三节）。反思性分析将回顾研究结果并考虑局限性，以探索未来研究的可能途径。随后的第四节将当前研究作为例证，设想网站文本的实证研究将成为让教学、研究和行业实践互为裨益的一个有前景的领域。最后，第五节总结本章。

第一节　工具

网站的文本分析反映了对集成式数据处理和管理框架的需求，该框架建立在深入理解文本和语言复杂性的基础之上。本研究从选定的网站下载符合研究条件的网页，再从指定网页上提取文本，最后对网站文本逐一应用常规文本的测量工具。像这样的跨平台操作会对数据分析的效率产生不利影响，且难以将这套测量程序应用于规模更大的网站数据集。

在技术程序上，与研究传统文本不同，网站文本的研究人员不仅需要选择额外的工具将网站数据转换为纯文本，还需要从提取的原始文本中去除不需要的文本噪声。当前研究中的文本噪声包括重复出现的图像替代（alt）文本①和用于跨层级网页导航的网站版块标题。

初看之下，似乎应该选择 R 而不是一组工具设计这样一个系统，以促进文本数据的生命周期管理，因为作为一种以统计计算和图形绘制而闻名的编程语言，R 拥有丰富的程序包，可实现数据收集、处理和分析等不同目标。假如 R 适用于当前研究，则与研究涉及的文本数据相关的每一项任务都将在 R 环境中执行，从而形成一个集成系统，提高数据分析的效率。然而，一个重大的技术挑战使研究人员在当前的研究中避开了 R。

---

① 替代文本为图像提供替代性信息，如果用户因故无法看到网站图片，在图片的位置会显示替代文本，以便用户了解图片的大致内容。

对本研究而言，R 编程的主要难点在于代码的可适应性。为了提取符合研究条件的网站文本，需要修改和定制 R 代码以适应每个组织网站的编码方案。由于在设计和格式方面存在差异，本研究分析的大多数网站对文本部分采用了不同的 HTML 标记设置。这意味着尽管改写 R 代码以满足某个网站提取相关“无噪声”文本的需求是可行的，但必须对应各个网站的具体情况逐个调整代码，因为网站很少遵循统一的文本格式设置，所以有必要开发“万能”代码来提取任何网页源代码中的正文文本。因此，本研究使用在线网络文本提取工具来完整提取网页文本，并手动去除每个网页文本中的文本噪声。

关于网站文本处理与传统文本处理之间差异的另一个发现是，广泛使用的文本分析工具的算法背后隐含着对一些文本特征的定义，在网站研究的背景下，需要重新审视这些定义。一个典型的例子是“句子”。大多数文本分析工具定义的句子是有序的单词序列，以三个标点符号之一作为结束，即以句号、问号或感叹号结尾。句子层面的计算和分析完全依赖于这个定义。这在传统文本的研究中可能不会带来太大的问题，因为每个句子都应该以一个终结点结束。然而，网站文本增大了定义句子这一问题的复杂性。例如，网站写作倾向于简洁明了，因此，要点符号或数字编号被视为组织和呈现信息的最佳方式。对于列表中列出的每一条文字如何结尾，大多数标点符号指南要求句子末尾需要写标点符号，但句子片段或单词则不用。然而在实践中，本研究涉及的大多数网站上的列举项都没有用标点符号结尾，不论句子完整与否。这种情况对传统文本分析工具得出的统计结果产生了很大影响。为了使工具算法与网站场景相协调，研究人员在手动去除文本噪声时在句子条目的末尾添加了一个结束标记。这说明了对文本特征进行自定义以及为分析网站文本定制工具系统的必要性。

虽然上述困难客观存在，但研究人员坚信，面向网站文本研究场景的具有数据收集、处理和管理功能的集成系统是可以实现的。依据这样的思路，未来研究将探索网络文本特征具有可操作性的定义以及对网站文本格式设置的编码方案进行分类，以便设计出基于 R 的一体化网站文本分析系统。这种系统的重要意义在于它可以跨行业和跨时间高效分析大规模网站数据集。此外，该集成系统的在线发布将促进研究程序的可复现，从而集结全球兴趣相近的研究人员，有助于全面了解以网络为媒介的组织传播。

第二节 数据

为了进一步展开第一节中扩大数据集规模的问题，本节重点讨论两种类型的网站文本——导航文本和内容文本，展望多样化程度更高、规模更大的数据集研究这一未来发展方向，与第四章的多维度比较思路保持一致。从目前的研究中可以看出，可比较的网站和网站版块的数量随步骤和阶段推进呈稳步下降趋势。这主要是由于研究预设的限制条件，即只分析一个网站的一级和二级网页以获取第一手概览信息。总体而言，未来的研究将关注更多行业、源语言为其他语言的本地化英语网站以及网站文本随时间更替的演变情况，将纵向和横向比较结合。此外，未来的研究在对较大数据集进行预处理时，将引入文本自动标记工具。

一、导航文本——网站规约的支柱

组织网站最重要的常规特征之一是版块标题中的导航文本，对相关网站版块给出简要的描述。对于像“关于我们”“联系我们”和“新闻”这样的常规版块，网站访问者在点击文本链接之前就已经对即将看到的内容有所了解，或者说已形成“通用心理模型”（Nielsen，Tahir 2012）。正如标题有助于文章其余部分展开切题论证一样，版块标题点明了相应版块中的内容文本的核心主题。因此，对于导航文本的分析，目前的研究主要关注代表导航文本的版块标题，因为版块标题在不同级别的网页中普遍存在，并且与内容文本密切相关。通过比较可以确定两种类型的版块：一种用于表征不同行业的组织网站，可以称之为行业特定的网站版块，另一种用于表征整个组织网站，可以称为组织特定的网站版块。表 5-1 列出了目前研究中确定的行业特定和组织特定的网站版块。这些版块是本研究涉及的大多数本地化和非本地化网站所共有的。

表 5-1 行业特定和组织特定的网站版块

<table>
<tr><th>网站版块
行业类型</th><th>行业特定</th><th>组织特定</th></tr>
<tr><td>语言服务提供商</td><td>What We Do (Services)
Technology
Featured Client Solutions
Industry Blogs and Resources</td><td rowspan="5">About Us
Contact Us
Join Us
News and Events
Legal Notices (e. g. , privacy policy, terms and conditions of use, and disclaimer)</td></tr>
<tr><td>电子商务</td><td>Product Classification
Deals
Help
Call for Partners</td></tr>
<tr><td>大学</td><td>Academics
Admissions
Campus Life
Call for Donations</td></tr>
<tr><td>政府</td><td>Education
Feedback
FAQ</td></tr>
<tr><td>旅游目的地</td><td>Recommended Activities
Accommodation
Routes and Tours
Neighborhoods</td></tr>
</table>

如表 5-1 所示，行业特定的网站版块能提示网站的行业类型；只要浏览行业特定的网站版块，就基本可以判断拥有该版块的网站所属的行业。在本研究中，一个值得注意的行业部门是语言服务提供商，其行业特定版块很可能与当前研究未涉及的其他服务行业部门有所重叠。此外，政府网站所特有的版块并不一定提示了政府特定的网站规约，这意味着政府网站尚未出现明显的常规化。组织特定的网站版块可以被视为组织网站的基本组成部分，因此可以为组织网站的内容规划提供很好的参考。不过，值得注意的是，不同的组织网站的“关于我们”版块可能在主题方面存在差异。未来的研究将提升数据集规模，对行业特定的网站版块进行行业内分析，追踪某个版块内容随时间演变的情况，或

对组织特定的网站版块进行跨行业分析，探索更多的行业和组织的网站文本特点。

还有一些网站其他文本特征可以用于进一步研究。首先，我们可以对更大数据集的主页导航提示“Home”的存在与否进行统计检验；MANOVA 检验也适用于分类因变量。同样，也可以对冗余链接的存在与否进行 MANOVA 检验，冗余链接可以定义为组织网站的一个共同特征，其中指向位于页面顶部的重要版块的链接通常会以不同的措辞再次出现在页面底部，以便再次争取访客的关注。最后，未来的研究也可以探索导航文本采用的语法形式分类，从而为本地化实践提供参考。

关于可比网站版块标题的实际措辞，本研究涉及的本地化网站和非本地化网站并未发现太大差异，即使是非本地化网站组内比较，在许多网站版块的标题措辞方面也存在很大差异。通过分组比较，可以确定四种以上介绍网站版块的方式（参见附录 B-E）。大学是导航文本标准化程度最高的行业部门。这在某种程度上表明，尽管有些网站版块已经常规化，但网站版块的文本呈现情况仍然因网站而异，不拘本地化与否。未来的定性分析可以继续记录描述网站版块的不同方式，并通过案例研究讨论在特定版块中选择某种表达方式的原因。

二、内容文本——规约初现

由于缺乏相关文献，导航文本的定量分析本是在没有前人研究参考的情况下完成的。与之不同的是，本研究分析的内容文本特征均来自之前的我国网站汉英翻译研究。其中两个文本特征——平均句长以及第一和第二人称句子所占比重——在本地化和非本地化网站组的比较中呈现出统计学上的显著差异，尤其是包括大学在内的几个行业。在国外的学术刊物中，关于中英语言对比的网站本地化和翻译的相关文献极为少见，未来的研究将参考关于翻译和非翻译英语文本比较的文献，进一步探索具有可操作性的网站文本特征。另一方面，未来的研究可以将来自英语非第一语言国家/地区的组织的英语网站与中美同业英语网站进行比较。下一步计划选择研究的一种源语言是日语，与印欧语系相比，它被认为更接近汉语，另一种是法语或德语，从欧洲语言的语言距离角度看，法语和德语应该是两种相对接近英语的主要语言（Elms 2008）。

另一个与内容文本相关的研究课题是明确英语变体的特征。如果美国组织的英文网站代表美国英语，那么非英语国家组织的英文网站代表什么样的英语？

未来的研究可以基于全球英语分类的特征研究①，评估全球组织的英文网站并探索现象背后的成因。

第三节 分析框架

未来的研究不仅需要为当前的分析框架增加细节和提升复杂度，引入本章第一节和第二节建议的更多特征，而且还必须让网站用户参与网站评估。可以根据网站产品的实证研究结果，规划和组织用户调查和焦点小组，用户研究获得的数据也会为面向产品的研究提供信息。

未来以产品为导向的研究还有必要超越计算机端网站媒介的局限，紧跟科技发展新趋势。随着手机端应用程序和有针对性的市场营销的发展，今天的组织还可以通过移动友好型网站和新闻通信来接触潜在客户，这些与时俱进的交流形式都是感受组织话语脉搏值得关注的研究课题。不过，"传统"的计算机网站是一个很好的起点，因为组织网站的移动端版本大多是其计算机端版本的概要或摘录。"不断发展的技术向我们抛出一个又一个刁钻的挑战，掌控我们的内容变得比以往任何时候都更加重要，无论内容在哪里，无论内容为谁服务。"(Halvorson, Rach 2012；笔者翻译)。

第四节 网站分析是产学研跨界合作的沃土——从"内容生产"到"内容策略"

从商业角度看，内容的定义（Halvorson, Rach 2012）是网站、应用程序、内联网或任何其他传播工具包含或交流的关键信息。内容创作本身并不是目的，遵循和实践统一的内容策略才是目的。内容策略指导我们创建、交付和治理内容的计划（Halvorson, Rach 2012）。制定内容策略需要组织中多个甚至所有团队的协作，这同样适用于组织网站的情况。广义而言，网站内容可以定义为在网站上发布的帮助读者和企业的任何内容（Fenton, Lee 2014）。作为语言和视觉效果的专业人士，网站内容的创建者和编辑者需要与其他组织单位密切合作，包括但不限于营销、传播、IT 和用户体验，以协商和协调不同利益相关者的期望

① HICKEY. R. Studying Varieties of English [EB/OL]. [2023-07-18].

和不同的关注重点。在网络上展示企业形象时，不应将文字和语言问题视为可以最后进行的回顾思考。相反，内容的规划、实施和审查应作为组织传播持续改进周期的一个有机组成部分，实时应对解决。

随着世人对内容和内容策略的日益关注，可以预见未来将有更多令人兴奋的机会，将教学与研究联系起来，弥合学术界和工业界之间的差距。例如，学习网络创作和网站本地化课程的学生可以学习内容审核的一般程序和指导原则（对所有当前发布的未来内容进行定量和定性审计，将所有详细信息记录在电子表格中；参见 Halvorson，Rach 2012）。具备理论知识后，学生可以练习完成设计流程（引导读者完成任务的一系列屏幕展示；参见 Fenton，Lee 2014），在真实或虚构网站上运行用户测试，采访行业从业者或阅读和讨论相关采访，在实践中对理论有更清晰的认识。通过调查在职专业人士对自己任职的组织的不同理解以及努力实现的企业形象，学生们参与了“组织人类学工作”（Fenton，Lee 2014）。未来与网站内容有关的课堂可以期待语言和非语言专业学生的共同参与，因为文本和非文本特征在网站上共存并相互作用，这需要不同学科合作学习，这与 Kiraly（2000）的社会建构主义模型相呼应。通过使用真实的材料和情景项目练习团队合作技能（Gouadec 2007），学生将学会理解有关内容创建和开发的实用观点，从而有利于他们的职业规划和未来的职业生涯。在以真实语言材料和分析结果为网页设计和创作课程提供教学素材的同时，网站本地化产品的实证研究结果可以为互联网语言学的研究以及网站内容开发的行业实践提供反馈，进而为相关学术培训和本地化教育提供参考。正如希门尼斯-克雷斯波（2013a：186）所预言的，这样的良性循环可以“提供本地化能力习得的最佳框架（笔者翻译）”。

大多数关于内容策略的作品都避开了多语内容方面的讨论。作为使用两种或多种语言的专业人士，本地化和翻译从业者可以在与业务中的其他职能团队合作开发、实施和审查国际组织的内容战略中，探索职业发展新的可能性。继语言项目经理之后，内容策略师极有可能成为下一个有前途的语言和翻译专业的职业选择。

第五节　本章小结

人们往往会忽略网站的语言方面，这与软件产品的情况类似，因为可以客观地评估网站的功能方面，因此网站本地化的过程被视为与工业制造类似

(Dunne 2006)。本研究重点关注组织网站的文本和语言，以期抵消上述趋势，呼吁关注网络体裁中广泛存在的文本、话语和传播问题（Jiménez Crespo 2013a)。

总体而言，在本研究涉及的一些文本特征方面，本地化和非本地化组织网站之间存在显著差异。本研究还发现，网站文本表现出的一些特征受到行业和本地化概况的影响。然而，如果就此得出一个行业的本地化或非本地化网站的某些文本语言特征已经常规化的结论，似乎过于仓促。考虑到当前研究采用了便利抽样策略，研究人员将在未来的研究中采取结构更加均衡的抽样策略。

同样重要的发现是，与非本地化的同业网站相比，一些选定的本地化网站，特别是大学、政府和旅游目的地等行业的网站，需要重新设计和建构。目前的研究发现了以下常见问题：链接失效，英文版网站加载速度慢，网页文件命名方式无法满足定期检索和更新的要求。然而，如果就此认为本地化网站不如非本地化网站，并且不假思索地全盘接受“本地化产品应呈现被目标地区所接受的本土外观和感受”的本地化箴言，将是相当草率的。我们需要将批判性思维应用于网站本地化，理由有二。首先，在当前研究中，并非所有的非本地化网站本身在文本特征和共有版块的标题方面都是标准化或常规化的。因此，网站本地化人员最好选择一个或多个基准网站，再根据具体情况开展用户需求分析。其次，应仔细考虑将所有“非本土”或对目标市场陌生的内容剔除出本地化网站的做法。一个典型的例子是大学、政府和旅游目的地的本地化网站上最常见的内容词之一——“中国”。相比之下，在当前研究的美国组织的网站上很少能找到包括“美国”在内的国名。然而，如果只是简单地有样学样，删去本地化网站上的“中国”一词，只会失去在推广国家特色方面的独特竞争优势。

目前的研究提出并实施了用于本地化和非本地化网站文本的多维比较的分析框架，并将定量和定性数据分析与描述和推论统计分析方法相结合。以目前的研究为基础，配备完善的方法，未来的研究将涉及更多的行业部门，并在更深层次上运用文本提取方法，从而深入了解投影到网络空间的产业集群，最终得窥门径，找到通往组织机构世界之门的钥匙。

第六章

本研究对我国英语课程思政教学的启示

关于中美组织网站文本的对比研究，为我国英语课程思政教学提供了重要启示——不同学段的英语教师可以充分利用丰富的网站资源，去芜存菁，结合课程标准，提炼契合本学段学习难度的思政元素和内核，引导学生在自主探索的过程中培养信息素养和思辨能力，通过团队协作完成综合性研学项目，全方位提升语言能力、学习能力和人际交往能力。本章引介并评析了面向英语教育全学段的网络探究式项目案例，旨在为英语学科育人探索有效途径提供参考。

第一节　我国英语课程思政及相关研究综述

课程思政于2014年首次提出，是指充分利用课堂教学主渠道，努力发掘课程自身蕴含的思想政治教育元素，坚持有机融合和春风化雨的原则，在系统、科学地讲授知识的同时，有意识地开展理论传播、思想引领、价值引导、精神塑造和情感激发的教育方式（张荣军、汤云晴 2020）。在英语教育中实施课程思政，是要把立德树人的教育任务渗透到英语教学各个环节，使课程思政有效融入英语教育教学全过程，从而实现育人的最终目的。

英语作为年轻学子接触外国思想和文化的窗口课程，亟须引导学生辩证理性地看待中外异同。经济全球化、文化多元化和传播媒介的迅猛发展不断地丰富当代青少年儿童的生活，同时也极大地影响着他们的思想意识。当代学子的世界观、人生观、价值观正处于形成时期，他们涉世未深，缺乏辨识力，无法辩证地思考新时期出现的各种矛盾和问题。因此，英语课程有必要引入社会主义核心价值观教育，重视对学生文化、道德、价值等方面的引领。

目前，关于英语课程思政的研究主要集中在实现路径的探讨，关注学段集中在中学和大学。相关教学研究主要探讨如何从教材和教学内容中提炼出思政元素，解决“教什么”的问题；在教学过程中通过精心设计教师提问和学生讨论等课堂活动，充分发挥思政教学培根铸魂的作用，即解决“怎么教”的问题。探索科学高效的英语课程思政实践形式，检验其实践效果方面，一些研究者已经有所突破。例如，英语课程思政建设的六大要素（黄国文、肖琼 2021）why、what、who、when、where 和 how，为英语课程思政建设提供了明确的思路。本章主要从网络语料库辅助英语教学的研究视角出发，引介并评析适合英语教育全学段的网络探究式项目案例，基于网络真实语料，以学生为中心，以输出型任务为导向，抛砖引玉，以期为彰显思政元素和内涵的教学内容和教学形式设计引入新的视角。

第二节 语料库辅助英语教学的相关研究综述

随着信息技术的快速发展，语料库越来越多地应用于我国外语教学实践。语料库是根据语言研究的目的，有计划、有针对性地收集并用电子形式保存的大量自然语言材料。随着计算机技术在教育教学领域的深入应用，语料库作为一门重要的语言研究科学逐渐发展起来，成为集语言学、计算机学、应用语言学、计算机语言学等多学科交叉而成的科学。国内语料库辅助英语教学研究已初具规模，研究主题涉及了学习者语料库、口语语料库、平行语料库、课堂话语语料库等多个领域，但基于语料库的英语课程思政教育研究还很薄弱。

语料库在英语教学中的运用转变了学生对英语学习活动本身的认识，语言输出不是为了接近标准答案，而是通过真实语料的对比、讨论去发现并解决语言使用存在的问题。近年来国内外学者结合英语教学实践，不断提出基于语料库的英语教学应用范例（宋云霞、张大伟、孙卓等，2011；张林影 2020；甄凤超 2020）。这些研究的共同点是从教学实践出发，探索如何将语料库的丰富语料和便捷的检索工具等优势服务于教学目标，并注重发挥语料库在培养学生的自主学习能力上的作用。目前，英语课程思政教学缺乏可供推广的语料库应用案例和教学模式。

与大规模语料库相比，网络语料更新速度快，具有开放性、即时性、灵活性等特点，是一种较易推广普及的高校英语课堂教学模式，故本章第四节通过引介基于网络语料的全学段教学案例，探索网络语料在英语思政教学领域的应用，为英语课程思政建设实践提供理论依据和实例参考。

第三节 网络语料库辅助英语课程思政教学的总体思路

语料库语言学自身存在一定的局限性，即语料库中发现的语言现象只在这个语料库里是真实的，却不能代表普遍的语言现象（McEnery, Xiao, Tono 2006: 103）。传统定义的语料库里所包含的数据是固定的，也就是建造者已经收集好并且给予分类的。而新型的语料库，如网络语料库，才是本书关注的重点。有学者（Kilgarriff, Grefenstette 2003: 333）对“网络作为语料库”（Web as Corpus）的概念进行了阐释，他们设想在语言学家的处理下，网络如何更有效地被使用而不是仅限于目前搜索引擎的范畴。

网络可以成为语言数据的重要来源，因为它体量巨大，囊括了许多不同类型的语言资源。然而，网络不像传统意义上的语料库，有良好的设计和周密的构造。语言学家应该致力于实际问题“所选择的语料库 x 是否对所研究的语言现象 y 有利”，而不是集中于本体论问题——“什么是语料库”（Kilgarriff, Grefenstette 2003: 333）。因此，语料库研究应该引入更具开放性的定义，在研究语言现象时，语料库只是一个文本的集合，而其他很多附加条件都不是必需的（Kilgarriff, Grefenstette 2003: 333）。除此之外，在计算机语言学和自然语言输出两个领域，科学家们分别以非常实际的观点定义了语料库，他们声称人们一般根据一定的研究范围，从语料库中收集一定量的数据，而不是关注它是如何建立的。拥有更多发展方向的数据通常比均衡性的考虑更有意义（Kilgarriff, Grefenstette 2003: 333）。

对语料库的开放性定义，是本章将网络资源作为真实语言资料的主要动因。然而，在探索网络语料用于英语教学的过程中，反对将网络作为语料库的声音也不容忽视。不能把网络用作语料库的最明显的理由之一就是网络并没有语料库的代表性（Kilgarriff, Grefenstette 2003: 340），对此质疑的具体回应如下：首先，固定语料库并不具有代表性。特别是固定语料库不能区分语言活动的接受和输出，如说话和写作的活动。进一步说，固定语料库里的说话活动与写作活动不在同一层次。其次，似乎很难区分背景语言和复制语言。所以人造语料库也不具有代表性。但必须承认对将网络作为语料库而言，“版本类型”被认为是一个无法解决的难题。网络并不具有全面的代表性，但至少网络能代表语言的实际以及真实的使用情况。

此外，搜索引擎结果存在以下问题（Kilgarriff, Grefenstette 2003: 340）：首

先，不能展示足够的例子。同样，每个例子也不能展示足够的内容。其次，网络搜索引擎不能用于搜索符合语言学标准如词类等特性的语言学信息。再次，网络搜索引擎搜到的结果是根据被曲解了的标准所选择的。最后，搜索引擎计数具有不稳定性和任意性。由于搜索引擎负载和其他因素，包含特定语言现象的网页往往会发生变化，因此根据数据所产生的统计结果是不可靠的。

在未来，语料库语言学家会继续探索和发展可以在网络中搜索特殊的词型和文体的方法。搜索引擎将不断优化，以满足语言学家的需要。简而言之，未来网络将成为语言学研究的语料库。

综上所述，网络作为语料库能够提供丰富的语言学习资料，主题内容与时俱进，完全能够满足提高英语教学内容多元化和丰富度的要求。然而，考虑到技术发展现状，网络资源使用尚存在较大的局限性，英语教育实践者不能在不加甄别的情况下对网络语料全盘接受，而必须紧密结合教材重点和课程标准，以课程思政为纲，精心筛选组织网络语料，将真实语料有机地融入教学实践。

依托网络语料的多模态属性，本章第四节关注的各学段网络探究式项目教学案例通过音视频、文本、图片动画等多种语言素材形式，真实反映语言在语音、语义、语用等方面的全貌，为学生构建全方位接触和使用英语的语言学习环境。学生个人独力或小组合作完成多个任务，产出最终项目成果，旨在达成任务型英语教学法培养语言输出能力和团队协作能力的目标。

第四节　各学段教案示例及简析

本书介绍的教案形式均为网络探究项目，选取网络语料作为英语学习的真实材料，鼓励学生运用高阶思维能力解决实际问题。教案编号格式统一为“n_1~n_2”，其中n_1表示学段，取值范围为1~6。1 表示3~4 年级，2 表示5~6 年级，3 表示7~9 年级，4 表示高中，5 表示大学（含研究生），6 表示英语专业；n_2表示各学段内的教案编号。

各案例均由内容分析、实施过程、案例评析和辅助资源四部分组成。“内容分析”概括了案例的教学主题和目标；“实施过程”分步介绍了案例的具体实现过程，为便于教师读者在英语课堂教学中参考，其用中文简述每一步骤的主要内容，用英文详述教师在课堂上介绍的具体内容和相关要求。为统一不同学段的表述，项目成果的评价标准均用中文列出，供教师评分参考和学生在项目进行过程中比照；“案例评析”解读案例的设计意图，提出了在课堂实践中拓展改编的思路；"辅助资源"列出了与案例项目关系最为密切的参考资源，考虑到网站链接具有时效性，未列出具体网站，教师可以根据资源类别，自行检索最新的相关网站，整理后可作为初级学习者的指定学习资料，或作为推荐给中高级学习者的参考资料。

本书案例的教学目标的确定主要基于教育部印发的《义务教育英语课程标准（2022年版）》以及《中国英语能力等级量表》(2018)，面向义务教育阶段（一至九年级）的案例教学目标设计主要参照前者，后者则是高中、大学阶段英语（含大学英语和研究生英语）和英语专业案例建设的重要参考。

一、3~4 年级

（一）教学案例 1-1　色彩黑皮书：我们的五感（2 课时）

项目主题：The black book of colours：Feeling through our senses

该主题属于"人与自我"和"人与社会"范畴，涉及"身边的事物与环境""个人喜好与情感表达"和"同伴交往，相互尊重，友好互助"子主题。

1. 内容分析

本案例的重点是通过故事《色彩的黑皮书》(*The black book of colours*) 来学习如何在没有视觉的情况下"看见"。此外，还可以复习有关感受和五感的词汇并了解看待事物的不同方式。和本书介绍的所有案例一样，本案例的主要目标是通过与儿童故事相关的概念和信息通信技术来改进英语课程教学。本案例涉及的概念有：视角——人们理解信息的方式各有不同；联系——人类所有的五感都是相通的；反思——有不同的认知方式；形式——可以通过不同方式观察到一切事物具备的特征。

眼睛告诉我们颜色。但如果你是盲人呢？你还能认识颜色吗？

《色彩黑皮书》展示了如何在没有视觉的情况下去"看"世界，以此来了解五感（听觉、嗅觉、味觉、触觉和视觉）以及它们引发的感觉和感受。

此外，它使学生拥有一段通常只有盲人读者才能经历的体验，从而能够设身处地为盲人着想。

2. 实施过程

学生需要逐一完成根据《色彩的黑皮书》的情景和人物设计的任务：

(1) 任务一——How would you react if you were blind?

学生假设自己是盲童 Tomas，思考以下问题：如果失明，会有什么反应/感觉？和同学大声说出对这个问题的看法，全班一起讨论。

然后，全班做一个游戏：两人一组，一个是盲人（用围巾遮住眼睛），另一个是引导盲人绕过各种障碍物的导盲犬。

学生完成游戏后，再次讨论之前的问题，看看学生的回答是否有所改变。

（2）任务二——Stimulation：Feeling *The Black Book of Colours*.

教师引导学生用味觉、听觉、嗅觉和触觉来阅读《色彩的黑皮书》。全班围成一圈坐下，用围巾蒙住眼睛。

在阅读时，教师将代表故事所讲述内容的不同物品在班级内传递。例如："According to Tomas，yellow tastes like mustard"（味觉）"But it is as soft as chick's feathers"（触觉）——每个孩子都会触摸到一点芥末和一些羽毛。"Brown cracks under his steps when the leaves are dry"（听觉）"It smells like chocolate"（嗅觉）——学生可以揉碎一些叶子，获得听觉体验，然后全班传递一杯热巧克力来闻一闻。完成阅读后将进行任务三，这是一个与五感有关的活动。

（3）任务三——Participation：Using your senses.

本活动需要学生继续蒙住眼睛，使用自己的五感。

举例说明如下：

味觉：学生们会尝到不同的味道（芥末、番茄酱、柠檬和巧克力），他们需要猜测味道，甜的、酸的、咸的还是苦的。

嗅觉：学生会闻到装有咖啡、大蒜、薰衣草和橙子的玻璃杯，他们需要猜闻的是什么。

触觉：学生会触摸砂纸、丝绸、棉花和海绵等材料，猜测摸的是什么。

听觉：教师给学生播放录音，如鸟、雨、汽车和烹饪的声音，让学生猜是什么物体或动作发出的声音。

（4）任务四——看图匹配活动。

为复习在本单元学到的词汇，学生将用计算机或平板电脑完成图片匹配活动，在该活动中，学生需要将五感与其适用的不同对象和情景一一对应。可以单人或两人组队完成。

（5）总结性活动：讨论与自评。

本活动是对之前活动的反思，学生先对自己在完成四项任务时的自信程度分别打分，给分范围为1-3，1为最低，3为最高。然后，全班围坐在一起，讨论并回答以下问题：

- How did you feel when you were a blind person?
- How did you feel during the reading of the tale?
- Was it difficult to guess the objects presented without seeing them?

- What would you do/feel if you couldn't use the principal sense for the objects in the matching activity?

（6）项目成果评价标准如表 6-1 所示。

表 6-1 教学案例 1-1 项目成果评价表

	1-待行动	2-待进步	3-合格	4-优秀	得分
故事理解	学生能够用基本的方式理解故事的某些部分	学生能够从故事中找出一些细节，给出具体的例子	学生能够使用故事中的具体例子来反映问题并支持其观点	学生能够专注于故事的重要细节，理解其中的寓意，并利用这些信息表达自己的观点	
确定中心思想、寓意或经验教训	学生无法理解故事的寓意 词汇的理解	学生能够以基本的方式理解故事的寓意	学生能够通过具体的例子理解故事的寓意	学生能够通过例子、意见和支持性的想法来理解故事的寓意	
词汇的理解	学生无法记住所学的词汇或仅仅几个单词	学生能够记住所学的词汇，但难以理解其含义	学生能够记住所学的词汇及其含义	学生能够记住和使用所学的词汇及其含义，并在词汇和含义之间建立联系	
识别相同点和不同点	对可识别性能特征的描述体现了初级水平	对可识别性能特征的描述有待进步	对可识别性能特征的描述体现了熟练水平	对可识别性能特征的描述体现了最高水平	

续表

	1-待行动	2-待进步	3-合格	4-优秀	得分
使用信息通信技术	学生使用计算机和完成图片匹配活动有困难	学生可以在指导下使用计算机和完成图片匹配活动	学生能够正确使用计算机和完成图片匹配活动	学生能够完美地使用计算机和完成图片匹配活动	
合作情况	学生不能很好地与他人合作	学生有一些与他人合作的问题，但试图克服这些问题	学生能够与他人合作，分享自己的意见并考虑同学的意见	学生与他人完美合作，帮助他人，以实现目标为目的解决分歧	
表达想法、感受和意见	学生无法表达自己的想法、感受和意见	学生能够以基本的方式表达自己的想法、感受和意见	学生能够表达自己的想法、感受和意见，并给出广泛的答案	学生能够通过支持性的想法和广泛的答案来表达自己的想法、感受和意见。同时始终积极参与	

3. 案例评析

通过体验五感，学生可以训练表达不同感受的语言能力，同时有机会更加细致地感知周围的环境。此外，通过体验失去视觉的生活，学生能够体会盲人或残障人士日常生活的不易，培养包容心和同理心。此案例还可以进一步拓展，引入为残障人士设计公共活动空间的活动，引导学生友爱互助，成长为有责任有担当的社会人。

4. 辅助资源

（1）英文绘本《色彩的黑皮书》。

（2）用于引导学生体验味觉、嗅觉、触觉的物品和体验听觉的音频，可以是绘本上介绍的物品，也可以选取其他物品。

（3）用于完成图片匹配练习的电子设备。

（二）教学案例 1-2　体验……的一天（4 课时）

项目主题：Experiencing a Day in the Life of...

该主题属于“人与自我”和“人与社会”范畴，涉及“家庭与家庭生活”“学校、课程、学校生活与个人感受”等子主题。

1. 内容分析

在本案例中，学生将选择一个国家进行研究。学生将从居住在该国家/地区的同年级学生的角度出发，展示自己发现的信息。学生将谈论当地儿童的日常生活、衣着和饮食、学校、责任、传统等。鼓励学生以创造性的方式展示了解到的信息，例如，穿着该国的传统服饰，或者制作他国的土特产，并与我国的同类情况进行对比。

2. 实施过程

（1）引入教学主题。

Have you ever thought about what it might be like to live a day in the life of a person from another part of the world?

With this activity, you will research what life is like in another country with a group of friends in your class.

You and your group will act as though you were children living in that country and present what you have found out about the country to the class with a poster or a web page.

（2）教师介绍任务内容。

学生四人一组，自行选择要展示的国家，或从老师指定的名单中选择。介绍那个国家的孩子的日常生活，回答以下问题：

-他们吃什么食物？

-他们穿什么样的衣服？

-他们如何上学？

-他们在家做什么家务？

-他们的家是什么样的？

与同伴一起制作海报或网页，像自己生活在那个国家一样，给全班同学展示自己找到的信息。小组成员共同制作海报或网页，向全班展示其他国家的信息，就好像是生活在当地的儿童一样。使用诸如“I'm from ...”和“In my country, I ...”之类的句子。课堂展示鼓励创新，例如，可以把自己制作的当地食物分享给大家，或者像当地人那样穿戴。

（3）回顾活动：课堂讨论。

教师引导学生小组开展讨论，探讨我国成人和儿童日常生活的异同，发现他国儿童与我国儿童日常生活的相同点和不同点，各组向全班汇报各自的发现。教师展示我国现代生活的图片和视频，引导学生正确看待各国差异，培养学生的民族自豪感和爱国热情。讨论问题举例：

Now, what do you think adults do in your country? How is that the same as what the children do, and how is that different?

How does what we do in China compare to what people in other countries around the world do?

（4）项目成果评价标准如表 6-2 所示。

表 6-2 教学案例 1-2 项目成果评价表

	1-待行动	2-待进步	3-合格	4-优秀	得分
关于食物的情况介绍	项目没有提到食物	项目提到了食物，但没有进一步的细节	描述了该国的食物类型	详细描述了指定国家的食物类型以及食物制备过程	
关于服饰的情况介绍	项目没有提到服饰	项目提到了服饰，但没有进一步的细节	描述了该国的服装类型	详细描述了衣服外观以及穿着场合	
关于学校的情况介绍	项目没有提到学校	项目提到了学校，但没有进一步的细节	描述了学校	详细描述了上学日和儿童在校时长	

续表

	1-待行动	2-待进步	3-合格	4-优秀	得分
关于家务的情况介绍	项目没有提到家务	项目提到了家务，但没有进一步的细节	描述了该国家庭生活通常涉及的家务	详细描述家庭常见家务，并说明一般由谁负责完成哪些家务	
关于居住环境的情况介绍	项目没有提到住宅	项目提到了住宅，但没有进一步的细节	描述了住宅及其外观	详细描述了住宅、外观以及居住者	
海报或网页	没有海报或网页	海报或网页包含的该国信息仅有三条或更少	海报或网页至少包含五条该国信息	海报或网页包含至少十条有关该国的详细信息	
课堂展示	没有课堂展示	有课堂展示，但没有图片或视频来吸引注意	展示在视觉上令人愉悦，展示者大声分享 75% 的信息	展示在视觉上令人愉悦，展示者大声分享所有信息	

3. 案例评析

学生通过自主探索发现，了解世界各地儿童的日常生活，同时学习了如何用英语介绍自己的日常生活。教师引导学生正确看待各国差异，在培养文化意识的同时，增强学生的民族自豪感和爱国热情。

4. 辅助资源

（1）教师指导学生通过书籍和网络寻找信息，如 Kids Around the World 网站介绍各国儿童的日常生活等情况。

（2）学生还可以参考网上的模板，利用 graphic organizers（图形化组织工具）组织信息和构思。

（三）教学案例 1-3 帝王蝶迁徙记（4 课时）

项目主题：Monarch Migration

该主题属于“人与自然”范畴，涉及“常见的动物，动物的特征与生活环境”子主题。

1. 内容分析

作为春季主题的一部分，本案例将探索北美帝王蝶的迁徙路径。在此过程中，学生将学习蝴蝶的生命周期，了解帝王蝶的外观以及它们如何保持体温。本主题旨在学习季节、天气、南北和中外地理。

2. 实施过程

（1）引入教学主题（教师可以展示帝王蝶图片让学生猜）。

To find the Monarchs, we need to know some things first.

What do Monarch Butterflies look like? Do they always look the same? When do they change?

Where do Monarch Butterflies live? Do they always live in the same place?

Why do Monarchs migrate? Where do they go? How long do they stay?

（2）Listen and Learn（观看 Monarchy Butterfly Song 儿歌音乐视频并回答关于帝王蝶的一般性问题）。

What do you know about monarchs?

（3）Make your butterfly（教师给学生展示帝王蝶的图片，然后学生独立或和同伴合作画出或制作蝴蝶）。

（4）How happy are you with your Monarch?

（自制蝴蝶完成后，教师引导学生关注帝王蝶的外观特征）

Is it orange and black?

Does it have 4 wings?

Does it have a body?

Does it have antenae?

（5）Caterpillar, Chrysalis, and Butterfly（观看 The Very Hungry Caterpillar 绘本视频，然后 ppt 展示帝王蝶从蛹到蝶的发育过程，引导学生了解帝王蝶的生命周期）。

（6）Migration.

（再次观看 Monarchy Butterfly Song 儿歌音乐视频并回答关于帝王蝶迁徙的问题）Where do the butterflies go?

（教师展示帝王蝶迁徙路线地图，解释帝王蝶迁徙原因）

Before the wintercomes the Monarchs Migrate to Mexico.

In Winter its too cold for the butterflies in Canada and the United States.

Mexico is down south. It is warmer there.

In spring and summer it gets warmer.

The Monarchs fly up North.

The go back to the United states and Canada.

（7）Make our maps（延伸活动：学生以帝王蝶为例，绘制地图，介绍我国一种动物的迁徙情况）。

（8）Review（回顾：回答问题）。

Do you know what Monarchs look Like?

Can you draw one?

What are its colors and body parts?

Do you know how a caterpillar becomes a butterfly?

What does a caterpillar look like? Can you draw one?

What does a caterpillar do to become a butterfly? Can you draw it?

What happens inside thecocoon?

What are the 4 seasons? Which one is the coldest?

What do the Monarchs do in autumn? Can you draw it?

What do the Monarchs do in winter? Can you draw it?

What do the Monarchs do in spring and summer? Can you draw it?

What else did you learn about Monarchs?

（9）项目成果评价标准如表6-3 所示。

表6-3　教学案例1-3 项目成果评价表

	1-待行动	2-待进步	3-合格	4-优秀	得分
认识帝王蝶的外观（颜色和身体部位）	基本不了解帝王蝶的外观，不知道各部位名称	了解帝王蝶外观的一些情况，知道一些部位名称	了解帝王蝶的外观，知道它的颜色和大部分部位名称	了解帝王蝶的外观，知道它的颜色和各部位名称	

续表

	1-待行动	2-待进步	3-合格	4-优秀	得分
认识变态发育过程（如何从蛹化蝶）	不了解帝王蝶从蛹化蝶的过程，不知道具体步骤和相关单词	基本了解帝王蝶从蛹化蝶的过程，知道一些相关单词	了解帝王蝶从蛹化蝶的过程，知道大部分具体步骤，并掌握大部分相关单词	了解帝王蝶从蛹化蝶的过程，知道具体步骤，并能用语言描述	
季节性迁徙	能说出一两个季节的单词，知道一两个季节特点	能说出四季的部分名称和一些特点，知道帝王蝶会飞往温暖的地方过冬	能说出四季名称和一些特点，知道帝王蝶会飞往温暖的地方过冬	了解四季有序且各不相同，并且清楚四季的区别，知道帝王蝶会飞往南方过冬	
独立完成学习任务	需要帮助，有时无法完成	在帮助下完成	能够独立完成大部分任务	能够独立完成	
团队协作	难以配合团队完成个人分工，总是需要帮助，在帮助他人或求助方面有困难	有时能够配合团队完成个人分工，有时能够帮助他人并向他人求助	基本能够配合团队完成个人分工，有时能够帮助他人并向他人求助	配合团队完成个人分工，能够帮助他人并向他人求助	

3. 案例评析

本案例属于英语和自然的跨学科实践活动，学生复习四季和方位相关词汇，练习用英语介绍帝王蝶的外观特征和季节性迁徙过程，同时了解美洲的地理概况以及一种美洲昆虫的迁徙和变态发育的习性。这些学习内容有助于培养学生的世界观和国际视野，提升科学素养。本案例可以进一步拓展：学生遵循相同的思路，介绍我国的一种迁徙动物或昆虫，在巩固语言知识技能的同时了解我国的幅员辽阔和地大物博，培养社会主义核心价值观。

4. 辅助资源

（1）帝王蝶相关图片。

（2）Monarchy Butterfly Song 儿歌音乐视频。

（3）帝王蝶迁徙路线地图。

（4）帝王蝶从蛹到蝶的发育过程。

（5）中外迁徙动物相关图片和/或视频。

（四）教学案例 1-4　凡·高的《星夜》（2 课时）

项目主题：The Famous Artwork “Starry Night” by Vincent Van Gogh

该主题属于“人与自我”和“人与社会”范畴，涉及“个人喜好与情感表达”和“文学、艺术与体育”子主题。

1. 内容分析

本项目旨在训练语言能力和培养艺术素养，引导学生了解著名画家文森特·凡·高和他最著名的艺术作品《星夜》的故事，进而对西方美术史初窥门径。在完成项目的过程中，学生能够发挥自己的创造力，对自己的想象力充满信心，同时还能学到 19 世纪西方美术史。和语言艺术一样，绘画艺术是一门鼓励独特性的学科，让学生可以用自己的方式表达自我，用自己最舒适的方式与外界沟通。

2. 实施过程

（1）引入教学主题：教师首先介绍文森特·凡·高及其成长背景和环境，展示 19 世纪拍摄的凡·高照片，再引导学生了解凡·高的著名画作《星夜》。教师将向学生展示真实的《星夜》临摹作品，并简要说明作品内涵。在介绍过程中，教师会通过提问了解学生对授课内容的理解情况。

（2）学生发挥想象力，画出自己心中的《星夜》，完成艺术活动后，在课堂上介绍自己的作品，说明其含义，并就课程体验撰写心得。

（3）在课程和艺术活动结束时，学生完成的《星夜》作品将挂在校园或教室里，他们将每人写半页学习心得，回顾自己学到的有关著名画家文森特·凡·高和他的《星夜》的内容。教师可以安排学生用五到十分钟的时间，分组讨论这位著名画家的故事的有趣之处以及他们最喜欢的情节。

（4）项目成果评价标准如表 6-4 所示。

表 6-4　教学案例 1-4 项目成果评价表

	1-待行动	2-待进步	3-合格	4-优秀	得分
课堂参与	完全没有参与，对课程不感兴趣	付出了一些努力，但很容易走神，未参与全程	付出了不少努力，但在课程结束前放弃，只在老师提问时有所参与	充分投入，认真完成艺术活动，对课程充满兴趣，积极回答问题	

3. 案例评析

儿童总是喜欢欣赏同学的艺术作品，了解其他同学对活动或课程的看法。这个关于艺术品的主题创作活动简单而有趣，任何孩子都会乐在其中。鼓励学生充分发挥自己的想象力进行创作，并用语言详细介绍自己的艺术创作，在训练语言表达能力的同时，有助于增强学生的自信心，提升其思维品质。

4. 辅助资源

教师需要事先制作关于凡·高生平与《星夜》的演示文稿，整合相关图片和/或动画视频；此外，还需要准备好儿童绘画常用的各类工具。

（五）教学案例 1-5　听故事（2 课时）

项目主题：Listen to a story

该主题属于“人与自我”和“人与社会”范畴，涉及“文学、艺术与体育”子主题。

1. 内容分析

学生通过多种方式学习一个故事：先观看视频，再阅读文字，最后完成练习。多角度接触故事可以扩大词汇量。同时，学生阅读寓言学习做人的道理，学习抵御贪欲的诱惑，理解独立思考的重要性。

2. 实施过程

（1）引入教学主题。

Do you like listening and reading story? It's a very good way to expand your vocabulary. Here I have an interesting story for you.

（2）学生用计算机或平板电脑完成故事同名游戏 The clever monkey，为学习故事做好准备。

（3）观看故事的视频，回答问题：Why couldn't the crocodile eat the monkey?

（4）阅读故事的文字版。

（5）阅读关于猴子习性的补充内容。

（6）完成关于故事的练习。

（7）教师引导学生回顾课程内容，讨论故事的寓意，教导学生知足常乐，鼓励学生分享自己听过的类似寓意的故事。

3. 案例评析

儿童故事总是用简单的语言和情节表达深刻的人生道理，在增添英语学习趣味的同时，闪烁着人生智慧的光芒，在孩子心中播下扬善抑恶的种子。本案例通过多角度学习哲理故事，启迪心智，培根铸魂。此形式可进一步推广，用于所有儿童故事或寓言故事的教学设计。

4. 辅助资源

（1）The clever monkey 故事同名游戏。

https：//learnenglishkids. britishcouncil. org/short-stories/the-clever-monkey

（2）The clever monkey 故事的视频。

https：//learnenglishkids. britishcouncil. org/short-stories/the-clever-monkey

（3）The clever monkey 故事的文字版。

https：//learnenglishkids. britishcouncil. org/sites/kids/files/attachment/short -stories-story-time-the-clever-monkey-transcript. pdf

（4）关于猴子习性的补充阅读材料。

https：//kids. britannica. com/kids/article/monkey/353485

（5）The clever monkey 故事的阅读理解练习。

https：//learnenglishkids. britishcouncil. org/sites/kids/files/attachment/short -stories-story-time-the-clever-monkey-worksheet. pdf

二、5~6 年级

（一）教学案例 2-1　健康食品与非健康食品（2 课时）

项目主题：Healthy and Unhealthy Food

该主题属于“人与自我”范畴，涉及“健康、文明的行为习惯与生活方式”子主题。

1. 内容分析

本案例以识别对健康有益和有害的食物为目的开展调查，让学生在探索过程中扩充饮食健康相关词汇，同时了解相关营养知识，通过饮食管理提升个人健康水平。

2. 实施过程

（1）导入性活动：用计算机或平板电脑完成在线练习（https://www.liveworksheets.com/bg10484vz），选出有益健康和妨害健康的食物。

（2）两人一组，用教师给定的单词（和/或规定不可说出的单词，即 Taboo Words）描述一种食物，在不说出食物名称的情况下，让全班同学猜。教师可以鼓励学生用给定的单词（Given Words）讲一个故事，给定的单词如 red，healthy，useful，sugar。

（3）两人一组，在图片中找出六种有益健康或妨害健康的食物，写出它们的名称。

（4）观看一段饮食健康的科普视频，然后在新的一组图片中找出有益健康或妨害健康的食物。

（5）根据食物图片，填写缺失的字母，把食物单词补全。

（6）教师展示儿童牙疼、头疼、肚子疼等漫画图片，引导学生思考：

What do you think? Are they OK? What is the problem?

（7）角色扮演活动：选择正确的单词补充完整医生和病人之间的对话，然后两人一组扮演医生和病人，练习对话，可以在给定对话的基础上自由发挥。

（8）单词复习活动 Disappearing Words：全屏展示今天的重点单词，然后单词逐个消失，到单词全部消失后，让学生尽可能多地回忆单词。还可以一次让多个单词同时消失。

（9）课堂展示：学生两人一组以 A Healthy Meal 为题，介绍健康饮食搭配，时长 5 分钟。

（10）项目成果评价标准如表 6-5 所示。

表 6-5 教学案例 2-1 项目成果评价表

	1-待行动	2-待进步	3-合格	4-优秀	得分
识别	未找到相应食物但付出了努力	找到 1~2 种相应食物	找到 3~4 种相应食物	找到 5~6 种相应食物	
对话填空	有部分空格未填	完成但出错且超时	完成但超时	准时完成	

续表

	1-待行动	2-待进步	3-合格	4-优秀	得分
课堂展示	未完成展示	展示内容形式枯燥	展示超时或较短	展示新颖有创意	

3. 案例评析

本案例集中展示了词汇学习练习和复习的活动，为学生构建单词使用的真实场景，通过不同练习方式接触单词。学习场景涉及健康饮食，有助于学生引导反思自己的生活方式，运用本案例学到的知识构建自己的健康生活，对自己的健康负责，就是对家庭负责，对社会负责。此形式可进一步推广，适用于学习任何主题意群的单词。

4. 辅助资源

（1）无文字的饮食图片若干。

（2）包含对应单词的饮食图片若干。

（3）包含不完整的对应单词的饮食图片若干。

（4）饮食单词若干。

（5）关于饮食健康的科普视频。

（6）儿童牙疼、头疼、肚子疼等漫画图片。

（7）不完整的医生与病人的对话文字。

（8）重点单词的幻灯片，单词可逐个或多个同时消失，用于复习活动。

（二）教学案例 2-2　了解同学（4 课时）

项目主题：Understanding Classmates

该主题属于“人与自我”和“人与社会”范畴，涉及“个人感受与见解，倾听、体谅他人，包容与宽容”子主题。

1. 内容分析

本案例以深入了解同学为目的开展调查，让学生在主动理解他人的过程中认识到大家的相同点多于不同点，团队合作应求同存异。学生为完成项目需要换位思考，积极了解自己的团队，定位自己在团队中的角色，与队友密切合作，为共同的目标努力，培养集体意识。

2. 实施过程

（1）背景介绍：学生 2~4 人一组，为城市的一个体育团队选定吉祥物。

Your city is going to be getting their very own [CHOOSE ONE SPORT] team.

The city is trying to decide on what the mascot for the team should be. It would be unfair to not include everyone from your great city in deciding what the mascot should be. The city wants the mascot to reflect the people of the city the team is from. Who could pick such a mascot, and this is were you come in!

You are the spokesperson for the newly foundedteam. You must pick a fellow classmate and learn all about them. I want you to learn their History, Culture, Differences, and Similarities. You will then give a presentation on the student you choose. Finally we will take all of our data and see how similar we all are! After we see our similarities we will accordingly pick A Mascot!

（2）选定研究对象：选择班上一名不熟悉的同学，了解他/她的情况，与自己的情况联系起来。

（3）开始研究：尽自己所能了解同学，并开始思考如何展示一个充满敬意和教育意义的项目，体现自己和同学的所有异同，以及如何使用这些异同点挑选吉祥物。在探索过程中，学生会意识到大家的相似之处多于不同之处，在图书馆或网上寻找更多关于背景文化及其影响的资源。

（4）提前规划：开始思考如何将收集到的信息呈现在演示平台上。学生可以选择 PowerPoint、Prezi 等任何平台。所展示的项目应该起到教育、启发和团结同学的作用。

（5）完成研究并制作项目：完成这一项目的前期数据收集工作的基本标准是“三个 10”——与同伴共同工作 10 个小时，开展 10 个小时的额外研究，确定 10 个同行评审的支撑性资源。下面，学生利用掌握的所有数据打造一份制作精美且鼓舞人心的演示文稿。学生需要做一个关于所调查的同学的演讲。通过所有演讲传达的信息，可以了解每个人的相似之处，并选择相应的吉祥物。

（6）演讲日：在正式展示前，根据评分标准对演讲做最后的修正。

（7）项目成果评价标准如表 6-6 所示。

表 6-6　教学案例 2-2 项目成果评价表

	1-待行动	2-待进步	3-合格	4-优秀	得分
时间日志	无时间日志记录。没有调查同学，对同学不了解	时间日志记录了基本信息。花 1 ~ 3 小时对同学做了一些调查。开始理解人与人之间的共同点	时间日志记录较好。花 3 ~ 5 小时调查同学。理解人与人之间的共同点	时间日志记录详细。花 5 ~ 10 小时调查同学。研究结果表明，人与人之间的共同点多于差异	
课堂展示	PowerPoint 或 Prezi 展示了基本内容，不清楚且无附加值	选定的展示平台为课堂展示增色，结构清楚，引人注目	演示长度和平台合适，制作精美，具有教育意义	演示平台带来附加值，制作精美，结构精巧，具有教育意义	
文字内容	日志、研究和演示文稿无可读性	日志、研究和演示文稿存在很多问题，但具有可读性	日志、研究和演示文稿存在 3 ~ 5 个问题，内容充实，不影响理解	内容非常充实，没有问题	
现实意义	观众未发现项目具有现实意义	观众了解到项目和现实世界之间的关联	促使观众思考项目的现实意义	项目可应用于校外的真实世界	

续表

	1-待行动	2-待进步	3-合格	4-优秀	得分
参与度	未做项目，未参与学习	参与了项目，认识到与同学之间的共同点，尊重彼此背景的差异	项目展示效果良好，对同学有了新的认识和尊重，开始考虑吉祥物的问题	项目充分体现了同学之间的相同点，根据相同点选定了吉祥物	
资源利用	未跟同学交流，未利用外部资源	跟同学有所交流 2~5 个同行评审的参考资源	花很多时间和同学交流，5 个同行评审的参考资源，为项目提供新观点	和同学密切交流 10 个同行评审的参考资源，为项目增值	

3. 案例评析

本案例让学生有机会了解他人，学习如何介绍同学的个人背景和经历，在介绍他人的过程中训练语言表达能力。团队吉祥物的设计需要发掘团队成员的共同点，各小组为完成项目需要求同存异，增强团队凝聚力，可以锻炼学生与人合作的能力。本案例可推广用于在教学过程中加强团队建设。

4. 辅助资源

（1）知名团队吉祥物的参考资料。

（2）记录团队合作进程的时间日志范例。

（三）教学案例 2-3　《夏洛特的网》：友谊与词汇学习（4 课时）

项目主题：*Charlotte's Web*：a Study of Friendship and Vocabulary

该主题属于“人与自我”和“人与社会”范畴，涉及“文学、艺术与体育”和“个人感受与见解，倾听、体谅他人，包容与宽容”子主题。

1. 内容分析

本案例以理解友谊的内涵和词汇学习为教学目标，通过学习《夏洛特的网》选段，让学生在自主探索过程中从不同角度接触新词汇，在扩充词汇的同时体会友谊的真谛，学习如何获得友谊。

2. 实施过程

（1）教师在课前布置学生自行阅读《夏洛特的网》绘本版。

（2）导入：教师介绍故事写作背景，通过提问了解学生对故事的理解情况。

Charlotte's Web was described by its author, E. B. White, as "a story of friendship and salvation on a farm." Since we've already read the book, we know about the friendship that grows between Wilbur, a runty pig, and Charlotte, a heroic spider.

E. B. White (Elwyn Brooks White) was born in New York in 1899. He worked as a writer, reporter, and editor. He wrote both Charlotte's Web (1952) and The Trumpet of the Swan (1970). In both books, the animals display human qualities as they talk and act like people. Mr. White also wrote Stuart Little.

（3）教师选取第10章的片段，介绍选段背景，带领学生阅读理解。该故事片段涉及单词humble的定义，由此引入单词训练任务。

In Chapter X, Charlotte weaves the word "Humble" onto a web to describe Wilbur.

（4）单词训练任务：

首先，书写多遍；其次，根据该单词画画；最后，搜索在线字典，列出humble的三条定义，写一个带有humble的句子，写出humble三个近义词。

（5）单词的情景式使用练习：教师引导学生说出一位humble的同学，并用例子说明。

（6）发散式思维训练：教师鼓励学生小组头脑风暴，想出尽可能多的描述人物性格品质的形容词，想得最多且不与其他小组重复的小组获胜。

（7）猜谜活动：学生使用相关形容词描述班上的一位同学，并举例说明。不透露其姓名，让其他同学猜。

（8）总结性活动：开展课堂讨论：具备哪些品质可以收获友谊？具体应该怎么做？课后可布置一篇100词左右的短文。

（9）启发式提问，预告下次课内容：

Now that you have discovered what the word humble means it time to think about it more carefully. Do you really think that Wilbur is humble? Are any characters in the story the opposite of humble? Be prepared to talk about this the next time we meet.

3. 案例评析

友谊是一笔重要的人生财富，如何获得友谊是少年学生非常感兴趣的话题。本案例通过阅读经典文学，探讨好朋友的重要品质。学生在探索过程中可以扩充描述人物的形容词词汇，同时反思自己的交友之道，思考今后如何与同学更好地相处。

4. 辅助资源

（1）《夏洛特的网》第十章文字。

（2）介绍故事写作背景的幻灯片。

（四）教学案例 2-4 热带雨林探险（2 课时）

项目主题：Exploring the Rainforest

该主题属于“人与自然”范畴，涉及“人与自然相互依存，绿色生活的理念和行为”子主题。

1. 内容分析

本案例以掌握单词分析策略和词汇学习为教学目标，学生通过科普网站学习关于热带雨林的基本知识，让学生在探索过程中尝试使用单词分析策略接触新词汇，在扩充词汇的同时理解保护自然环境的重要意义。

2. 实施过程

（1）教师播放幻灯片，用多幅图片引入话题。

What does the picture tell? Do you like to explore? Do you want to explore the rainforest? You can learn about the animals that live in the rainforest. See many of the different plants in the rainforest. Join me in a journey into the tropical rainforest.

（2）了解雨林概况：学生通过浏览儿童版热带雨林科普网站（见“辅助资源”），回答以下问题：What is a rainforest? Where is the rainforest? What are some animals that live in the rainforest? 在学生探索的过程中，教师可以对新单词做简单梳理，引导学生学习或回顾单词分析策略，如上下文线索、词根词缀、同音词等。

（3）教师在课堂上使用 quizlet live 词汇训练网站，让学生独立或组队完成将动物单词与对应图片相匹配的测试，综合速度和正确率，评选出表现最佳的参与者。

（4）总结性活动：教师展示相关图片，引导学生讨论如下问题：Why can we find so many types of animals in the rainforest? Why is the area of the rainforest becoming smaller and smaller? How would you feel if the rainforest totally disappears one day and why? What should we do to protect the rainforest?

（5）让学生完成一篇关于热带雨林的短文填空，答案均为本课的重点单词，以此评测教学效果。

3. 案例评析

学生在学习热带雨林相关知识的同时，扩充了有关词汇。热带雨林与整个地球的生态环境息息相关，学生在了解热带雨林相关概念的同时，培养环境保护意识，共建绿色地球、和谐家园。此案例可用于环保主题教学的引导环节，有助于学生树立世界观和培养国际视野。

4. 辅助资源

（1）热带雨林图片。

（2）介绍热带雨林的儿童科普网站 https：//kids. mongabay. com/。

（3）关于热带雨林的短文填空。

（五）教学案例 2-5　电影院（2 课时）

项目主题：The Cinema

该主题属于“人与自我”“人与社会”范畴，涉及“学习与生活的自我管理”和“个人感受与见解，倾听、体谅他人，包容与宽容”子主题。

1. 内容分析

通过本案例，学生学习在以下情况下使用英语：如何计划去电影院，如何决定看哪部电影，电影的类型是什么以及有哪些类型的电影小食。学生可以了解英语电影文化。

2. 实施过程

（1）引入教学主题。

You are going to plan a date at the cinema with your friends. You will decide the genre of the film, the film, and the cinema in London where you want to go. GOOD LUCK!!

（2）学生自选五部现代英语电影，分别写出故事概要。

Find five films, write a summary why or why not you want to see the film. Explain the subject of the film and whether you like or dislike this subject.（2-4 sentences for each film please）

（3）确定每部电影的类型。

Choose two films with different genres, tell the genre of each film and explain why you like each film（5 film genres）

（4）确定观影时品尝的小食。

Search for the different snacks to decide what kind of snack you want to eat during the movie. Write down the kind or kinds of snacks you want to buy at the cinema and explain WHY. Write 1-2 sentences.

（5）确定观影活动细节。

Choose the best film, choose the cinema and the date and time of the film. Please be specific. To find the locations (the cinema) and the time of the film, check the website for film ticket booking. Give DETAILS!!!

（6）两人一组角色扮演在电影院相聚的朋友。

In pairs role-play the scene of two friends meeting at the cinema. Imagine what they would say to each other and act out. (Now you can go to the cinema in an English-speaking country!)

（7）项目成果评价标准如表 6-7 所示。

表 6-7 教学案例 2-5 项目成果评价表

	1-待行动	2-待进步	3-合格	4-优秀	得分
电影情节概要	讲解不到 5 部电影，细节很少；解释了学生愿意或不愿意看细节很少的电影	讲解 5~10 部电影，细节很少；解释了学生愿意或不愿意看细节很少的电影	讲解了 10 部电影的一些细节；解释了学生愿意或不愿意看细节很少的电影	详细讲解 10 部电影；解释了学生愿意或不愿意看电影	
根据个人喜好的五类电影写句子	学生选择自己喜欢的电影类型少于 5 种，未做解释说明	学生选择了自己喜欢的 5 种电影类型，未做解释说明	学生选择了自己喜欢的 5 种电影类型，并做了一定的解释说明	学生选择了自己喜欢的 5 种电影类型，并做了详细的解释说明	
关于电影小食的一两句	学生选择了一种或多种电影小食，未做解释说明	学生选择了一种或多种电影小食，解释说明空泛	学生选择了一种或多种电影小食，解释说明有一定细节，句式结构完整	学生选择了一种或多种电影小食，解释说明细节充分，句式结构完整	

续表

	1-待行动	2-待进步	3-合格	4-优秀	得分
观影活动的书面计划	学生给出了观影活动的一份书面计划，但缺少关键信息	学生的观影活动书面计划细节极少，如电影名称、影院情况、观影时间等	学生的观影活动书面计划细节不足，如电影名称、影院情况、观影时间等	学生的观影活动书面计划细节充分，如电影名称、影院情况、观影时间等	
角色扮演	学生未完成任务	学生扮演了不同角色，但角色互动无法体现观影场景	学生完成了不同角色在观影场景中的互动，但细节不足	学生细致有创意地完成了不同角色在观影场景中的互动	

3. 案例评析

学生不仅练习了电影相关词汇和介绍自己的电影好恶的主要句式，还通过制定观影计划，体验了如何安排休闲活动，从而学习如何管理安排自己的生活。本案例可以进一步推广，教师可引导学生自主设计安排其他活动，培养其独立进行生活决策的能力。

4. 辅助资源

电影相关词汇和谈论电影话题的主要句式。

三、7~9 年级

（一）教学案例 3-1　制作健康餐食指南手册（4 课时）

项目主题：Creating Healthy Meals and Snacks Pamphlet

该主题属于“人与自我”范畴，涉及“身心健康，抗挫能力，珍爱生命的意识”子主题。

1. 内容分析

本案例以制作健康饮食科普手册为目的开展调查研究，让学生在探索过程中了解并传播饮食管理相关知识，对有效传播的概念形成感性认识，同时丰富强化饮食词汇。此外，中美膳食指南的比较有助于学生深入了解我国国情，理解因地制宜的重要性，树立文化自信，培养独立思考的能力。

2. 实施过程

（1）引入教学主题。

Have you ever heard your mom or dad ask you what you wanted to eat? Have you ever heard them say "I don't know what to make" or remind you to eat something healthy?

You have seen some food vocabulary with your teachers and now it is time to take it a step further.

Having a healthy and balanced diet is important. It can be very hard to find meals and snacks that are healthy and balanced all while tasting delicious and being appreciated by yourself and your loved ones. Following the completion of this assignment, you will become better able to determine if a meal is adequate based on the official dietary guidelines.

（2）学生分组比较中美膳食指南。

Did you know that there is a guide as to how much of each different food group you should eat per day? It is called the dietary guidelines. Compare "Dietary Guidelines for Americans（2020-2025）" and "中国居民膳食指南（2022 版）", and share your findings in class. Then give possible explanations for the differences found in the comparison. Which guide do you think should be followed by Chinese families, the American or the Chinese?

（3）教师介绍小组项目。

After online research and information collection, you will create a brochure/pamphlet with three meals, three snacks, and drinks that follow the official dietary guideline.

This project will be done in teams of 4-5 students. You must work together to complete the research needed for your brochure. Make sure that every member contributes to the project!

Your Challenge: Make the tastiest and healthiest brochure/pamphlet! Your friends and their families will be the judges!

First, you will learn about and explore the concepts of portions and servings, the different food groups, and healthy eating.

Then you will explore various food, drink, and cooking vocabulary to help you come up with ideas for the brochure/pamphlet using the correct vocabulary.

You will also have links to some kid-friendly recipe websites to help you look for ideas if you need some help.

Finally, your team will use the brochure/pamphlet website link provided to create your suggestions using all that you have learned here.

In the brochures/pamphlets, your team will practice using imperatives, synonyms, and practice using different sentences.

These brochures/pamphlets will be shared in class. Every week you will get a new team's brochure/pamphlet to bring home for your family to try out! After that, you are encouraged to share them with your other friends and family to give them healthy ideas.

Please be reminded of the following tips:

- Take note of portions/servings.
- Take note of your favorite foods.
- Do not forget about DRINKS in your brochure/pamphlet.

（4）学生自主探索学习表示重点概念的单词。

Take some time to explore "Dietary Guidelines for Americans (2020-2025)" and "中国居民膳食指南（2022 版）" and notice the different food groups, the different portions, and the difference of things for people of different ages.

After asensible comparison of food guide from USA and China, you will have new healthy meal, snack and beverage ideas that you can cook up and feel good about eating!

For help understanding portions, portions are the size of each serving in a more visual way.

（5）教师播放健康饮食的视频。

Not only is it important to eat different foods in a day, but it is important that the food you eat is healthy. Eating healthy helps you have enough energy and nutrition to get you through your day! To learn more on healthy eating as a group watch the following videos on healthy foods.

（6）教师提供制作指南的参考词汇并带领学生练习。

Here is where you can find great food and drink words to use as ideas for the final project. Most of them have pictures to help you understand the words. Get creative and use different ones! The Quizlet lists include fruits and vegetables, grains, meat and meatless proteins, and dairy.

Some foods may be used for lunch/breakfast/dinner. These are just labeled this way to HELP you organize them and find ideas more quickly.

Also here are somevocabulary for food preparation for your reference.

Now, let's do some (Quizlet or Kahoot) quizzes to show what we have learned about related vocabulary!

(7) 教师提供参考网站供学生检索信息制作手册(见“辅助资源”)。

Here are some helpful cooking websites where you will find inspiration for your brochures!

(8) 学生(用 Canva 或其他工具平台)制作手册。

Now that you know the dietary guidelines, portions, servings, and a lot of food and drink vocabulary, we are going to put it all together.

As a group, you will come up with three meals and three snacks that fit with Chinese dietary guidelines. The goal is to share these ideas among classmates, friends, and family so everyone can have new ideas for healthy meals and snacks.

Group Roles - 3 members

-1 member makes sure all elements are included.

-1 member makes sure it adds up to the Chinese Dietary Guidelines standard.

-1 member makes sure the wording is clear, appropriate, varied, and uses imperatives.

You must include:

-1 breakfast

-1 lunch

-1 dinner

-1 morning snack

-1 afternoon snack

-1 night snack

= 6 suggestions in total

ALSO

Don't forget about drinks! A glass of milk can count as a serving of dairy!

In your brochure, you must include:

All 6 suggestions

Drink suggestions

1 picture per meal/snack = 6 pictures minimum

A clear and relevant cover

Cleartitles for when each suggestion should be eaten (example: breakfast)

The general serving sizes of each suggestion (example: one bagel, a handful of rice, 1 pork chop)

Synonyms

Imperative Words

Different sentence formats

Take some time to work with a friend and share ideas.

Write a rough draft to help you make sure you have all the elements.

Have a friend read it over to make sure you are ready to make the brochure.

(9) 总结展望。

Now that you are an expert in food vocabulary in English, take advantage of this and share your brochures with your classmates, exchange them every week!!

After that share them with your family.

Take some time to help your parents with grocery ideas and making dinner since you are a healthy eating expert!

(10) 项目成果评价标准如表 6-8 所示。

表 6-8 教学案例 3-1 项目成果评价表

	1-待行动	2-待进步	3-合格	4-优秀	得分
小册子/手册的整体外观	没有标题，图片缺失或不相关，间距和字体过小或平淡。标题和说明缺少或很难找到	有标题但用语模糊或不完整，有一些图片且与主题相关。间距和字体大多是合适的。有标题和描述，但不容易找到/区分	有标题且基本清楚，提供的大多数图片与主题相关，间距和字体适当。标题和描述大多很清楚，且基本能够找到	标题清晰，图片全部与主题相关，间距和字体吸引人且适当。标题和描述很容易找到	

续表

	1-待行动	2-待进步	3-合格	4-优秀	得分
小食、饮料和餐点的数量与质量	未列出三餐、饮料或零食	涉及1餐、1份小食和一些饮料。非常相似，数量适当	包括两餐、两份小食和一些饮料。餐食大多不同，数量适当	包括三餐、三份小食和全部饮料。餐食各不相同，数量适当	
与膳食指南的关联	每餐/每顿点心的各食物组的分量不符合中国膳食指南标准。所有4个食物组均缺失，且并未散布于任何餐点、小食和饮料中	每餐/每顿点心的各食物组的分量在一定程度上符合中国膳食指南标准。手册基本包含了所有的4个食物组，基本散见于一些膳食、零食和饮料中。每餐/每顿点心的各食物组的分量大部分符合中国膳食指南标准	所有4个食物组都包括在内，并且大部分分布在大多数膳食、小食和饮料中。每餐/每顿点心的各食物组的分量准确符合中国膳食指南标准	包括所有4个食物组，并分布于所有膳食、小食和饮料中	

续表

	1-待行动	2-待进步	3-合格	4-优秀	得分
创意与变化	饭菜和小食都是相似的，没有提出新的想法，说明没有努力探索新的想法	餐点和小食有所不同，提供新的想法，说明在寻找新想法方面付出了一些努力	膳食和小食基本做了调整，大多不同，提出新的想法，说明在寻找新想法方面付出了努力	餐点和小食各不相同，富有创意，提供新想法，说明在寻找新的美味创意方面付出了巨大的努力	
拼写与语法	有十二个或更多的拼写/语法错误。 很少或未正确使用可数和不可数名词	有九到十一个拼写/语法错误。 使用可数和不可数名词的情况略好	有五到八个拼写/语法错误。 大多数情况下正确使用可数和不可数名词	有三个或更少的拼写/语法错误。 正确使用可数和不可数名词	
句式丰富程度	所有句子都遵循相同的格式，未使用形容词或同义	有些句子使用不同的格式。 在某些句子中使用了形容词和同义词	大多数句子使用不同的格式。 大多数句子都使用形容词和同义词	所有的句子都使用不同的格式。 每个句子都使用形容词和同义词	

续表

	1-待行动	2-待进步	3-合格	4-优秀	得分
祈使句的使用	介绍膳食或小食时均未使用祈使句	一些正餐和小食的介绍使用祈使句。各祈使句有些不同，与主题相关且书写正确	一些正餐和小食的介绍使用祈使句。祈使句大多是多种多样的，与主题相关且书写正确	每餐饭和点心的介绍均使用祈使句。祈使句多种多样，与主题相关且书写正确	

3. 案例评析

在本案例中，学生比较中美膳食指南的异同，确定最适合中国人的健康饮食结构。小组合作制作健康饮食指南手册，有助于学生形成健康生活理念的同时，对技术传播形成初步认识。

4. 辅助资源

（1）制作手册的参考网站（面向儿童的烹饪教学网站）。

Spatulatta

http：//spatulatta. com/

Fit For a Feast

http：//fitforafeast. com/kids_ cooking. htm

The Kids Cook Monday!

http：//fitforafeast. com/kids_ cooking. htm

（2）关于健康饮食的视频。

（3）健康饮食指南的参考词汇。

（4）补充活动。

与家人练习在餐厅点健康食品，查看家人的选择，看看是否订购了健康食品；

查找食品图片并判断是否健康，解释原因以及如何调整；

练习/学习阅读英文食品标签和“每日摄入量”（daily serving）；

介绍不同文化的食物；

让学生介绍/解释自己文化中的传统食物，并要求学生确定其所属的食物类别，以及如何将这些传统食物组合成有益健康的膳食。

（二）教学案例 3-2　童话改写（4 课时）

项目主题：Fractured Fairy Tales

该主题属于“人与社会”范畴，涉及“文学、艺术与体育”子主题。

1. 内容分析

在本案例中，学生将使用传统童话故事中熟悉的角色、情节和场景来创作新的版本。通过改变故事情节、添加意想不到的转折或创造引起当代人共鸣的“曲折”，学生将扩充英语词汇和培养阅读理解能力。在分析和评估众所周知的童话故事时，学生将和同伴交流、协作、合作翻译，并在写作和口语练习时做出语言选择。学生将通过本案例探索和审视一个改版的童话故事；使用多媒体和桌面出版工具，向特定的观众和/或社区开发和呈现（扮演故事讲述者）部分或全部“改版的”童话故事（编写剧本/表演）；还可以在线分享已完成的故事。

2. 实施过程

（1）教师介绍模拟情景（为杂志社的改编童话版块供稿），引入教学主题。

You work for a children's magazine called "Fairy Tale Footnotes" . Your team writes short stories for the magazine. This is not a paper magazine, but an electronic magazine. The magazine would like to feature a "fractured" fairy tale section in next month's issue to increase online subscriptions of readers. You and your team will present your "fractured" stories to the board of directors. If your teams' story is exceptional, your team will be up for a bonus and will become department head leaders. Good luck to everyone!

Your team will also have to research background knowledge on the origin of fairy tales and answer questions such as: Where do Fairy Tales come from? What was their purpose? Are morals involved with fairy tales and if so how? Why are fairy tales so prevalent as a form of storytelling? How have illustrations been used to make fairy tales more enjoyable?

Today, some authors still like to retell and invent new fairy tales. JonScieszka's fractured fairy tales in *The Stinky Cheese Man* and *Other Fairly Stupid Tales* are an excellent example of a retelling fairy tales but with humor.

So jump in and find out what makes these fairy tales so enduring, and write a unique fractured fairy tale that our readers will enjoy!! Good Luck!

(2) 教师引导学生思考童话需要具备的特征。

Is it a Fairy Tale?

In order for a story to be a Fairy Tale it must have 6 or more of these characteristics:

①Begins with Once Upon a Time, Once long ago; Long, long ago etc.

②Story setting is usually in a castle, forest, or town

③Story has good / nice characters

④Story has mean / bad characters

⑤Many of the characters are animals or members of royalty

⑥Story has magic

⑦Story has the numbers 3 or 7 in it

⑧Story has a problem

⑨Problem in the story is solved

⑩Good wins /outsmarts bad

⑪Ending is "happily ever after"

(3) 安排学生四人一组，教师发布小组任务。

Teams will need to research on the Internet finding out the origin of fairy tales and why they were written. Teams will need to view and read traditional fairy tales and decide which fairy tale you plan to "fracture." Hold a brainstorming session to create a graphic organizer (bubble map) about your new fractured fairy tale using the computer program *Inspiration*. Use your creativity to produce a top notch fairy tale for our magazine.

(4) 学生小组讨论组内分工。

Discuss what you know about fairy tales from previous stories you have written for the magazine. Based on experience, select your role within your team.

Editors (a thinker who will help the group key in on the task, and an organizer who knows the English language)

Note Takers and Writers (the individual will tell you what notes are important and will guide the writing of the story)

Computer Operator and URL Manager (this person will take care of all your computer needs)

Publishers (this person will prepare the story for publishing)

Illustrators (this individual will create drawings to accompany the story)

Presenters (the person needs to present the new story to the board of directors and earn a good evaluation on the presentation- great speaking skills are a must!)

(5) 课程总结。

All team stories were outstanding!! The board of directors decided to use ALL stories in the magazine. The fractured fairy tale stories were published and Fairy Tale Footnotes Magazine has won an award for Best Children's Magazine!!! This award has increased online subscriptions and our readers are very happy. Expect to see a bonus in your paycheck. Great team effort and outstanding work! Keep up the good work!!

"Imagination is more important than knowledge." Albert Einstein (1879—1955), German born US physicist.

(6) 项目成果评价标准如表 6-9 所示。

表 6-9 教学案例 3-2 项目成果评价表

	1-待行动	2-待进步	3-合格	4-优秀	得分
故事地图	学生尝试绘制改编童话的故事地图	学生开始绘制改编童话的故事地图	学生完成了改编童话的故事地图	学生完成了改编童话的详细故事地图	
对故事地图的改动	故事偏离原版	故事大致遵循原版	故事流畅，与原故事相比，改变显而易见	故事流畅，与原故事相比，改变明显且恰当	
语言	改编童话几乎没有描述性语言	改编童话包含一些描述性语言	改编童话包含描述性语言	改编童话包含描述性语言，为故事增色	

续表

	1-待行动	2-待进步	3-合格	4-优秀	得分
组织	想法和场景似乎是随机排列的	这个故事有点难以理解。过渡有时不清楚	故事安排得很好。一个想法或场景可能不合适。使用清晰的过渡	故事组织得很好。一个想法或场景按照逻辑顺序跟随另一个想法或场景，过度清晰	
写作过程	学生在写作过程中投入的时间和精力很少。似乎不太在乎	学生在写作过程中投入了一些时间和精力，但不是很充分。得过且过	学生在写作过程中投入足够的时间和精力（写前准备、起草、审查和编辑）。努力完成任务	学生在写作过程（写前准备、起草、审阅和编辑）上投入了大量时间和精力。努力使故事精彩	
解决方案	未尝试给出解决方案或解决方案无法理解	人物问题的解决方案有点难以理解	人物问题的解决方法很容易理解，有一定的逻辑	人物问题的解决方案很容易理解，而且合乎逻辑。没有未交代清楚的情节	

3. 案例评析

本案例的组织形式适用于创意写作教学。学生在语言输出实践中把握童话的特点，学习用故事地图开展叙事构思的方法，充分发挥想象力和创造力，各司其职，合作编织出一个设计精巧、组织严密、富有创意的故事。团队合作过程也能让学生提前感受创意文案团队的工作状态，体会合作式写作的魅力，培养团队精神。

4. 辅助资源

著名童话故事传世的不同版本及其改编版示例

（三）教学案例 3-3　有客到访——为学校客人安排欢迎会（4 课时）

项目主题：Someone is coming to your school!（Welcome Party Planning）

该主题属于“人与社会”范畴，涉及“跨文化沟通与交流，语言与文化”子主题。

1. 内容分析

本案例专为中学英语学习者设计。学生将通过完成现实世界中的真实任务，运用口语、听力、阅读和写作技巧，同时学习如何与同学一起安排欢迎会。

2. 实施过程

（1）引入教学主题：为到访嘉宾安排欢迎会，全班投票选出最期望接待的嘉宾。

Someone（to be decided by the whole class）and his family are coming to your school to speak to the students about culture and heritage of his/her native country at a school-wide assembly. You are in charge of putting together a welcome party for the visitors that will include the student body as well. The welcome party will take place before the assembly in the gymnasium. You are in charge of food, music, decorations and activities that all reflect the visitor's native country. Make sure you explore the target culture and heritage so that the party is correctly themed.

（2）教师发布小组任务，然后安排学生分成五个组。

Your task is to research, plan and develop a welcoming party for the visitors before an assembly about the culture and heritage of the visitor's native country. Your groups will create an actual welcoming party to display their finished products for enjoyment and for a grade.

Group #1: Builders（Symbolic Building Creation）- Your team will research, plan and create a model of a symbolic building in the target country with supplies of your choice. The model is to be made of 3-D materials and must have similar qualities of the actual symbolic building that were created long ago.

Group #2: DJs - Your team will research, plan and create a playlist of songs that are traditional songs along with current popular songs in the target country. Make sure music is appropriate to the taste of the visitors who are mostly adults. The playlist will be played at the party.

Group #3: Chefs - Your team will research, plan and create a food item to be eaten at the party. The food item is to be a traditional dish of the target country. You must list the ingredients, purchase the ingredients, and cook the food prior to the party.

Group #4: Decorators – Your team will research, plan and create decorations for the party. The decorations are to be appropriately themed and must be hung up and displayed prior to the party.

Group #5: Game Planners – Your team will research, plan and create activities/games for the party goers. The activities are to be traditional games or games that would be currently played in the target country during a party.

If you are interested in being a part of a certain group please let the teacher know and they will see if your request can be fulfilled. Also, if necessary affordable items need to be purchased, groups must let their teacher know in advance. Remember, not all items requested will be purchased.

（3）学生分组明确各自的任务，收集并讨论资料。

You will be working with your team to get ready for the welcome party. Each group has a specific task that is not easy and needs research, planning and time to develop. Use teamwork to get your task completed in time for the party.

The whole team should first research the visitors so they know about the family they are creating the party for.

Group #1: Builders – Your job is to build a symbolic building of the native country. Your group will research online and come up with a unique way to build it. You will be graded on the creativity along with the sturdiness of the building. Make sure to also make your building pleasing to eye; this is important because the building is for the party and all the party-goers are going to be looking at it. Lastly, make sure there is a way that candy can be put inside and then make sure the candy is put inside before the party starts.

Group #2: DJs – Your job is to create a playlist of songs that will be played at the party. You will first need to research traditional music and current popular songs of the target country. Then you will need find the songs and make a playlist of the songs. Your team can determine how you want to make a playlist and play the songs. Some examples could be the use of a computer with speakers or smart phones. You will also need to create a written/typed playlist of all the songs, artists, and years the songs were created along with an explanation of two traditional songs. You will need to choose a minimum of 5 traditional songs and 5 current popular songs. Your playlist will be played during the party and your group will share the information you gathered at one point during the party.

Group #3: Chefs - Your job is to create a food choice for the party. You will first need to research popular foods of the target country and determine if it is something that is possible for your group to make. You will need to look at the ingredients and preparation to determine the possibility. Keep in mind the utensils, pans, and cooking method needed. Once your group has decided on the food choice, you will need to create the food to be ready for the party. Make sure you have enough food for all the guests. During the party you will give a brief summary on what food was chosen, its ingredients and how it was prepared.

Group #4: Decorators - A party isn't a party without decorations and your job is to decorate for the party. You will need to first research typical and traditional decorations of the target country. You will need to determine a decoration plan that includes wall decorations, ceiling decorations, table decorations, party favors for guests, and anything else that you decide. You will be responsible for a sketch/computer illustration of your decoration plan prior to actual decorating. Next, you will create the decorations with classroom supplies and use of the internet. Make sure your decorations are set up prior to the start of the party. You will be graded on how nice the decorations look and that you have all of the above mentioned components.

Group #5: Game Planners - Your job is to create two activities that the guests can participate in during the party. The activities must be traditional party games of the target country. You will need to research the games, find out how they are played, get the necessary supplies and be prepared to engage the guests in the games during the party. During the party you will be responsible for explaining the games and getting the guests engaged in the games. You will also give a summary of how the games relate to the heritage of the target country. You will be graded on your presentation of the games during the party.

（4）课程总结。

Your team has done it! You've put on a top-notch welcoming party for the visitors! You should feel proud of the hard work your team has done to make this party a success. The visitors have formally thanked all of you for your diligence and has invited you to take a vacation to their country free of charge! Keep in mind the skills you have learned by completing this task: teamwork, perseverance, attention to detail and the ability to engage others in a group. You have learned a lot by participating in this task and I hope that you will use the skills you gained one day when the time comes for another party!

（5）教学效果评测标准如表 6-10 所示。

表 6-10 教学案例 3-3 教学效果评价表

	1-待行动	2-待进步	3-合格	4-优秀	得分
建筑组	模型看起来和实物有点像，但不够美观。模型不坚固，有一个放置糖果的开口。团队没有准备好，欢迎会期间的演示遇到了很多麻烦	模型看起来和实物有点像，颜色正确，造型立体。模型较为坚固，有一个放置糖果的开口。团队做了一些准备，欢迎会期间做了很好的介绍	模型看起来很像实物，外形美观，颜色准确，立体造型具有创意。模型较为坚固，有一个放置糖果的开口。团队做了一些准备，欢迎会期间做了很好的介绍	模型看起来很像实物，外形美观，颜色准确，立体造型具有创意。模型十分坚固，有一个放置糖果的开口。团队准备充分，欢迎会期间完成了出色的展示	

续表

	1-待行动	2-待进步	3-合格	4-优秀	得分
音乐 DJ 组	播放列表包含 1~2 首传统歌曲和 1~2 首当代流行歌曲。小组介绍了一首传统歌曲的概况或未介绍。欢迎会期间播放列表歌曲时遇到很多问题	播放列表包含 3 首传统歌曲和 3 首当代流行歌曲，并附有手写/打印说明，介绍每首歌曲的演唱者和创作日期。小组介绍了一首传统歌曲的概况。欢迎会期间使用播放列表时播放遇到了一些困难	播放列表包含 4 首传统歌曲和 4 首当代流行歌曲，并附有手写/打印说明，介绍每首歌曲的演唱者和创作日期。小组介绍了两首传统歌曲的概况。欢迎会期间播放了播放列表	播放列表包含 5 首传统歌曲和 5 首当代流行歌曲，并附有手写/打印说明，介绍每首歌曲的演唱者和创作日期。小组清楚地介绍了两首传统歌曲的概况。欢迎会期间成功播放了播放列表	
美食组	小组勉力制作了当地菜肴，味道尚可，欢迎会上略做介绍	小组参与制作了当地菜肴，味道不错，欢迎会期间做了介绍	小组承担了制作当地家常/传统菜肴的大部分工作，味道很好，欢迎会期间做了介绍	小组独力制作了当地家常/传统菜肴，味道出众，欢迎会期间做了详细介绍	

续表

	1-待行动	2-待进步	3-合格	4-优秀	得分
装饰组	视觉效果图完成情况不理想。欢迎会装饰品仅包括以下四项中的两项：墙壁、天花板、桌子和礼物。这些装饰与当地的传统文化遗产关系不大	视觉效果图可以转化为实景。欢迎会装饰品仅包括以下四项中的三项：墙壁、天花板、桌子和礼物。这些装饰与当地的传统文化遗产有关	视觉效果图可以转化为欢迎会装饰实景，包括以下所有项目：墙壁、天花板、桌子和礼物。这些装饰比较漂亮，富有创意，且与当地的传统文化遗产有关	视觉效果图很有巧思，可转化为欢迎会装饰实景，包括墙壁、天花板、桌子和礼物。装饰十分精美，富有创意，且与当地的传统文化遗产有关	
游戏策划组	小组安排了一场与当地文化有些关联的游戏。游戏缺乏组织，客人基本没有参与感	小组安排了一场与当地文化有关的游戏。游戏缺乏组织，客人有一定的参与感	小组安排了两场与当地文化有关的游戏。游戏很有趣，客人一定程度上参与了游戏	小组安排了两场与当地文化有关的游戏。游戏富有巧思，很有趣，客人充分参与了游戏	

3. 案例评析

组织安排对外交流活动能够锻炼学生多方面的能力，包括语言表达、团队协作和跨文化交际。同时，学生通过研究特色建筑、音乐、饮食、游戏，深入了解了目标国家或地区的文化特色。本案例可以要求学生在最终展示中体现具体的语言点和文化概念，以巩固之前课程学到的语言和文化知识。

4. 辅助资源

到访嘉宾及目标国家/地区情况简介

（四）教学案例 3-4　以中美教育制度为主题给笔友写信（4 课时）

项目主题：Schooling in China and the United States (writing to a pen pal)

该主题属于“人与社会”范畴，涉及“跨文化沟通与交流，语言与文化”子主题。

1. 内容分析

本案例旨在帮助我国的初中学生将自己的教育经历与美国的同龄人进行比较，进而正确理解不同教育体系之间的异同，同时培养跨文化交流能力。学生将分组选择学习 5 个探索主题之一，并在课堂上展示小组学习成果。

2. 实施过程

（1）引入教学主题。

VIRTUAL VOYAGE

You will be writing your first letters as pen-pals to students in the United States!

These pen-pals know little about schools in China, so it is your job to learn from each other about what school is like in your own country. You will watch the video about schooling in the United States and will choose to learn more about one of the five Discovery Topics that were in the video. You will take notes about the topic you picked, and will share this learning with your classmates. Using what you have learned, you will write your first letter to your American pen-pal!

Create a new Journal page and take notes on the video.

（2）教师公布可选的探索主题，安排学生作出选择。

Now you need to choose one of the following topics:

School subjects

What subjects do they learn in school?

What subjects do students learn in different grades?

Can you describe subjects that may be unfamiliar to us?

Schedule

When does the school year start and end? Why?

What does a typical school day look like?

Can you describe a flag ceremony and its importance?

Sports, Extra-Curricular

What do students like to do for fun?

What kind of sports do they do?

What types of programs do they participate in?

Style, Trends, School Clothes

What do they wear in school? Students? Teachers?

What are the rules about school clothes?

Is there a trend in the type of clothing and shoes that students wear?

School Layout, Classroom Setting

What does a typical American school look like?

What are some different things about the classrooms?

How many students are usually in a class?

（3）学生分组查找相应探索主题的相关信息，记录重要信息。

（4）教师提示学生整理信息后可以思考的问题，再安排组成新的小组。

Before breaking into new groups, go back in your journal and ask yourself:

Did I answer the key questions from the task?

Do I have enough information to really understand the topic and represent my topic in the small group?

How well did I communicate with my fellow researchers?

Can I make a valid and well-thought connection or comparison to the educational experiences of American students?

（5）原来的所有小组需要派出一名成员加入每个新小组，学生在新小组内分享自己的发现。

（6）小组讨论结束后，教师引导学生反思如下问题：

After representing your topic in the small group discussion, ask yourself:

How did I do with sharing relevant information?

Did I respond to peer presentations with juicy (not flat) questions about their research?

What new things did I learn about education in the United States? (take notes on peer presentations, if you have not done so already.)

Do I have new questions I wonder about?

（7）学生和全班同学分享自己的发现，每人说出至少一个希望进一步了解的问题。

（8）教师布置写作任务，让学生写信给笔友，了解美国中学的基本情况，在信中需要提出那个自己最想了解的问题。

（9）项目成果评价标准（给笔友写信之前的所有活动）如表 6-11 所示。

表 6-11　教学案例 3-4 项目成果评价表

	1-待行动	2-待进步	3-合格	4-优秀	得分
笔记质量	笔记杂乱无章，学生未在语言选择上投入全部努力	笔记内容简略呈碎片化，表明学生为正确使用英语付出了一些努力	笔记内容简略有条理，表明学生为正确使用英语付出了最大努力	笔记非常透彻，条理清晰，并尽可能使用正确的英语	
恰当使用技术工具和资源	尝试使用技术工具，但未使用在线资源	恰当使用技术工具和某个主题的相关资源，但未访问其他主题的相关资源	善用技术工具，使用其他主题的资源以扩充常识储备	灵活运用技术工具，参考其他主题的资源以加深对自己负责主题的理解	
向新小组展示主题信息	未准备好与小组分享。比较/建立联系的内容不能引起小组成员的共鸣	对话题信息有一定的敏感度，展示时比较胆怯。比较/建立联系的内容与小组成员有一定关联	关注并对要分享的重要信息有一定了解。比较/建立联系的内容与小组成员有比较紧密的关联	对记录的所有信息有深入的理解，展示形式生动，展示内容能够引起小组成员的强烈共鸣	
回应小组成员提问的能力	无法回应同组成员的提问	回应同组成员的提问十分困难	通常能够对同组成员的提问给出很好的回答，并且能引述相关笔记内容支持自己的观点	能够非常自然地回答同组成员，言之有物，且能引述相关笔记内容支持自己的观点	

续表

	1-待行动	2-待进步	3-合格	4-优秀	得分
对他人展示予以回应，通过提问营造组内对话氛围	几乎不参与小组对话	偶尔对他人展示作出回应，提出基本问题	对他人展示作出回应，提问有创意	对他人展示作出回应，提问体现高阶思维能力	
尊重他人的观点、文化和经历	缺乏对美国学生的经历和同学努力的尊重：不专心、分心、不认真倾听、缺乏同理心	基本尊重美国学生的经历和同学努力：基本专注、基本感兴趣、通常认真倾听、有一定同理心	真正尊重美国学生的经历和同学努力：总是专注、总是感兴趣、认真倾听、有一定同理心	真正尊重美国学生的经历和同学努力：专注、积极投入、认真倾听、富有同理心	
提出关于中学教育情况的真正有意义的问题	提出的问题得到了笔友的一个词的回答	提问引出了和笔友之间的常规对话	提出有趣的问题，和笔友展开良性对话	提出高阶思维问题，和笔友展开真正的对话	

3. 案例评析

学生结合自身的教育经历，与笔友就不同国家的教育制度展开对话，通过正确认识社会之间的异同，树立身份认同，培养爱国热情。通过同伴讨论和教师引导，学生学习如何在跨文化交流的书信中提出开放式问题，从而开展深入而有意义的对话。

4. 辅助资源

关于中美教育的视频（用于引入分组研究的五个主题）

(五) 教学案例 3-5　租客找房（2-4 课时）

项目主题：House Hunting

该主题属于“人与自我”和“人与社会”范畴，涉及“职业启蒙，职业精神”和“跨文化沟通与交流”子主题。

1. 内容分析

在本案例中，学生将以房产经纪的身份，为英语国家客户研究我国的三处房产，他们将使用真实的在线资源和学到的房屋相关词汇来完成最终的课堂展示任务。

2. 实施过程

（1）引入教学主题。

You are a real estate agent with a new client that's expanding a business into China! You get to explore houses and apartments in many cities to help your client choose the best place!

（2）教师介绍任务内容：按客户要求寻房。

You will need to look through real estates listings to narrow down the options for your client. Your client wants to move to China, but doesn't have time to travel to endless cities.

Before you begin the search, your client gives you a budget and a list of requirements.

-Your client wants to rent, not buy.

-The budget is between $1, 500-2, 500 a month.

Wish list:

-at least 2 bedrooms/2 baths

designated parking spot or close to public transportation

-outdoor space

-space for entertaining

Your client wants to be surrounded by the locals and NOT in the touristy area. As your client is busy with the business, you've been asked to present three properties from one city to choose from.

You can present the houses and/orapartments in either a video/slide show presentation or a printed brochure or poster.

（3）教师安排学生编成两人组，给予任务提示。

Use the real estate websites to look at listings.

Remember that your client has a budget you are expected to meet. Use the online exchange rate converter to ensure that the mortgage in the local currency does not exceed the $2500 budget.

Use the following template to keep track of your research.

	#1	#2	#3
Property Name			
Property Type (House/Condo/Apartment)			
City and Province			
Price ($)			
No. of Bedrooms			
No. of Bathrooms			
Outdoor Space?			
Parking Lot?			
Close to Public Transport?			
Type of Public Transport			
Tourist Area?			
Area (m^2)			
Level/Floor			
Furnished?			

（4）课程总结

Congratulations! You successfully presented your research to your client and guided them in making the best choice in housing for the country. Along the way you have learned about the differences in houses in various Chinese cities and about how to explain these information in English. You also learned about currency and the exchange rate. In the future, when planning to study abroad or perhaps a vacation, you will have a greater idea on what you can expect to find!

（5）项目成果评价标准（给笔友写信之前的所有活动）如表 6-12 所示。

表 6-12　教学案例 3-5 项目成果评价表

	1-待行动	2-待进步	3-合格	4-优秀	得分
内容	未能遵照要求完成任务	遵照部分要求完成任务	遵照大部分要求完成任务	遵照所有要求完成任务	
创意	未付出努力，项目既不清楚也没有创意	项目投入不足，组织不够清楚	项目内容基本完整，有一定创意和趣味	项目内容翔实，富有创意，生动有趣	
语法	词汇和拼写错误超过5个	词汇错误超过4个	3~4 个词汇和拼写错误	没有词汇和拼写错误	
用时	迟交	按时完成项目有困难	项目准时完成	时间管理出色，准时完成项目	

3. 案例评析

对外交流包括为来华定居经商的外国旅客提供信息咨询服务。学生在扮演房产经纪这一职业角色的过程中，可以对我国各地的居住状况进行一定了解，锻炼与房产主题有关的英语表达能力，练习相关词汇和表达。本案例可扩展为研究其他国家的房产情况，学生在自主探究的过程中会对当地的日常生活有一定了解，培养国际视野和独立生活能力。

4. 辅助资源

我国和英美国家常用的房产资源网站。

四、高中（10~12 年级）

（一）教学案例 4-1　中美家庭比较（4 课时）

项目主题：Comparison of Chinese and American Family

该主题属于“人与社会”范畴，涉及“和谐家庭与社区生活”子主题。

1. 内容分析

这个家庭主题的教学案例包括团队和个人的能力展示，这些学习活动的目的是引导学生训练和展示关于家庭主题的语言技能，并比较中美家庭之间的文化差异。

2. 实施过程

（1）引入教学主题：跨文化家庭比较。

Dear students,

The goal of this activity is to present your language integration, application and cultural awareness. You will work in small groups and research family structures and lifestyles in the American community and compare them to your own.

You will create a poster to present your findings. Your group also needs to perform a 3 minutes' skit in English to show your knowledge about the differences and similarities between Chinese and American families. Afterwards, Each student will write a reflection about what has impacted you from this activity. Enjoy working together and ask for assistance as needed.

（2）学生以 4 或 5 人为一组，研究在线资源，收集整理相关信息。

Work with your peers collaboratively to discuss how to divide and conquer the tasks and come up with a procedure to fulfill all assignments.

I will ask for a summary of your plan to distribute labor.

（3）比较中国家庭与美国家庭的结构和理念。

Compare American family structures and your own family structures, and come up with some ideas about the differences and similarities. Be creative and objective.

- Analyze positive and negative stereotypes

-Compare how norms and beliefs lead to behaviors and practices

-Construct your own concept of the structures based on your research

（4）制作彩色海报，比较中美文化之间的异同。

The poster/PPT/Presentation may include pictures, drawings, characters, phrases and sentences to address your point of view.

Post your completed work in Schoology and be prepared to explain and answer questions from classmates.

（5）排演 3 分钟英语短剧，比较中美家庭。

Work as a group to create a skit to show your understanding about families across cultures.

Performance duration is about 3 minutes. Refer to the vocabulary and sentences you have learned so far, apply and create your own script.

Make the skit fun to watch, and present your point of view.

Language usages and fluency are graded.

Each group member has to produce meaningful language usage.

（6）各人独立写一份书面小结，记录本次活动的学习心得。

Write a paragraph or two of personal experience about this project including what you have learned about Chinese family and American family. Evaluations and suggestions about this activity will be appreciated.

（7）项目成果评价标准如表 6-13 所示。

表 6-13　教学案例 4-1 项目成果评价表

	1-待行动	2-待进步	3-合格	4-优秀	得分
海报	仅有 1～2 个异同点，思路欠清晰，无创意	3～4 个异同点，思路基本清晰，提供论据支持	至少 5 个异同点，思路清晰，论据充分	至少 5 个异同点，结构清楚，富有创意	
短剧	内容偏离主题，努力不足	内容与主题基本相关，付出了一定努力	内容与主题相关，有一定趣味性	内容与主题紧密相关，富有创意，生动有趣	

3. 案例评析

语言学习就是培养沟通技巧和了解其他文化的过程。学生通过短剧表演，展示跨文化家庭比较过程中的所学所感。本案例让学生有机会与同伴合作创造有趣的学习体验，通过小组合作，学生能够进一步了解中美两国的家庭文化，进而培养文化意识。此形式可推广为比较中美两国社会生活的其他方面。

4. 辅助资源

比较中美家庭的短视频（用于引入教学主题）

（二）教学案例 4-2　理想的学校（4 课时）

项目主题：Ideal Schools

该主题属于“人与自我”范畴，涉及“多彩、安全、有意义的学校生活”

子主题。

1. 内容分析

在本案例中，学生将检索互联网资源，研究世界各地的多种教育制度。然后，他们将利用这些收获描述自己心目中理想的教育制度并解释其优缺点。

2. 实施过程

（1）引入教学主题。

China's public school system was created in the 20th century. It affects tens of thousands of students everyday, and yet few of those students take the time to think about what exactly the system is, or why it exists. In fact, nearly every "civilized" nation around the world has a public education system. Interestingly enough, these systems vary just as much as religious and political institutions.

Do you think the system would be different if it were developed by us today? How might it look if it were designed by students?

（2）学生在课堂上讨论中国的公立教育体系，提出优点和缺点。

（3）学生研究不少于 4 个其他国家的公立教育体系，其中 2 个为"一带一路"国家/地区，1 个为欧洲国家，1 个为美洲国家。

（4）学生以小组为单位分享研究成果，就每个教育体系的优缺点达成共识。

In the groups you will decide which role you want to take. The roles are mediator, note-taker, zealot, devil's advocate.

（5）各小组设计一个优点最大化且缺点最小化的教育体系，收集整个过程中的收获，完成随后的小组演示项目和个人写作任务。

Now that you have researched and begun discussion it is time to come to some decisions. Remember the questions:

①What is your ideal school system?

②How would you design it?

③Who would attend?

④When will they attend?

⑤What will they learn?

⑥Who will teach it?

Your group must come to a consensus on the what your groups ideal system will be like.

Make sure you write everything down. This will be essential to building your paper as well as your final presentation.

In groups of 4, you will create a 5-6 minute presentation for the class that answers those questions and includes a representation of your school. (Chart, PPT).

Group presentation:

①5-6 minutes.

②each students speaks about 1-2 minutes.

③must answer all of the questions.

④must provide references.

⑤must have at least 1 visual aid.

Individually you will write a 2 pagepaper describing your chosen school system. It will describe the pros and cons, that explains why your system is the best choice.

You individual paper.

①2 pages

②references (at least 4 in total, 1 European country, 1 American country, and 2 other countries from "One Belt One Road" initiative)

③answer all questions.

④correct grammar/spelling/structure.

(6) 小组向全班展示本组的观点，运用视觉辅助工具（PowerPoint 或海报或 Prezi）描述本组所做的工作，给出具体理由

(7) 每个学生写一篇关于自己设想的教育体系的两页纸论文，描述利弊，解释为什么这一教育体系是最佳选择。

(8) 课程回顾总结。

After finishing this project think about the following questions. Write down 1-2 sentences (or more) on each in you journals. Feel free to elaborate if you wish, but please at least give a simple answer.

What did you learn while doing this project?

How would you approach it differently next time?

What did you think about the way your group worked together?

After seeing your peers' presentations which ideal school system do you like the best? Why?

（9）项目成果评价标准如表6-14所示。

表6-14 教学案例4-2项目成果评价表

	1-待行动	2-待进步	3-合格	4-优秀	得分
研究	完成或参考的研究最少，参考了1个信息来源	完成了基本研究，参考了2个信息来源	完成了足够的研究，参考了3~4个信息来源	完成并引用了示范性研究。参考了4个以上的信息来源，来源质量“过硬”	
演讲用时	实际用时与规定用时相差4分钟以上	实际用时与规定用时相差2~3分钟	实际用时与规定用时相差1~2分钟	实际用时与规定用时相差少于1分钟	
课堂展示质量	团体参与很少，只读讲稿，缺乏视觉辅助	有一些团体参与。读稿而非现场演讲展示。设计感不强，视觉辅助不足	良好的团体参与。主要是现场展示而非读稿。足够的视觉辅助	所有小组成员现场展示时间相同。全程不读稿。优秀的视觉辅助	
论文	参考资料很少或没有。许多语法和结构错误。在多个方面不完整或存在明显不足	缺少1~2个参考资料。存在一些语法和结构错误。完整但缺少一些要件	参考资料完整但引用格式有误。很少有语法和结构错误。完整但不够出色	参考资料完整或数量超过要求。没有语法和结构错误。完整且出色，工作量超出要求	

3. 案例评析

通过描述理想的教育制度，学生有机会反思自己近十年的教育经历，了解不同国家教育制度的异同，最终体会到世间没有完美的教育制度，各国不同的教育体系都是顺应各国历史发展过程的结果。搜集相关资料，确定论题，在小论文中表达观点，提供论据，展示论述过程，学生将完成研究论文的雏形，口头介绍自己的研究成果，对学术研究的完整过程形成初步认知，培养严谨治学的学术精神。

4. 辅助资源

介绍现代教育制度的短视频（引入教学主题）

（三）教学案例 4-3　为中国电影设计数字广告牌海报（4 课时）

项目主题：Digital Billboard Poster for Chinese Movies

该主题属于"人与自我"和"人与社会"范畴，涉及"丰富、充实、积极向上的生活"和"影视作品的文化价值和赏析"子主题。

1. 内容分析

本案例围绕年轻人喜闻乐见的电影主题设计，旨在训练演讲能力和团队协作能力。同时，通过为中国电影设计和宣传英文海报的活动，培养青年一代的爱国热情和民族自豪感，未来助力中国电影走向世界。

2. 实施过程

（1）引入教学主题。

Think about the movie that you love. What makes you watch it? News about it? A poster or a trailer?

Do you know how advertisers make movies more stunning? Most of people decide whether they will watch a movie or not by considering its posters.

Throughout the project, you will learn how to release a movie by creating a digital billboard poster about it.

（2）介绍项目要求（设计用于数字广告牌展示的电影海报）。

You are an advertiser of a big movie company. Your manager wants you to watch the trailers of the movies which will come out soon. Then you are asked to prepare a billboard poster according to the movie which you choose (it can be horizontal or vertical). When your billboard poster is ready for displaying, you share it with your colleagues (other learners). Then you will present your movie by using your poster and answering the below questions:

When will the movie be released?

What kind of the movie is it?

Which actors/actresses have starred in the movie?

Why should people watch the movie?

Do not forget to be persuasive.

（3）学生观看四部中国电影的英文预告片，选择其中一部，小组合作设计海报。

After having information which you need, you can watch the trailers of the given movies by clicking their name. Then choose one of them and do not forget to take notes you will need in the process of designing its digital billboard.

（4）项目成果评价标准如表6-15所示。

关于所选电影及其数字广告牌海报的演示文稿应提供足够的信息，在进行演示时，学生应该畅所欲言并使用适当的语言。

项目作品（数字广告牌海报）应具有原创性和吸引力，语法正确，并且应包含有关所选电影的足够的信息。

表6-15　教学案例4-3项目成果评价表

	1-待行动	2-待进步	3-合格	4-优秀	得分
课堂演讲语言	许多错误，理解困难	可能会出现一些令人困惑的错误	一些不影响意思的小错误	近乎完美的语言	
课堂演讲技巧	只读稿	时而读稿，时而畅所欲言	犹豫时会看下笔记提示	无需稿子，全程畅所欲言	
课堂介绍信息	太多不必要的信息/重要信息太少	有些不必要的信息，有些重要的信息	不必要的信息较少，主要是重要的信息	足够的信息	
海报语法	许多错误，理解困难	可能会出现一些令人困惑的错误	一些不影响意思的小错误	近乎完美的语言	

续表

	1-待行动	2-待进步	3-合格	4-优秀	得分
海报信息	太多不必要的信息/重要信息太少	有些不必要的信息，有些重要的信息	不必要的信息较少，主要是重要的信息	足够的信息	
海报设计	没有明显的创造力/独创性	既不乏味也不吸引人	有吸引力但并不出色	出色且有吸引力的原创作品	

（5）课程总结。

Consider the feedback your classmates and teacher have given to you.

Now you know how to create a digital billboard poster of a movie. If you're really interested in it, keep improving yourself. Who knows, maybe one day you will find yourself really preparing a movie poster.

3. 案例评析

电影是传播大众文化最有力的媒介之一，英文的宣传推广活动有助于塑造一个国家的国际形象。学生既可以锻炼用英语介绍自己喜爱的中国电影的语言表达能力，还可以培养家国情怀，树立文化自信，为将来作好准备，在世界舞台上代表中国发声。可对本案例做适当改编，要求学生推介最新的中国电影和其他文艺作品，讲好中国故事，让世界更加了解当今中国。

4. 辅助资源

中国电影的英文海报和预告片示例（可引导学生评论）

（四）教学案例 4-4　社交网络依赖问题（4 课时）

项目主题：Social network... are you addicted to?

该主题属于“人与自我”“人与社会”范畴，涉及“自我认识，自我管理，自我提升”和“社会热点与国际事务”子主题。

1. 内容分析

本案例在帮助学生训练英语综合能力的同时，反思青少年使用或过度使用网络的社会现象。在课堂讨论和同伴交流中，学生将培养批判性思维能力，理性思考社会问题，提出解决方案，逐步成长为勤思考有担当的社会人。

2. 实施过程

（1）引入教学主题。

Technology is great... but how addicted to Facebook (or socials) are you?

We are going to reflect on the use of social network and technology through this project. Then you will critically decide how dangerous it can be or not... keep an eye open!

（2）教师介绍项目任务概况。

Dear students,

You are going to work and read about the topic of technological features, in particular Social Network like Weibo, Wechat, or QQ.

May you already use them, or not. Nobody will be judgemental about it.

I'm expecting to know your honest opinion about the social network, and we will compile at least a leaflet with the usage instructions to use them and be safe.

The leaflet will be posted on the class chat group and the school website.

Good work! Enjoy!

（3）学生描述相关动漫图片。

Describe a cartoon related to computer, then find online a funny gif image about PC or social media. Then post it on the class chat group and explain why did you choose it. (what does it represent?)

（4）学生阅读社交网络相关主题文章，完成学习活动。

Read the article (about Social Network) given by your teacher and do the activities.

（5）学生自测对社交网络的依赖程度，提升学习探究的兴趣。

How addicted are you to the social network?

Do the test and post the results in the class chat group.

（6）学生完成相关主题的听力练习。

Do the listening activity (choose the level and the speed that is better for you).

Listen to the article and answer the given questions.

Post the answers in the class chat group.

（7）学生阅读网络欺凌相关主题文章，完成学习活动。

Read the article on Cyberbulling, given by the teacher, and do the activities.

Post the answers in the class chat group.

（8）学生分组讨论阅读心得，然后合作撰写青少年社交网络使用说明，最后教师带领学生在课堂上讨论各组的说明。

Groupwork：in team（4/5 students）discuss what you understand from the activities you've done. Then write a list of things teenagers should do or not accessing to a social network.

Post the list in the class chat group (with all group members' names)

Discuss the lists in class.

（9）项目成果评价标准如表 6-16 所示。

表 6-16　教学案例 4-4 项目成果评价表

	1-待行动	2-待进步	3-合格	4-优秀	得分
参与	被动参与，无个人贡献	贡献很少，全靠团队合作	积极参与，和他人密切合作	积极参与，有独特贡献，帮助基础较弱的队友	
语言能力	语言能力不足	具备基本的语言能力。错误很少，不影响理解	良好的语言能力	准确使用语言，具备出众的语言能力	
任务	未完成任务	在指定时间内完成部分任务	在指定时间内完成任务	在指定时间内完成任务，且有额外发挥	

3. 案例评析

学生通过多种方式接触社交网络这一社会热点问题，由语言输入任务逐步过渡到语言输出任务，最终实现对社会热点问题发表自己观点并言之有物的教学目标。本案例形式可进一步推广，适用于与探讨社会问题有关的网络探究式项目。对社会问题的思考和表达有助于提升公民素养，培养学生的家国情怀和社会责任感。

4. 辅助资源

（1）与社交网络有关的动漫图片。

（2）社交网络相关主题文章及阅读理解练习。

（3）社交网络依赖自测题。

（4）社交网络相关主题听力练习。

（5）网络欺凌相关主题文章及阅读理解练习。

（五）教学案例 4-5 一本见证了两百年历史的旅行日志（4 课时）

项目主题：The Journal

该主题属于“人与自我”和“人与社会”范畴，涉及“家乡和社会的发展，历史的变迁，对未来的畅想”和“跨文化沟通与交流，语言与文化”子主题。

1. 内容分析

本案例虚构了一本日志在尘封一个多世纪后被世人发现的场景。学生必须自行创作这本关于从一地到另一地（从东到西）旅行的日志。这项活动是关于美国的西进运动（Western Expansion，1801—1861）和人们在旅途中使用的生活技能。学生们自行决定这些旅行者是谁（虚构的或真实的）、他们要去哪里、他们在路上看到了什么，以及他们到达目的地后会做什么。学生必须介绍旅途上遭遇的阻碍、地标和旅行计划。他们将想象（或自行创造）笔下的角色在旅途中可能捡到的物品。

2. 实施过程

（1）引入教学主题。

Your trunk is found over a century after your death in the attic of your great, great, grandchild's house. They are earnestly examining all of the objects in your trunk. They find a journal that tells the story of how your came to settle in this special location. They also find a map that you made as well as some items you picked up along your journey.

（2）教师介绍任务概况。

Your job is to create a journal with at least 20 entries. Make sure your entries are accurate and explain in detail everything the reader needs to know about your journey. You must attach notes and a bibliography. To do your journal you must do the following things：

①Choose a character，your current location，and your desired location.

②Research what conditions in the eastern settlement that might cause you to find a new home in the west.

③Research what conditions were at the new settlement that made it exciting for you to go westward. Include: what kinds of obstacles you have to overcome, what dangers your may face, what kinds of risks will you take so you can achieve success in your new location, how you will get your food, what kind of shelter you will have on the way, what kind of landforms and natural landmarks you will see on the way, and what kind of transportation you will use.

④Things to think about: How will you prepare for the journey? What kinds of food, clothes and other supplies will you need.

⑤Explain what you will do once you get to your new location. What does it look like? What kind of job will you have? Tell about your new job.

You will create the trunk with 5-10 items that you gathered during your trip.

Include a handwritten map of your journey.

You will use the big six checklist as you do your research.

Big6 #1: Task Definition

What am I supposed to do?

What information do I need in order to do this? (Consider listing in question form.)

Big6 #2: Information Seeking Strategies

What are the best sources I can use to find this information?

If using web sites, how will I know that they are good enough for my project?

Big6 #3: Location, Access

Where will I find these sources?

Who can help me find what I need?

Big6 #4: Use of Information

How will I record the information that I find?

How will I give credit to my sources?

Big6 #5: Synthesis

How will I show my results?

How will I give credit to my sources in my final product or performance?

Materials I will need for my presentation or performance (list, separating by commas)

How much time do I estimate it will take to find the information and create the product?

Timeline for assignment

Ideas for project (task definition) completedby:

Information searching (note taking) completed by:

First draft due:

Completed assignment due:

Include here any additional information needed to successfully complete the assignment:

Big6 #6: Evaluation

How will I know if I have done my best?

Before turning in my assignment, I need to check off all of these items:

What I created to finish the assignment is appropriate for what I was supposed do in Big6 #1

The information I found in Big6 #4 matches the information needed in Big6 #1

Credit is given to all of my sources, written in the way my teacher requested

My work is neat

my work is complete and includes heading information (name, date, etc.)

I would be proud for anyone to view this work

(3) 教师介绍项目要求和提示。

Use the Big6 Checklist as a guideline. You do not have to fill in all the blanks. This is the checklist I will use when I do your interview.

For your Powerpoint presentations or notecards, remember to only use one topic on each slide. (You may have more than 1 slide for each topic) Don't forget to put the citation at the bottom of the page. After you have the slides filled out, put all the slides with the same topic together. After you take your notes and put all the same topic together use the template to make your journal entry.

Write your final draft of your journal. It must be handwritten. Use the sources you got for your report and put them in Easybib to make a bibliography.

Make a trunk with items from your trip. Be creative. Include a map of your journey.

（4）项目成果评价标准如表 6-17 所示。

表 6-17　教学案例 4-5 项目成果评价表

Big 6 研究（25 分）	视觉辅助（25 分）	创意（25 分）	现场展示（25 分）
具体题目——老师指定 研究：10 分 5 分：5 个信息来源，必须包括：书籍、视听资料、互联网 5 分：笔记卡片或笔记 PowerPoint 记录重要的单词、短语和引用，不要照搬所有内容 每张卡上列出信息来源的标题、页码、版权日期、出版商 每张卡片记录一个观点，这样便于重新排序 日志：10 分 编辑文章显示更改以及版本更新过程 最终版包括： 使用 Easybib. com 制作的参考书目 收尾工作——最终日志、笔记模板或笔记卡片 评价：5 分 教师或同学根据 Big 5 检查清单开展访谈，了解项目实施的具体情况	与主题相关， 对介绍主题有帮助， 满足视觉辅助要求， 内容完整， 体现学生所做的工作， 作品给人的第一印象很好	简洁明了， 组织体现学生付出了最大努力， 反映了学生的创造性想法， 使用不同的材料	关注他人的演讲， 眼神接触， 通过详细信息和示例深入介绍主题，展现出出众的学科知识水平， 现场展示流畅有趣，说明经过精心排练，吸引观众的注意力

（5）课程总结。

Your family has learned so much about you and your journey. They want to share your story with everyone. They are donating it to the local museum so everyone can learn about your journey.

3. 案例评析

想象自己身处真实的历史事件中，扮演某个角色，以角色的视角撰写日志。

在日志撰写过程中，学生不仅能够深入了解历史事件，还能够系统了解并实践人文研究收集使用资料信息的全过程，培养信息素养。本案例形式可进一步推广，适用于解读中外重大历史事件的网络探究式项目。

4. 辅助资源

（1）介绍美国西进运动的幻灯片或短视频（用于引入教学主题）。

（2）旅行日志的记录内容示例（可用历史老照片举例）。

（3）Big 6 人文研究检查清单。

五、大学阶段英语（大学英语与研究生英语）

（一）教学案例 5-1 语言学习心得分享（4 课时）

项目主题：Learning Languages

该主题属于“人与自我”范畴，涉及“积极的学习体验，恰当的学习方法与策略，勤学善思”子主题。

1. 内容分析

在本案例中，学生将讨论很多与语言学习有关的重要问题，听取彼此的意见，最后结合自身体会，给初学者一些建议。

2. 实施过程

（1）导入教学主题：大学专业学习阶段是否应该重视外语语言学习？

Welcome!

Before we start, here is something for you to think about:

“... As Chinese universities offer more instruction to Chinese students in English, study abroad administrators and their students will start to de-emphasize language learning on programs. The same phenomenon is happening in all parts of the world. I think the natural trend will be to overlook the incredible benefits of language learning, and to more quickly embrace programs that require very little in terms of language. This is what we have to work against...”

MarkLenhart

Executive Director of CET Academic Programs

（2）学生分成三组，分别讨论关于语言学习的不同问题。

Brainstorming in groups

Group #1: In which situation you think the more effective learning is taking place?

Group #2: Which situation you think is more enjoyable for the student involved?

Group #3：If you wanted to improve your spoken English which of the situations would you prefer?

（3）学生阅读同一篇文字，各组完成不同的任务。

Mattia：

I wanna talk about learning languages. I've lived in many different countries, both in Western Europe, Middle East, and now here, in Hong Kong. And during all of that time, I've learned five or six different languages, to one degree or another. I love learning languages. Not only are they important when you move to a country, I just find them fascinating.

Before I came to Hong Kong, I lived in Barcelona Spain for ten years. And when I first arrived, the most important thing was being able to communicate with people locally. I don't attend classes. I don't think I'm particularly good in classes. I prefer to learn by just talking to people, finding out what I need to say by looking at dictionaries and listening carefully.

Other things that helped me when I first moved to Spain, were watching the typical kinds of programs we see every day on channels around the world. For example the weather. This is great because they always say the same things. So you can really quickly hear the same words repeated again and again. And the pictures helped of course.

Anyway, by far the best practice I ever had was just talking to people in the street, or in shops where I'd rehearse in my head what I wanted to say beforehand before I went in. Usually, I'd make a right mess of it first of all, but, after you get over the embarrassment, it's quite funny really. And people are very sympathetic and support in most cases.

Group #1：Translate the text；

Group #2：Retell the text；

Group #3：Prepare questions to ask the speaker.

（4）各小组经过讨论，给语言（英语或中文）初学者提一些建议。

The final task

All together Wecreate the list of advice which you can give to the person who is starting to learn a language.

（5）项目成果评价标准如表 6-18 所示。

表 6-18 教学案例 5-1 项目成果评价表

	1-待行动	2-待进步	3-合格	4-优秀	得分
团队合作	合作效果差	试图合作，但存在很多分歧	所有成员积极参与	彼此配合默契	
使用资源	不会使用电脑和浏览网站	知道如何使用电脑，但不清楚如何访问相关网站	操作电脑没有问题，但使用网站遇到很多困难	电脑和网站使用均没有问题	
做笔记和完成任务	不做笔记不提问题	做了一些笔记但不给出答案	做了一些笔记，准备了一些答案	认真做笔记和准备答案	
回答问题	没有回答任何问题	回答了一些问题	回答了大部分问题	回答了所有问题	

3. 案例评析

本案例的主题是给语言初学者一些建议，这能够帮助学生反思自己的语言学习经历，以己度人；同时，通过和同学关于语言学习经验的交流，有助于加深对自己英语学习现状的了解，明确自己近期的努力目标。本案例适用于大学开学伊始，可帮助学生厘清过去，面向未来。此外，通过向中文学习者提供建议，学生还能够培养跨文化交际能力，学习换位思考。

4. 辅助资源

关于语言学习的简介性文章或短视频（用于引入教学主题）

（二）教学案例 5-2 提高阅读能力（4 课时）

项目主题：Reading Better

该主题属于“人与自我”范畴，涉及“积极的学习体验，恰当的学习方法与策略，勤学善思”子主题。

1. 内容分析

本案例旨在通过引导学生研究文章的形式，定位主要思想、要点和结论，以提高学生的阅读水平。完成本课程后，学生将成长为专业型读者，无须通读整篇文章，即可掌握需要的信息。

2. 实施过程

（1）导入教学主题。

What role does reading play in English learning? Would you like to become a professional reader? In this lesson we will together find out how. You will read several texts to know:

Where does the main idea locate?

Where do the supporting sentences appear?

Where does the conclusion appear?

How to find the main idea without reading the whole text?

（2）教师介绍任务概况。

Three tasks are designed for this lesson.

Task 1.

Students should read a paragraph within 200-250 words without supporting sentences or conclusion, then retell the main idea to the teacher.

Task 2.

Students should read an article within 300-350 words, then find supporting sentences and retell the main idea to the teacher.

Task 3.

Students should read an academic article more than 1000 words, then discuss main ideas, supporting sentences of every paragraph and conclusion.

（3）任务一：阅读 100~150 个单词以内的文本。

首先，学生将有 5 分钟的时间阅读这篇文章，并与同伴讨论文章的主要思想。

然后，老师讨论主要思想的位置，通过提问引导学生寻找主要思想。

最后，学生再读一篇相同级别的文本，不读完全文，只需找出主要思想即可。

（4）任务二：阅读 300~350 个单词以内的文本。

首先，学生阅读 300~350 个单词以内的文本，大约 15 分钟。

然后，老师讨论主要思想和支持性句子的位置。

最后，学生再读另一篇同级别文本，在不读完全文的情况下找到主要思想和支持性句子。

（5）任务三：阅读1000个单词以内的学术文章。

现在学生可以阅读长篇学术文章了。首先，他们可以阅读整篇文章，找出主要思想和支持性句子。

然后，老师教给学生定位主要思想和支持性句子的方法。

最后，教师给学生另一篇学术文章，要求他们根据所教的规则找出每个段落的主要思想和支持性句子。

（6）项目成果评价标准如表6-19所示。

表6-19 教学案例5-2 项目成果评价表

	初级阅读者	成长中的阅读者	合格阅读者
了解一篇文章的结构	了解一篇200~250个单词的文章的组成部分	了解一篇300~350个单词的文章的组成部分	了解一篇学术文章的组成部分
定位主要思想、支持性句子和结论	定位一篇200~250个单词的文章的主要思想	定位一篇300~350个单词的文章的主要思想、支持性句子和结论	定位一篇学术文章的主要思想、支持性句子和结论
实操	在较短时间内定位另一篇200~250个单词的文章的主要思想	在2分钟内定位另一篇300~350个单词的文章的主要思想、支持性句子和结论	定位另一篇学术文章的主要思想、支持性句子和结论

3. 案例评析

“授人以鱼不如授人以渔”，学习能力和策略的习得是大学教育的重要内容。为面向未来培养终生学习者，大学阶段的英语课程有必要引导学生反思自己的学习习惯，掌握重要学习技能。本案例旨在提高英语学习者的阅读能力，老师教学生定位文本主要思想、支持性句子和结论的规则，学生将在完成任务的过程中潜意识地习得这些阅读技能。

完成本课程后，学生将能够定位文本的不同组成要件，快速把握文章主旨，提高阅读效率。

4. 辅助资源

（1）一篇用于阅读示范的文章，单词数为200~250个，教师在课堂上和学生一同定位主要思想、支持性句子和结论。

（2）三篇用于阅读训练的文章，单词数分别为200~250个、300~350个和900~1000个，主题相近。

（三）教学案例5-3　口头分析图片（2课时）

项目主题：Picture Analysis Quest

该主题属于“人与自我”范畴，涉及“积极的学习体验，恰当的学习方法与策略，勤学善思”子主题。

1. 内容分析

这个口头分析图片项目旨在让学生通过介绍分析照片来提高英语流利度和批判性思维能力。除了在语言学习中提升词汇能力外，看图说话还可以训练语言流利度和批判性思维。通过口头分析图片，大学阶段英语学习者可以描述所看到的内容，推测与特定背景相关的某张照片拍摄前、拍摄时或拍摄后可能已经发生、正在发生和将要发生的事件，以展示自己在看图讲故事方面的创造力。

2. 实施过程

（1）导入教学主题。

As the saying goes, a picture is worth a thousand words. In different people's eyes, a picture can say different words. For this lesson, we would like you to show a picture in your eyes. We will practice describing a picture, guess what happened before the picture was taken, and predict what would happen after the picture was taken.

（2）教师介绍任务概况。

Individual students will go online to download pictures of their choice, related to their chosen topics or situations. After selecting their pictures, they will get online help on how to speculate on a given picture. Later on, they will read a picture analysis evaluation rubric for them to know what are expected from them. Then, they will have picture analysis practices, accordingly, until they are ready to record their own voices commenting on their chosen images using voice- recording software. Finally, students will electronically save for themselves and send their recordings, with the pictures as attachments, to peers and their teacher for evaluation/ criticism.

（3）学生从网上下载自选或指定主题的图片。

（4）学生描述图片，猜测拍摄前后发生的故事并录音。

（5）学生将录音与图像文件上传至共享空间，供教师和同学评价。

（6）项目成果评价标准如表 6-20 所示。

表 6-20　教学案例 5-3 项目成果评价表

	5 分	3 分	1 分
描述选定图片	场景+人物+活动 = 3 要素	2/3 要素	只介绍了人物或场景
录音内容	人物及其感受、时间、地点、活动 = 5 要素	3/5 要素	仅有 2 个要素
叙事质量	连贯且有逻辑	有逻辑但不连贯	无逻辑且不连贯
猜测的内容	过去、现在和未来可能发生的事件=3 要素	2/3 要素	仅有 1 个要素
词汇使用	广泛	足够	不足
连接词	频繁使用	经常使用	很少使用
口语表达	流利清楚	清楚但不流利	很难理解

3. 案例评析

看图说话是一项基本的口语训练活动，为帮助一定英语基础的大学阶段学习者提升口头表达能力，本案例不仅提出了口头描述的具体要求，还设计了全面的评价标准。可以通过变换活动形式，增加看图说话的难度，或者考虑实施差异化教学，给英语水平高低不一的学习者布置不同难度的任务。难度较低的看图说话任务，可以提供部分配图文字和问题作为提示；难度较高的任务，则可以让学生对教师或同伴给出无配文图片进行描述，甚至还可以暂时只展示图片的局部，鼓励学生发挥想象。看图说话既可用于密集型口语训练活动（可以参考本案例介绍的评价标准进行口语评价），也可以用于引入教学主题或有争议的热点问题。图片主题包罗万象，动静态图片与文字的有机组合容易给观者留下深刻印象，是提炼思政元素的有力抓手。

4. 辅助资源

教师可以预先准备一些与当前教学主题相关的图片，用于活动示范，之后再鼓励学生自行检索下载图片进行口语练习。

(四) 教学案例 5-4　电话演变的历史 (2 课时)

项目主题：Evolution of the Telephone

该主题属于“人与社会”范畴，涉及“科学技术与工程，人类发明与创新”子主题。

1. 内容分析

展示多种形式的资料，回顾电话技术的发展史，自 1876 年至今的电话演变，电话的发明人及发明过程，电话获得专利的始末，电话对我们的日常生活的影响，以及电话在未来的改进方向。本案例旨在引导学生运用历史视角认识科技，调查中国企业发展现状，了解我国取得的科技成就。

2. 实施过程

(1) 介绍荒岛求生的虚构情景，引入教学主题。

You are stranded on a desert island without any technology to call for help. As you are wondering the island looking for food and shelter, you stumble across a time capsule machine that will allow you go back in time to the late 1800s, when the first telephone was invented. You find a letter next to the capsule with instructions on how to use the time capsule machine.

The instructions on how to use the time capsule machine

When you find this capsule, climb inside and explore how the telephone has dramatically change over time and have impacted our lives. You will be discovering artifacts and exploring the evolution of the telephone from the late 1800s to present day through websites, videos, audios and pictures and discovering the impact it have on our daily life. Afterwards, you will answer questions about what you have learned about the evolution of the telephone. When the task is complete, the time capsule will allow you to make one phone call for help to get off the deserted island.

Good luck!!

Don't Be Stranded!!

(2) 四人一组，在网上查找以下问题的答案，用完整的句子回答，可以分

2-3 次分批发布以下问题。

FROM 1876 to 1976

You jump into the time capsule machine and travel back to 1876. While in the time capsule, answer the following questions:

①Who invented the telephone? When was it invented?

②What was the conflict about the patent before Alexander Bell received it?

③What major technology breakthrough happened during this era?

④What technology innovations are used today that were invented during this era? Describe the impact they have on your life today.

FROM 1977-1997

①List at least 10 technology innovations the telephone have had over time.

②Describe how the innovations improve everyday life.

③Name and describe some technology innovations that are obsolete, or not in existence today.

FROM 1998- PRESENT DAY

①Finally, Describe how technology has improved telephones in the last five years.

②What impact does it have on your everyday life?

③What features do you think the telephone will have in the future?

④If you could improve the telephone, describe one thing that you would have the telephone do to enhance your life.

⑤Name 2-3 leading Chinese companies in telephone technology, cite their major achievements, and discuss the significance of their contributions.

⑥Use the online resources to answer your questions.

（3）项目成果评价标准如表 6-21 所示。

表 6-21　教学案例 5-4 项目成果评价表

	1-待行动	2-待进步	3-合格	4-优秀	得分
列举科技创新	列举出 0～3 项技术创新	列举出 4～6 项技术创新	列举出 7～9 项技术创新	列举出 10 项技术创新	

续表

	1-待行动	2-待进步	3-合格	4-优秀	得分
介绍科技创新	未对技术创新做进一步介绍	技术创新的介绍欠清楚	对技术创新进行了有效的介绍	详细介绍了技术创新并提供事例支持	
答题情况	未回答问题，未使用完整句	问题回答欠清晰，使用了1～2句完整句	问题回答有效，使用了3～4句完整句	问题回答详细，使用了3～4句完整句并举例	
完成情况	未答完全部问题，或未使用完整句	回答了部分问题，部分使用完整句，存在语法错误	部分问题的回答使用了完整句，有些问题回答有误	所有问题的回答均使用了完整句并举例说明。	

3. 案例评析

如今，手机电话已成为人们生活不可或缺的日常用品。从童年到老年，手机见证了我们的人生岁月。回顾电话发展史这一教学主题贴近学生生活，与时俱进。同时，回顾知名企业代表我国取得的科技成就，有助于培养学生的爱国热情，增强对民族工业的信心。本案例可为所有以科技发明为主题的大学阶段英语教学单元提供必要的语言实践活动。

4. 辅助资源

不同年代的电话图片以及电信系统设备图片，用于导入教学主题。

（五）教学案例 5-5　儿童何时能够使用手机？（4 课时）

项目主题：When should kids use phones?

该主题属于“人与社会”范畴，涉及“社会热点与国际事务”子主题。

1. 内容分析

在本案例中，教师引导学生从少儿家长的角度出发，探讨少儿如何合理使用手机。通过换位思考，学生能够更加深刻认识手机的影响，推己及人，反思自己使用手机的情况，并通过社会问题的讨论，在训练语言能力的同时，培养独立思考能力和社会责任感。

2. 实施过程

（1）导入教学主题。

Nowadays, I see that you have already become adults with good jobs, your own family and a lot of responsibilities… sorry…! One day, you see yourselves waiting for your kids at the school entrance. You are chatting with a group of parents of your children's class. You are worried about the use of technology and the freedom that children have to use mobile phones and social networks. Some of you have read articles, other have listened to podcasts or watched short videos; some agree, others don't… So, you have decided to prepare a campaign to raise awareness among parents and families about the responsible use of mobile phones.

There's a lot of ground to make up!

（2）教师介绍任务概况：两人一组制作视频，向少儿家长宣传如何合理使用手机。

In pairs you'll have to create a video aiming at raising awareness of the misuse of the mobile phones among children and teenagers.

In this video you should explain, from your own experience, how dangerous can be mobile phones if they are not used in a responsible way.

You have to address parents and families and make them think critically about their own role in using mobile phones and possible consequences it may have.

（3）录制视频前的准备活动（个人研究和分组练习）。

You need to research a little bit to collect some information before starting your work. Researching is not necessarily boring, you can be well informed watching videos. So, this is your first step. Watch the videos about the use of mobile phones and the experience with the first telephone. After that, each of you should look for, as much as possible, pros and cons of mobiles phones among teenagers. Then, in pairs you can comment and share your work doing a brainstorming.

Well, a good researcher is known for using a wide range of resources. Now, we will change the format of the information.

You have a text with a similar structure to the videos. Read it individually to be concentrated and then you can complete the activities in pairs.

（4）教师介绍录制视频的要求和提示。

Now you are prepared to record yourselves. You have to film a video about your experience with mobile phones. Try to add the ideas you have commented about the text and the videos and be confident: you are persuading parents and families to be critical and responsible with their own use and the use their children make. You can use as many resources you need and you want, but remember that it is a campaign, what means it should impact people and it shouldn't be so long, no more than 4 - 5 minutes.

(5) 项目成果评价标准如表6-22所示。

表6-22 教学案例5-5 项目成果评价表

	1分(待进步)	2分(合格)	3分(良好)	4分(优秀)	
流利度(语音和语调)	学生的演讲听不懂,或者发音不好。讲话不流畅,有很多处犹豫和中断	讲话有些部分不清楚,表现出发音和语调的不足。讲话不流畅,有些地方有犹豫和中断	两个学生同时说话,但说话不够清晰,语调和发音都不够好。说话流畅,有些犹豫	成员的演讲时间均等。讲话很清楚,语调和发音良好。演讲非常流畅	
内容(给出的信息)	学生不理解视频和文章内容,不使用词汇(手机、新技术、应用程序)和语法(情态动词)	学生已经了解大部分相关内容,但使用基本的词汇和语法	学生已经理解相关内容,可以使用基本的单词和结构以及一些词汇(手机、新技术、应用程序)和语法(情态动词)	学生已经理解了相关内容,可以广泛使用与主题(手机、新技术、应用程序)和语法(情态动词)相关的词汇	

续表

	1分（待进步）	2分（合格）	3分（良好）	4分（优秀）	
活动完成和小组合作情况	学生常常忘带材料，不与同学合作，不愿意做活动	学生带来材料，与同学的合作不多，也不太愿意做活动	学生常常带来材料，经常与同学合作，通常非常愿意做活动	学生总是带来材料，与同学积极合作，愿意完成活动	
视频	视频没有或很少剪辑，不是很直观，展示有点困难，音效非常糟糕	视频有一些剪辑，比较直观，但观众有的地方不容易理解展示，音效可以接受	视频剪辑得很好，直观且易于理解，音效非常好	视频剪辑得非常好，非常直观，有趣且易于理解，音效清晰	
总体印象	观众难以理解	观众有时需要努力尝试理解，不过可以把握总体意思	观众基本能理解视频传达的所有信息，不需花费太大精力	观众可以非常轻松地理解视频传达的所有信息	

（6）课程回顾与反思。

Well, well, well...

We are interested in your impression! We are all ears and eyes!! Tell us what you have learned throughout this process! How do you feel after advising parents about this issue?

WOULD YOU ALLOW YOUR CHILDREN TO USE THE PHONE FREELY?

At what time do you consider kids can start to use mobile phones? Have you run into some disagreements?

It should be legally established?

We think there are so many interesting opinions out there regarding this topic, which is particularly timely. Who knows? Maybe, we will do further researches about what people think about it!

We want to thank you all for your participation and we hope you enjoyed!

3. 案例评析

本案例的形式可以进一步推广，适用于大学阶段英语学习者的社会热点话题讨论活动。视频是当代年轻人喜闻乐见的传播方式，用视频作为展现语言输出能力的媒介，可以鼓励大学生使用英语，用英语分享感受，表达自我，进而调动英语学习的积极性。

4. 辅助资源

（1）关于手机使用体验的视频，便于学生熟悉话题。

（2）关于手机使用体验的文章以及阅读理解练习，便于学生进一步熟悉话题。

（六）教学案例 5-6　爱情观测试（4 课时）

项目主题：Love Actually Test

该主题属于“人与自我”和“人与社会”范畴，涉及“自我认识，自我管理，自我提升”和“良好的人际关系与人际交往”子主题。

1. 内容分析

在本案例中，学生将通过设计调查问卷，了解年轻人对爱情的看法。在设计问卷的过程中，学生不仅能够学习量化研究方法和如何提出并检验假说，了解社科研究的基本过程，还能在培养学术英语能力的同时，树立正确的爱情婚恋观。

2. 实施过程

（1）导入教学主题。

Nowadays, most of you have free access to internet and free applications. You might have seen a dating website or an affinity test. However, if you have not seen one, you can imagine it!

Now, it’s your turn to elaborate the best love questionnaire in order to attract people’s attention.

（2）教师介绍任务概况。

During the previous sessions you have worked on lexicon related to love and relationships, you have also revised how to express hypothesis and you have learned about British and American cultural and linguistic differences.

Now, it’s turn to use the content learned so far and include it in the love questionnaire.

Options:

The project can be done either in groups (you create the groups with a maximum of four students) or individually.

The final product can be done either in a digital or a physical version. Both options must be sent to the teacher. In case you choose the digital version, you can use resources as Canva. On the contrary, if you choose the physical version, you can use materials such as cardboard and colours. Then, take a picture and send it.

Instructions:

The questionnaire must have, at least, 15 questions with open or multiple choice answers. Furthermore, after the questions there must be some affinity results. The questions and the affinity results should include the following content:

The lexicon learned so far during the previous lessons.

Hypothesis structures in order to show you now how to express hypothesis in context.

British or American cultural and linguistic aspects. The questionnaire must be devoted to a specific audience. Therefore, by including some British or American cultural and linguistic aspects, the questionnaire will be devoted to British people or people from the US.

(3) 检索相关网络资源。

In order to do a quick research, you should visit the following websites where there are useful examples of love questions or tests.

Questions for couples

Love Lab Tru Love Tester

True Love Calculator

In the websites given above, there are examples of useful questions and some affinity results.

ATTENTION!!

You can use them to inspire yourself but not to copy the questions!

(4) 自行设计问卷问题。

Once you have done the research, it's your turn! You must write your own love-questionnaire using the content learned so far. In addition, you must take into account the websites just visited.

Remember to include the lexicon learned, express hypothesis and devote the questionnaire to an specific culture（British or American English-speaking people）.

（5）介绍最终成果并制作视频记录展示过程。

Finally, for completing the task you must film yourself presenting the final product. You must explain what you have done and what people can expect from your love questionnaire. In addition, talk about whether your product is devoted to British English-speaking people or, on the contrary, to American English-speaking people and how that is presented in the final product.

There are two options for the video:

In groups: the video must last 5 minutes as minimum and each member of the group has to appear in it. Therefore you can film yourself separately and then, edit the video with online editors tools.

Individually: you must film yourself explaining the product for a minimum of 2 minutes.

The video must be sent to the teacher after completion.

（6）项目成果评价标准如表 6-23 所示。

表 6-23　教学案例 5-6 项目成果评价表

	1-待行动	2-待进步	3-合格	4-优秀	得分
引入学过的词汇并提出假说	学生引入了一两个学过的概念，未提出假说	学生引入了几个概念，在三分之一的问题中提出假说	学生引入了很多概念，在超过一半的问题中提出假说	学生引入了学过的各种概念，在大多数问题中提出假说	
成品面向英美受众	学生在最终成品中引入了几个学过的词汇概念	学生在最终成品中引入了一些学过的词汇和拼写概念	学生在最终成品中引入了一些学过的词汇、拼写和文化概念	学生在最终成品中引入了各种学过的词汇、拼写和文化概念	

续表

	1-待行动	2-待进步	3-合格	4-优秀	得分
清楚介绍作品	学生很难解释清楚作品目的	学生使用基本词汇解释作品目的	学生轻松流利地解释了作品目的	学生清楚、流利、准确地解释了作品目的	
有效传达意见和想法	完成项目后，学生很难清楚表达自己的想法	完成项目后，学生使用基本词汇表达自己的想法	完成项目后，学生轻松流利地表达自己的想法	完成项目后，学生流利、准确、清楚地表达自己的想法	

3. 案例评析

本项目的主要目的除了按照任务给出的步骤完成调查问卷的设计外，还有清晰、流畅、准确地表达最终作品体现的思想。就某话题对同学进行调查是一种常见的英语课堂活动，过去多关注学生如何汇总归纳搜集到的信息，口头介绍调查结果，本案例聚焦调查问卷的设计，学生需要介绍设计思路和设计成品，突出社科研究的过程而非结果，有助于学生对调查问卷这种常见的社科研究方法的构思和设计形成初步认知。

4. 辅助资源

英文婚恋观自测网站，学生设计问卷时可参考其中的问题。

(七) 教学案例 5-7　选择职业 (4 课时)

项目主题：Selecting a Career

该主题属于“人与自我”范畴，涉及“自我认识，自我管理，自我提升”和“职业启蒙，职业精神”子主题。

1. 内容分析

本案例介绍的自测工具可以帮助学生缩小自己感兴趣的职业范围，确定自己的优势和劣势、性格类型、学习风格以及实现目标的阶段规划过程。

2. 实施过程

(1) 导入教学主题。

Have you decided what job you will do in the near future? This lesson is designed to identify your “Career” of choice. Whether you want to pursue a new career or advance in your career, you must complete some of the exercises presented here. Students and professionals can use this lesson as a starting point to set achievable goals and make appropriate plans or to check progress and reevaluate their current status over time.

（2）教师介绍任务概况。

Your task is to identify the careers you would be interested or fields you prefer to work in. Identify what it would take to gain access to such careers. For instance determine the type and the level of education required. This is accomplished through series of self evaluating tests, questions, and answers using available web resources.

（3）在线自测 MBTI 人格测试。

Check the explanation for your four letter personality type（ISTJ, ESTP, etc...）.

After completing Myers－Briggs personality type you should be able to discover paths to enrich you life through having a better understanding of your preferences and choices.

（4）根据模板列举自己的优势和劣势。

The list of strengths and weaknesses provides you with a platform to build upon the weaknesses and better utilize the strengths. This can help narrow down professions that best fit your strengths and would help develop the weaknesses.

（5）自测学习风格。

（6）制作一份基本个人简历。

A resume has to be specific to a job. However, having the information handy in a desirable format can be a great time saving tool.

（7）列一份自己感兴趣的职业清单。

You must search for matching careers and analyzing different professions with pros and cons to be able to make sound decisions in planning your future. Through this type of analogy you would be able to differentiate between fantasy and reality. You would be able to decide what type and level of education is needed for the career of you choice and plan accordingly as early as possible.

（8）列一份常见面试问题清单。

Interview skills are great asset. You must practice and prepare to be able to compete and succeed in acquiring a desirable position. Reviewing the most commonly asked questions in an interview is a starting point. The applicant should come across as the best fit for the position. Employers look for attitude, communication skills, aptitude, matching skills and education. Not being able to confidently express how an employer can benefit from your skills and abilities may allow your seat to be lost to candidates with less qualifications than yours.

(9) 课程回顾总结。

Hopefully these exercises provided you a better understanding of your learning styles, your personality type, and enabled you to identify your career or careers of your interest. Creating resume and reviewing interview questions should prepare you for the competitive world of employment.

3. 案例评析

职业规划是大学的重要一课，英语在大学生求职中也是常见的考查环节。本案例将英语学习与职业规划相结合，引导学生了解自己的职业兴趣，树立奋斗目标，为求职过程中的英文表达环节做好准备。

4. 辅助资源

(1) MBTI 人格测试。

(2) 个人优势劣势模板。

(3) 学习风格自测题。

(4) 简历模板。

(5) 求职网站（用于制作职业清单及查看岗位要求）。

(6) 常见面试问题示例。

(八) 教学案例 5-8 最佳电影具备的特质（4 课时）

项目主题：What a Film Needs to be the Best

该主题属于“人与社会”范畴，涉及“电影的文化价值与作品赏析”子主题。

1. 内容分析

本案例设计了电影节的场景，学生通过英语宣传展示电影的精彩之处，在训练英语输出能力的同时，从年轻人的视角出发，为中国电影走出去献计献策。

2. 实施过程

(1) 导入教学主题。

Do you like watching movies? What is your favorite movie? Are you interested in attending a film festival? Today we are holding a film festival for you. To celebrate the festival, you will work in groups to promote a given movie.

(2) 教师安排分组，介绍任务概况。

①Create groups of 5.

②Assign roles to each member of the group: manager, speaker, writer, designer and time-keeper.

③Think of the best English speaking movie of the year and write its name on a piece of paper. Put all the papers in a pocket/bag. The manager in each group will pick one of the pieces of paper. This will be your movie. (If two or more groups have chosen the same movie, the teacher will intercede by repeating the process with the managers of these groups).

From now on you will work together to research about your film and present it to the public (your classmates). Take into account that your goal is to argue that your film is the best one and must be voted.

（3）搜集影片相关信息。

Please take into account aspects such as:

①Trailer.

②Synopsis.

③Actors and actresses.

④Nominations and awards.

⑤Other relevant information that makes your movie more attractive: costume design, make up and hairstyling, music...

（4）准备课堂展示。

In this session you will create a (Prezi) presentation (of 5 slides) with the relevant information you have gathered about your film. Videos and songs are allowed but never longer than 2 minutes.

The correct use of past simple and present perfect tenses will play a main role in your presentation. A wide variety of regular and irregular verbs will improve your speech. (Review how and when to use them). And bear in mind to include specific vocabulary related to cinema: gender, actor, actress, ost, red carpet, festival, script, and so on.

And do not forget that your presentation should keep a ceremony style. Therefore, your speech must be written according to the event.

Remember that this is an independent Film Festival and your movie will win if your presentation is convincing enough for the audience.

Some smart details are welcome to create the appropriate atmosphere!

（5）庆祝电影节（课堂展示）。

You have eight minutes for your presentation.

Teacher will assess each group following the rubric you used todesign the presentation（up to 70%）. Your classmates will also assess each group（up to 30%, among which appealing design accounts for 10%, appealing speech 10%, and the best film 10%）.

（6）课堂展示评价标准如表 6-24 所示。

表 6-24　教学案例 5-8 课堂展示评价表

	1-待行动	2-待进步	3-合格	4-优秀	得分
流利度	读稿，有多处较长停顿	未读稿，有几处较长停顿	状态放松，有多处短停顿	状态放松，有几处短停顿	10%
发音	很难理解，口音重	可以理解，但需要一些努力	可以理解，语音语调标准	发音和语音语调非常清楚	10%
语法	几乎未使用过去时和现在完成时，错误很多	使用过去时和现在完成时有困难，有一些错误	频繁使用过去时和现在完成时，但不规则动词缺乏变化	频繁使用过去时和现在完成时，不规则动词使用多变，几乎没有错误	25%
词汇	未使用特定场景的相关词汇	使用特定场景的相关词汇存在一定困难	频繁使用特定场景的相关词汇	广泛使用特定场景的相关词汇，富有创意	25%

（7）全班投票选出“最佳电影”。

所有课堂展示结束后，学生将投票选出最佳电影。投票将由各小组内部协商决定。每组的经理会写下本组一致推选的电影名，交给老师，老师计票后宣布获奖电影。

（8）课程回顾与反思。

Now that we have enjoyed all the presentations about some fantastical movies, what do you think does a film need to be the best? Any lesson learned for Chinese films?

3. 案例评析

本案例基于年轻人喜闻乐见的电影主题，模拟电影节评选电影的场景，调动学生用英语表达的积极性，向同学推介自己欣赏的电影，最后鼓励学生为中国电影走向世界出谋划策。此形式适用于大学阶段所有英语演讲活动的设计：各学生小组认领一个研究主题，课堂展示研究成果，全班根据各组展示情况投票支持。这种小组竞技的方式，有助于培养学生的团队精神，让团队成员有机会各展所长，全组为达成同一目标共同努力，在此过程中使用英语的能力也会得到锻炼。

4. 辅助资源

（1）电影节及其评选程序的介绍性 ppt，用于引入教学主题 。

（2）电影英文资讯网站：The Oscars，Filmaffinity，IMDB。

（九）教学案例 5-9　音乐表演会场（4 课时）

项目主题：Musical Venues

该主题属于“人与社会”范畴，涉及“跨文化沟通与交流，语言与文化”子主题。

1. 内容分析

在本案例中，学生将扮演一支中国乐队的经理，决定乐队将在哪些场地演出。学生将研究美国纽约市四家音乐场馆的信息。学生收集分析信息以决定为乐队预订哪家场地。本案例旨在引导学生浏览网站以获取初步信息，熟悉纽约的音乐活动场所，以便向旅游会务行业提供建议。在培养语言表达能力的同时，学生将从年轻人的视角出发，为中国文艺的对外交流献计献策。

2. 实施过程

（1）导入教学主题。

When musicians go on tour, there are many venues to choose from in cities that they have never been to before. Where is the venue located? How many people can it accommodate? Are there seats or open standing? Is the venue indoor or outdoor? What other artists have performed there? These are all important questions in deciding which venue a band will play at.

As band managers, it is important to do the research in choosing the right venue for the band. You are currently looking into New York City venues to help determine which venue the certain band should choose to play at.

（2）学生四人一组，比较备选音乐会场之间的相同点。

Students brainstorm a list of questions in order to compare similar points across the four venues.

Example questions include, but are not limited to:

How many people does the venue accommodate?

Is the venue indoors or outdoors?

What other musicians and bands have played here?

Do concertgoers sit or stand?

Is the venue accessible to people of different physical abilities? (e.g. wheelchair accessible or has an elevator?)

Who can we contact for more information?

（3）组内成员每人选择一家音乐会场进行深入研究，针对小组集体整理出的问题寻找答案。

（4）小组集中讨论，各人分享研究发现，共同整理出四家音乐会场的比较结果。

（5）根据掌握的信息，小组讨论适合在某家音乐会场表演的中国乐队，并给出理由。

（6）项目成果评价标准如表 6-25 所示。

表 6-26　教学案例 5-9 项目成果评价表

	1-待行动	2-待进步	3-合格	4-优秀	得分
研究问题	未回答所有问题，也未提出新问题	回答了一些问题，提出了一两个新问题	回答了大多数指定问题和新增问题	出色地回答了所有指定问题和新增问题	
搜集信息	未使用资源，为搜集到所需信息	基本搜集到了研究问题的答案	使用推荐的资源，找到了大部分所需信息	对所有问题作出回答，并提供了额外信息	

续表

	1-待行动	2-待进步	3-合格	4-优秀	得分
团队协作	未开展团队协作，任务未完成	团队协作情况不佳，但完成了部分任务	团队合作完成了部分资料的阅读和研究，展示了搜集到的信息	团队密切合作，完成了资料的阅读和研究，展示了搜集到的信息	
介绍适合在各个音乐会场演出的乐队	选择适合某会场演出的音乐家/乐队没有合理解释支持	选定了适合某会场演出的音乐家/乐队，但未给出解释	解释了选择音乐家/乐队的原因	解释了选择音乐家/乐队的原因，并得到了团队成员的一致认可	

（7）课程总结。

I hope you all learned a bit about the four listed music venues. People travel often to see musicians they are fans of, and now next time you have a guest travelling for a concert, or wondering the difference between certain venues, I hope you are able to highlight some benefits of each venue and help them determine which option might be best for them.

Further your curiosity: What special events are coming up at these venues? What other music venues are in New York City? How do they differ? Which do you prefer? Why?

Thank you for your collaborative hard work and participation!

3. 案例评析

本案例不仅锻炼学生检索信息、搜集信息、分析信息和做出决策的能力，还引导学生去了解中国的乐队生态，以及特定乐队对演出的音乐会场的不同要求。学生不需要具备很高的音乐鉴赏水平，但需要通过此项目体会到，跨文化交流的主要场景之一是服务业从业者推出定制化服务方案，以满足自己所服务的特定人群的需求。模拟学术报告会、国际竞赛的会务安排等真实场景的网络探究式项目同样可以考虑采取让学生选择场地这种形式。

4. 辅助资源

（1）选择音乐会场的注意事项。

（2）音乐会场相关信息。

（十）教学案例 5-10 打造自己心中的超级英雄（4 课时）

项目主题：Create Your Superhero

该主题属于“人与社会”范畴，涉及“志愿服务与公共服务”和“对世界、国家、人民和社会进步有突出贡献的人物”子主题。

1. 内容分析

本案例聚焦广受年轻人欢迎的超级英雄主题，学生将描述自己心目中的超级英雄，以提升创造力。同时，教师还将带领学生联想到生活中的“超级英雄”，关注那些为维护社会和谐稳定作出贡献的平凡而又伟大的职业，探讨真实英雄和虚构英雄的异同，引导学生树立爱岗敬业的思想。

2. 实施过程

（1）导入教学主题。

Have you ever dreamed of being a superhero?

Imagine being a superhero! How would it feel?

In today's class, our dream will come true thanks to our creativity.

You will choose an existing superhero (e. g. Spider-Man, Batman, Wolverine) and write an essay about it.

Then you will create your own superhero, draw it, and write an essay about it.

（2）观看相关视频，集体讨论超级英雄的形象特点。

（3）学生各写一篇关于某位超级英雄的短文，文中不能出现超级英雄的名字。然后两人一组互换短文，阅读后猜出短文所描写的超级英雄。

（4）集体讨论超级英雄的魅力所在。

（5）学生创造自己理想的超级英雄形象，画出该形象并撰写短文。

（6）教师引导学生联想现实中的“超级英雄”，比较现实和虚构的异同，鼓励学生思考如何成为掌握自己人生的超级英雄。

（7）项目成果评价标准如表 6-26 所示。

表 6-26 教学案例 5-10 项目成果评价表

	1-待行动	2-待进步	3-合格	4-优秀	得分
超级英雄作文	超级英雄诞生的故事	超级英雄的人物动机	超级英雄的超能力	相关电影和动漫作品	40
自创超级英雄作文	超级英雄诞生的故事	超级英雄的人物动机	超级英雄的超能力	相关画作	60

(8) 课程反思

In your journal, please write down the answers to the following questions:

Why are superheros so attractive?

Do superheroes exist in our real life? Who are they? Why do you think they are superheroes?

Is it necessary for us to become superheroes in our own life? How?

3. 案例评析

通过描绘心中的理想形象，学生对“英雄”和“超级英雄”的概念会形成更加具体的认知。“能力越大，责任越大。”能力必须由责任感和使命感护航，才能“用之有度，用之有道”。为国家和人民贡献一生的平凡而又伟大的劳动者，逆风而行的抗议者，是真实生活中的“超级英雄”。只要积极培育和践行社会主义核心价值观，我们都可以成为自己生活中的超级英雄，迎接丰富多彩的充实人生。

4. 辅助资源

(1) 超级英雄的电影图片，用于引入教学主题。

(2) 生活中的“超级英雄”图片，用于最后的课程反思。

六、英语专业

(一) 教学案例 6-1 ELL 有效英语教学的研究与策略（1-2 课时）

项目主题：Research and Strategies for Effectively Teaching ELL Students

该主题属于“人与社会”范畴，涉及“积极的学习体验，恰当的学习方法与策略，勤学善思”和“职业启蒙，职业精神”子主题。

1. 内容分析

英语学习者（ELL）是指英语非母语或第一语言的英语学习者。在本案例中，语言教育方向的英语专业学生从英语学习者的视角出发，思考他们可能面临的英语学习问题，通过网络调研，针对特定问题提出教学策略。

2. 实施过程

（1）导入活动：回顾自己学习英语的经历。

教师和学生共同回忆自己作为英语初学者的经历和体会，分享英语学习印象最深的英语学习故事。教师引导学生认识到英语学习者（ELL）在新环境中学习英语可能会面临的挑战，作为未来的英语教育工作者，学生应该帮助英语学习者尽快融入学习环境，找到适合自己的学习节奏。

（2）阅读相关介绍性文章并讨论如何为英语学习者准备欢迎礼包。

Welcome kits for ELL students and their parents/guardians is an excellent way to get new students into the swing of things and inform caretakers about the ins and outs of the school and classroom. Read an article about welcome kit and pick 5 things you would include in a welcome kit that would best accommodate a new ELL and their parents/guardians. After choosing those 5 things, add 2 more that you feel would be beneficial. Jot down how each informational item will make the transition easier.

（3）面向 ELL 学生的英语教学策略：观看关于 differentiated instruction（差异化教学）的视频后回答问题。

Watch the video and consider the following questions:

How does the inductive strategy help teachers reach their goals with ELL students?

How can you enhance new ELL students' background knowledge?

Does giving ELL children a different text or providing a slower speaking video effectively help in the learning process?

（4）阅读介绍英语教学新策略的文章后填表。

Read the article and fill in the following chart with reasons why each of these strategies would be effective. If there are any you feel would be ineffective please state the reason why. Then list at least one way you can apply this strategy in your own classroom.

Strategy	Reason for effectiveness	Way to apply this in your own classroom
Cultivate relationships and be culturally responsive		

续表

Strategy	Reason for effectiveness	Way to apply this in your own classroom
Teach language skills across the curriculum		
Emphasize productive language		
Speak slowly – and increase your wait time		
Differentiate – and use multiple modalities		
Incorporate students' native languages – and don't be afraid of technology		

（5）课堂表现评价标准如表6-27所示。

表6-27　教学案例6-1课堂表现评价表

	1-待行动	2-待进步	3-合格	4-优秀	得分
参与状态	学生表现出不自在	学生表现出一定的舒适感	学生表现出较多的舒适感	学生表现出自然大方的状态	
理解和学习	学生没有表现出对任务的理解并且似乎没有在学习	学生表现出一定程度地对任务的理解并开始学习	学生表现出对任务的较多理解，并学到了较多内容	学生表现出对任务的充分理解，并掌握了大部分或所有学习内容	

续表

	1-待行动	2-待进步	3-合格	4-优秀	得分
参与度和社交情况	学生没有表现出参与的意愿，也没有建立社交关系	学生表现出一些参与的愿望，并试图建立社交联系	学生表现出较多的参与愿望，并进行了较多的社交互动	学生充分参与并与多名学生建立联系	

3. 案例评析

英语学习者是指学习英语的个人，通常是将英语作为第二语言习得的学生。在美国等很多英语国家，已有相当数量的学生将英语作为第二语言学习。身为英语教育工作者，我们有义务适应变化，与时俱进，努力成为来到教室学习的任何学生的优秀老师。我们应该为英语学习者投入更多的关注和时间。英语教学策略和方法多种多样，有些是适用于任何学生和教师的。这种形式的课堂学习和讨论可以帮助所有现在和未来的教师确定每个学生的优劣势和特定的学习方式。我们教师要坚信通过这样的付出，每个孩子都能成功。

4. 辅助资源

（1）英语学习欢迎礼包的介绍性文章。

（2）关于差异化教学的视频。

（3）关于教学策略的文章。

（二）教学案例 6-2　计算机技术辅助英语学习与学习工具的选择

项目主题：Learning English with Technology - which tools to use?

该主题属于“人与社会”范畴，涉及“积极的学习体验，恰当的学习方法与策略，勤学善思”和“职业启蒙，职业精神”子主题。

1. 内容分析

本案例旨在引导学生了解在线可用的英语语言教学资源和工具，为今后从事语言教育工作做好资源储备，计算机辅助语言教学也为有意从事语言教育研究的学生提供了一种大有可为的思路和方向。

2. 实施过程

（1）情景介绍，引入教学主题。

Context

You have been hired by a private language school to teach English. The Director of the school has just invested in "state-of-the-art" technology - there is a fast wifi connection to each classroom, interactive whiteboards in every room, enough tablets for each learner to use in class etc. However, despite spending a lot of money, she has no clear idea how all this technology should best be used. She has called on you as a group to research what to recommend to teachers and expects you to give a set of recommendations at the next staff meeting.

（2）教师介绍任务概况。

You will each choose to focus on a different one of the following aspects of language learning: listening, speaking, reading and writing.

You will get together with others interested in that aspect and develop three criteria for adoption of learning technology tools.

You will then work with your original group to evaluate a number of language learning tools that can be found on the Internet, trying as far as you can to make sure that the criteria you have been decided are respected and that your aspect of language learning is fully catered for.

As a group you will find a tool that you think the Director of your school should recommend to teachers. You will have clear reasons for your choice linked to the various aspects of language learning that you have focused on.

（3）学生分组后，教师发布任务的相关提示。

What is the name of your school? Choose something that everyone is happy with.

You will each be responsible for a different aspect of language learning.

①Listening Leader

②Speaking Expert

③Reading Researcher

④Writing Representative

Then get together with those with a similar role.

For the Listening Leaders:

Look at some discussion of how listening skills can be supported, and then with that and your own understanding of the listening skill decide on three criteria for choosing an online tool for listening support. You have 15 minutes.

For the Speaking Experts

Look at some discussion of how speaking skills can be supported, and then with that and your own understanding of the speaking skill decide on three criteria for choosing an online tool for speaking support. You have 15 minutes.

For the Reading Researchers

Look at some discussion of how reading skills can be supported, and then with that and your own understanding of the reading skill decide on three criteria for choosing an online tool for reading support. You have 15 minutes.

For the Writing Representatives

Look at some discussion of how writing skills can be supported, and then with that and your own understanding of the writing skill decide on three criteria for choosing an online tool for writing support. You have 15 minutes.

Back with your original group, remind yourselves of criteria for CALL (Computer-Assisted Language Learning) task appropriateness:

①Language-learning potential

②Learner fit

③Meaning focus

④Authenticity

⑤Positive Impact

⑥Practicality

As well as the characteristics of good materials:

①Interaction

②Motivation

③Autonomy

④Collaboration

⑤Feedback

⑤Creativity

Bearing these in mind as well as the criteria that each of you bring for the various skills, choose ONE of the following websites/tools that you feel fulfills MOST of your criteria for MOST of the language aspects you have been researching OR if you think that one skill is more important than others, a tool that supports that skill - make sure you are all in agreement about which skill and why.

You have 40 minutes. Make sure that everyone's opinion is taken into consideration. Agree on a system to help make your decisions.

Candidate websites/tools: Quizlet, Breaking News English, Tubequizard, Simple English Videos, Duolingo, Voicethread, Lyricstraining, Voki, YouGlish, and Speech-

Ling.

Once you have decided, nominate one of your group to explain which one you chose and why in the next staff meeting.

（4）项目成果评价标准如表 6-28 所示。

表 6-28 教学案例 6-2 项目成果评价表

	1-待行动	2-待进步	3-合格	4-优秀	得分
选择在线英语学习工具的标准制定	制定的标准不足三条，或者理由薄弱或无关	制定了三条标准，一些理由有一定关联	介绍了三条标准，给出的理由清楚且恰当	介绍了三条标准，给出的理由均十分有力	
选择英语学习工具的团队合作过程	未始终处于合作状态，有些意见分歧未得到解决	大部分时间保持合作，能够解决大多数意见分歧	始终保持合作，能够以较为满意的方式解决意见分歧	始终密切合作，通过有效讨论达成理想的决议，得到全体成员的认可	
选定工具并给出合理解释	未选定工具或解释无法令人信服	选定了工具，解释基本相关	选定了工具，解释基本令人信服	选定了工具，解释非常具有说服力	

（5）课程回顾与反思。

You have chosen your tools and given your presentation, justifying your choices - the Director of the school is very pleased with all your hard work!

Now reflect on what you learned in the process of this activity. Did you learn more about language learning skills? Did you learn about the variety of resources available online for English Language Teaching? Did you learn about being part of a team and negotiating a conclusion when everyone has a different agenda? Did you find a good system so that everyone's point could be taken into account?

Also reflect on the way the task itself was structured. This was a task designed around a Comparative Judgement framework. It was also a jigsaw task - each person in each group had a specific role and contribution to make - the task could not have been successful without each person's involvement. What are the benefits of this kind of task? What are the possible drawbacks? You might want to reflect on these issues and use this experience to support comments in your assignment.

3. 案例评析

本案例适用于以探索语言教学方法为主题的语言教育方向的本科高年级或研究生课程，也可用于本科阶段的英语学习预备课程。

4. 辅助资源

(1) 常见的英语学习问题示例（用于引入教学主题）。

(2)《中国英语能力等级量表》，帮助学生了解英语学习涉及的诸多方面。

(3) 在线英语学习工具/网站示例。

（三）教学案例 6-3 应对校园欺凌（4 课时）

项目主题：Warding off Bullying

该主题属于“人与自我”范畴，涉及“多彩、安全、有意义的校园生活”和“职业启蒙、职业精神”子主题。

1. 内容分析

近年来，校园欺凌受到社会广泛关注，这一社会问题对构建安全和谐校园带来巨大挑战，也是每位正在或即将从事语言教育工作的教师需要防范和应对的重要问题。本案例旨在唤起语言教育方向的英语专业学生对校园欺凌的重视，引导学生探讨具有可操作性的解决方案，为今后工作中防范遏制校园欺凌做好准备。

2. 实施过程

(1) 导入教学主题。

Bullying is a fast growing problem in the US school system. About 160, 000 students miss school every day to avoid bullying. There are 2. 7 million students bullied each year.

Bullying is not ok. Bullying is not just another “joke” . Bullying does not make people feel part of a group. It is not acceptable under any circumstances

“Bullying builds character like nuclear waste createssuperheroes. It's a rare occurrence and often does much more damage than endowment. ” - Author Zack W. Van

The GOOD news is that YOU can make a DIFFERENCE!

Use this Bullying module to educate yourself on the issue and start to make a difference in your classroom, your school, and your community.

（2）研究并探讨校园欺凌，撰写小论文。

Research what is the definition of bullying? Research online or print media a recent bullying incident that has made local or national news. What happened? How was the student being bullied? What were the consequences for the person (s) who was the bully? Write a short essay that describes bullying is and answers the questions about the incident. Include conclusion that discusses how you would react if you were in the situation of the student who was bullied. (minimum 1 page double spaced)

Step 1: Get into groups of 2 students. Do all the steps with your group.

Step 2: Research the definition of bullying and what behavior is considered bullying (use links and sources provided on credits page).

Step 3: Research a recent bullying incident that made national or local news. Find out what happened with the incident. How was the student that was bullied? What were the consequences for the person engaged in the bullying (if any)?

Step 4: Synthesize your ideas of steps 2, 3 in a 1-2 page paper (double spaced) to be turned into class. In your conclusion write about what you would do if you were in the shoes of the student being bullied. How would you react if you were being bullied in the way described in the incident? Make sure to provide the source of your article/incident using APA format.

（3）制定政策遏制校园欺凌。

Create a new bullying policy for the school that the incident occurred. For policy include a detailed list of what behavior in considered bullying. In addition to the list include consequences for students who violate aspects of the bullying policy. You can have zero-tolerance policy, a tiered approach (progress consequences), or some other methods of consequence (be creative!). Make sure your policy would address the problems that were encountered in your researched incident. This may require some research into other schools policies for examples. (minimum 1 page double spaced)

Step 1: Research other school policies on bullying (look at examples on credits page). These sources are very detailed. Your policy does not need this level of detail, but needs to address all the necessary components.

Step 2: Make a detailed list of what behavior is considered bullying in your new school policy. Make sure your policy list included the behavior that occurred in your researched incident. The policy list should make clear that all the behavior mentioned is unacceptable in and outside of school.

Step 3: Create a system of consequences for students who have violated your new policy list. This system should fully address what happens to a student who brakes the policy rules. Be creative in your consequences! (Should not have to be just suspensions/detentions). What consequences that you think would be appropriate for a school to implement and also deters students from bullying in the first place.

Step 4: Synthesize steps 2, 3 into a written policy to be turned in to class (1-2 pages double spaced).

（4）项目成果评价标准如表 6-29 所示。

表 6-29　教学案例 6-3 项目成果评价表

	达到预期	接近预期	低于预期
研究欺凌事件（满分 5 分）	5 分：介绍了一个近期发生且相关的欺凌事件，通过可靠的消息来源获取相关信息	3 分：研究了一个欺凌事件，但不是近期发生的（近五年内），或不相关，消息来源可靠	0 分：没有证据表明研究了一个欺凌事件
欺凌事件小论文（满分 10 分）	10 分：论文定义了欺凌，充分清楚地回答了所有关于欺凌的问题，结论展现了对被欺凌者的感受的理解和共情	6 分：论文定义了欺凌，未回答所有关于欺凌的问题，有些答案考虑不够充分。结论未展现对被欺凌者的感受的深刻体察	0 分：未定义欺凌，未回答相关问题，未明确给出结论
反欺凌政策（满分 20 分）	20 分：政策明确定义并列出了哪些行为被视为欺凌行为，包括当前研究事件中存在的行为。对后果的推断经过深思熟虑，展现了创造力	12 分：政策列出了哪些行为被视为欺凌行为，未包括当前研究事件中存在的行为。对后果的推断未展现创造力	0 分：政策未定义欺凌，也未列出哪些行为被视为欺凌行为。政策未说明欺凌需要承担的主要后果

续表

	达到预期	接近预期	低于预期
语言组织与语法（满分5分）	5分：事件论文和政策的说明有效清晰。写作没有语法错误。资料来源真实存在，引用格式正确	3分：事件论文和政策都包含一些语法错误。文章的部分内容不够清晰。资料来源真实存在并且注明出处	0分：事件论文和政策都写得不好，不够清楚。没有注明资料来源

（5）课程总结与回顾。

“What if the kid you bullied at school, grew up, and turned out to be the only surgeon who could save your life?” – Lynette Mather

Congratulations on completing the bullying module!

This DOES NOT mean your work is done. Bullying is a problem that requires you to be vigilant and be aware during all your time in school. All it takes is one incident to effect someone and change their lives!

To end this activity please reflect on how bullying may have affected your life or someone who you know. Let this motivate you to do more on the issue!

“If you are neutral in situations of injustice, you have chosen the side of the oppressor. If an elephant has its foot on the tail of a mouse, and you say that you are neutral, the mouse will not appreciate your neutrality.” – Desmond Tutu

In the end no policy will be truly effective without students holding themselves responsible and stepping up to help stop this problem that affects their own community of peers. YOU can make a difference.

“Knowing what’s right doesn’t mean much unless you do what’s right.” – Theodore Roosevelt

3. 案例评析

在应对校园欺凌问题方面，教师的作用不可或缺。通过场景模拟、角色扮演和制定政策等活动，本案例让未来的英语教师可以未雨绸缪，更好地应对走上工作岗位后可能面临的现实情况。除了校园霸凌这一重要议题，本案例形式还可以进一步推广，适用于引导语言教育方向的英语专业学生探讨英语教学工作可能需要解决的各种具有挑战性的问题。

4. 辅助资源

（1）介绍校园霸凌的短视频，引入教学主题。

（2）中外校园霸凌案例，用于课堂讨论校园霸凌的危害。

（四）教学案例 6-4 F. 斯科特·菲茨杰拉德是盖茨比的原型吗？（4 课时）

项目主题：F. Scott Fitzgerald：The Real Gatsby?

该主题属于“人与社会”范畴，涉及“中外文学史上有代表性的作家和作品”子主题。

1. 内容分析

在本案例中，学生将对 F. 斯科特·菲茨杰拉德进行深入研究，并完成两页双面篇幅的日志来比较菲茨杰拉德和盖茨比。然后，学生将制作演示幻灯片并就“F. 斯科特·菲茨杰拉德是盖茨比的原型吗？”这个问题表达自己的看法。

2. 实施过程

（1）导入教学主题。

He had one of those rare smileswith a quality of eternal reassurance in it, that you may come across four or five times in life. It faced, or seemed to face, the whole external world for an instant and then concentrated on you with an irresistible prejudice in your favor. It understood you just as far as you wanted to be understood, believed in you as you would like to believe in yourself.

The truth was that Jay Gatsby, of West Egg, Long Island, sprang from his Platonic conception of himself. He was a son of God—a phrase which, if it means anything, means just that—and he must be about His Father's business, the service of a vast, vulgar, and meretricious beauty. So he invented just the sort of Jay Gatsby that a seventeen year old boy would be likely to invent, and to this conception he was faithful to the end.

（2）教师介绍任务概况。

Many critics suspect that F. Scott Fitzgerald's *The Great Gatsby*, is actually an autobiography based on Fitzgerald's life and Fitzgerald is Gatsby. You are to create a double sided journal comparing and contrasting the life of Fitzgerald and the life of Gatsby. To write your journal entries, you will research Fitzgerald and use detailed evidence from the book. At the end of your project, you will present your findings to the class using a PowerPoint and you will also pick a position on this long-time debate.

（3）学生网络调研。

Spend some time online researching F. Scott Fitzgerald. Locate at least 5 credible sources.

Make a detailed list of what you have learned about Fitzgerald. You may use any format you like, outline, notecards, graphic organizer, but you must turn in this portion with your final project.

Now create a similar set of notes about the character of Jay Gatsby. Use the text to find specific evidence.

Use the online library resources and journals to find critical essays or reviews commenting on the comparisons between Fitzgerald and Gatsby. You must find at least three critical writings.

Organize what you have found on the theory that Fitzgerald is Gatsby.

Create a chart of information comparing and contrasting Fitzgerald and Gatsby in terms of this theory.

（4）学生撰写日志。

Your are to create 5 double sided journal entries of Fitzgerald and Gatsby.

These entries are to be well written and are your evidence for your presentation.

Consider writing entries on elements such as childhood, education, family and personal life, education, place in society, values, and opinions on society.

（5）学生根据日志内容准备课堂展示的幻灯片。

You are to create a PowerPoint presentation showing your findings and taking a position on this issue.

You may choose any position, but you must prove your reasoning in your journals and you must center your presentation on your position.

Your goal is to convince your classmates that you have the correct position.

（6）项目成果评价标准如表6-30所示。

表6-30　教学案例6-4项目成果评价表

	1-待行动	2-待进步	3-合格	4-优秀	得分
写作体现出研究的努力成果	几乎没有研究，作文全部是个人观点的罗列	1-2处用到了研究内容	完成了研究工作，但与观点的结合不够紧密	使用了8个信息来源，有效加强了项目的可信度	

续表

	1-待行动	2-待进步	3-合格	4-优秀	得分
对盖茨比和菲茨杰拉德进行了均等评述	未遵循双面日志的写作格式，只关注其中一人	遵循双面日志的写作格式，但只关注其中一人	遵循双面日志的写作格式，但介绍了两人不同方面的特点	遵循双面日志的写作格式，且有效比较了二人特质	
作文的总体情况	存在一些语法错误，未做有效校对	5-6 处技术性细节错误，做了一些校对	3-4 处技术性细节错误，有证据表明做了校对	技术性细节错误很少，显然做了校对	
引用格式	未遵循 MLA 格式	3-4 处 MLA 格式错误	遵循 MLA 格式，3-4 处技术性细节错误	严格遵循 MLA 格式，仅有 1-2 处技术性细节错误	
幻灯片	未展示研究发现，创意很少	体现研究发现和创意的证据很少	展示的知识和主题增强了演讲的可信度，有创意	出色地展示了相关知识，增强了演讲的可信度，有创意且流畅	
课堂演讲	未事先准备，未有效使用 PowerPoint，或未切题演讲	使用了 PowerPoint，但总体组织欠妥或内容错误过多	有效使用 PowerPoint，演讲经过事先准备	有效使用 PowerPoint，演讲组织巧妙，自然流畅，令人信服	

续表

	1-待行动	2-待进步	3-合格	4-优秀	得分
学生提出观点并用论据支持	未陈述观点	陈述了观点，但没有证据支持	清楚陈述观点，有一些证据支持	清楚陈述观点，支持证据有效	

(7) 课程回顾总结。

Congratulations! You have now successfully completed your project! Some things to think about as we wrap up aresuggested below:

What did you learn through this process?

Did you feel you gathered enough research to take a position?

After hearing all your classmates' speeches, what is your position now? Is it the same? If it is different, whose project most influenced your position?

3. 案例评析

本案例形式适用于所有外国文学课程的人物分析环节，引导学生通过自主探究了解人物生平，运用不同视角理解人物动机和成长历程，培养批判性思维。通过课堂展示自己的研究过程，学生可以有效整理反思研究思路和方法，对今后的文学研究写作大有裨益。

4. 辅助资源

(1) 盖茨比电影片段，用于引入教学主题。

(2) 日志撰写示例。

(五) 教学案例 6-5　古罗马之旅 (4 课时)

项目主题：A Trip to Ancient Rome

该主题属于“人与社会”范畴，涉及“历史、社会与文化”子主题。

1. 内容分析

在本案例中，学生将展开一段跨越时空之旅，通过自主探究，深入了解古罗马历史。英语很多词汇来源于拉丁语，学生在探索古罗马历史的同时，还将接触到一些拉丁语词汇，初探英语的语言发展史。

2. 实施过程

(1) 导入教学主题。

During this project, you will be “traveling” to ancient Rome! While there you will learn about its history, geography, people, cultures, and more. You will learn about the famous architecture as well as the government system that ruled the empire and be able to compare and contrast what you learn to things you see today.

Keep an eye out for some Latin words throughout this project. Find the definitions for some extra credit!

（2）教师介绍任务概况。

Writea poem, song, rap, or essay about the people and cultures the existed in ancient Rome.

Use a venn-diagram to compare and contrast the government of ancient Rome to the United States government today.

Choose a famous building or structure from ancient Rome. Draw a replica of it or create a model, write a brief explanation of its history, and label the important aspects of it.

Pick a topic of of your choice, related to ancient Rome, and write a short story about it.

（3）学生分组后讨论分工，小组成员分头研究这个项目的各个方面。各人负责研究的内容各有不同，但最终项目仍是团队合作，所有人都将与队友分享自己的研究发现。评价标准可以提前发给学生，让学生了解对这个项目的预期。

（4）教师给出提示性问题，供学生研究过程中参考。

①Why do you think Rome is known as the "Eternal City"?

②Who were the legendary founders of Rome?

③According to mythology, how old is the "Eternal City"?

④Who were the patricians?

⑤Who was considered upper class? Middle class? Lower class?

⑥What was the Forum? What building is like today?

⑦If the former American President Obama or Donald Trump lived in ancient Rome, would he be considered a patrician or plebeian?

（5）项目成果评价标准如表6-31所示。

表 6-31 教学案例 6-5 项目成果评价表

	5分	4分	3分	2分	1分
团队贡献与合作	学生承担了开展研究和寻找答案的职责。此外，学生对小组做出了贡献，欢迎队友做出贡献，用尊重他人的方式表达不同意见	学生承担了开展研究和寻找答案的大部分职责。此外，学生大部分时间都在为小组做出贡献，并欢迎他人做出贡献。学生在表达不同意见时需要对他人更加尊重	学生承担了开展研究和寻找答案的一些职责。此外，学生和小组队友坐在一起，但没有充分参与。学生回应他人但未自愿承担工作。学生不会干扰同伴的工作	学生在开展研究和寻找答案方面的贡献不大。学生大部分时间不参与和/或发表无关或分散注意力的言论	学生没有为项目做出贡献。学生不参与，有时会离开小组。学生会对他人进行人身攻击
语言规约（拼写、语法、标点符号）	语法、拼写和单词使用正确，有助于提升清晰度和风格	语法、拼写和单词使用方面的错误极少	经常出现重复性错误	存在重大错误	存在干扰沟通的重大错误
最终成果	信息准确全面。所有材料和信息都井井有条，清晰而有逻辑地呈现	信息大多是准确全面的，几乎不包含无关的细节。大多数材料和信息都体现了组织性、清晰度和逻辑性	信息较为准确和全面。有些材料和信息展示了组织性或清晰度或逻辑性	信息较为准确和全面。包含无关的细节。有些材料和信息展示了组织性或清晰度或逻辑性	信息很少或根本没有提供信息。材料缺乏组织，很少或根本不注意清晰度或逻辑性

续表

	5分	4分	3分	2分	1分
资源使用	项目使用了提供的许多资源。学生们还不落窠臼，自行找到其他资源来支持本组的成果	使用了一些提供的资源。学生们还找到了一两个可以使用的外部资源	使用了一些提供的资源。学生没有自行寻找其他资源	很少使用提供的资源。没有找到外部资源	学生只使用一两个提供的资源来收集所有信息

（6）课程回顾总结。

Create a list of the Latin words and definitions your group found, put all group members' names on them, and turn in for extra credit!

Individually, please write me a brief summary of your experience with this project. In the first half, explain some things that you learned. In the second half, explain a few things you liked about this project, as well as any suggestions you may have to improve it.

3. 案例评析

本案例引导学生自主探究古罗马历史文化，与英语发展史的学习相结合，最终整合为历史文化和语言的跨学科实践活动。本案例形式适用于外国历史文化课程的阶段性回顾复习环节，以及国别区域研究方向课程的学生自主研究环节。

4. 辅助资源

（1）古罗马图片或影视剧片段，用于引入教学主题。

（2）源于拉丁语词汇的常见英语词汇示例。

（六）教学案例 6-6　体验演员的一天（4 课时）

项目主题：An Actor for One Day

该主题属于“人与社会”范畴，涉及“跨文化沟通与交流，语言与文化”和“中外影视的文化价值和作品赏析”子主题。

1. 内容分析

在本案例中，学生将通过自主式探究，深入热门电视剧的内核，通过角色扮演理解电视剧人物的成长经历和言行动机，发挥想象力和创造力，以跨文化视角重构经典剧集。

2. 实施过程

（1）导入教学主题。

Have you ever thought about being famous? A model, a writer, a football player, a singer...?

What about being an actor at least for a day? What a wonderful idea!

Imagine you are the protagonists of one of the most famous TV series of the world!

In this project you will explore the wonders of the seventh art from the inside. Are you ready to enjoy? This is one of the main goals: ENJOYING WHILE LEARNING.

（2）学生分成6组，通过网络检索深入研究电视剧人物。

First of all, you have to search information about the main characters of the TV series The Big Bang Theory (Sheldon, Leonard, Howard, Raj and Penny). Once you have enough information, what you have to do is to create a draft in which you specify: a) characteristics of the protagonists (physical appearance and behaviour), b) relationship between the different characters, c) context of the series, d) useful vocabulary.

The draft will be handed in the next day of class.

Group 1: "Pilot"

Group 2: "The Big Bran Hypothesis"

Group 3: "The Fuzzy Boots Corollary"

Group 4: "The Luminous Fish Effect"

Group 5: "The Hamburger Postulate"

Group 6: "The Middle-Earth Paradigm"

（3）改写剧集剧本，分角色演绎新剧本，录制视频。

Each group has to write their own script based on their episode. Do not reproduce exactly what appears in the episode, you have to be creative. Try to imagine you are within the screen, living the same situation of your episode, and design a new plot.

Now, it's your turn! It's time to see your actor side. With the scripts you created in the previous task, each group has to record themselves reproducing the situations of their scripts.

Each member of the group has to adopt a role: one of you will be Sheldon, another one will be Leonard, another one will be Penny, another one will be Howard and another one will be Raj (it doesn't matter if there are no girls in the group, or if there are more girls than boys, because you have to customize) .

Be careful: EVERY member of the group has to APPEAR AND SPEAK in the video.

Timing: each video has to be 5 minutes maximum and 2 minutes minimum.

We will play all the videos the last day in class.

(4) 项目成果评价标准如表 6-32 所示。

表 6-32　教学案例 6-6 项目成果评价表

	待行动 (5%)	待进步 (10%)	合格 (15%)	优秀 (20%)	得分
表演质量和用时 (20%)	并非所有成员都出现在视频中。人物塑造粗心大意，表演不够专业。视频时长不到 2 分钟	所有成员都出现在视频中，但有的角色台词极少。表演较为专业，但舞台呈现出现一些错误，视频时长为 2~3 分钟	所有成员都出现在视频中，台词均等。表演专业，角色改编适当，视频时长为 3~4 分钟	所有成员都出现在视频中，台词均等。表演非常专业，角色改编巧妙，视频时长为 4~5 分钟	
语法和词汇使用 (20%)	存在一些语法和词汇错误，学生未掌握之前学过的语法点和词汇	所有成员都用到了之前学过的语法结构，但存在一些错误，词汇使用也有一些错误	所有成员都用到了之前学过的语法结构，使用情况几乎完美，同时也用到了之前学过的词汇	所有成员都完美使用了之前学过的语法结构，同时也用到了之前学过的词汇，还增加了新词	
发音 (20%)	学生发音情况不佳，表演难以理解	学生发音水平一般，频繁出错，表演可以理解	学生发音水平良好，不常出错，表演易于理解	学生发音完美，表演易于理解	

续表

	待行动（5%）	待进步（10%）	合格（15%）	优秀（20%）	得分
流利度（20%）	学生经常停顿，停顿时间较长（超过4秒）	学生未出现明显停顿，不常停顿（不超过3秒）	学生停顿较难察觉，停顿不超过3次，每次不超过2秒	表演流畅，没有停顿	
创意（20%）	学生照搬了部分原剧本，没有体现创意	学生照搬了部分原剧本，但加入了一些变化	学生创设了新情景，但起承转合欠自然（照搬部分原剧本）	学生根据剧集的背景信息，创设了全新情景录制视频	

3. 案例评析

角色扮演是一种常见的口语练习活动，学生能够学习换位思考和团队协作，训练语言输出能力。本案例以年轻人喜闻乐见的影视剧为主题，鼓励学生发挥创造力和想象力，改编经典剧集，并尝试加入华人角色，探索中国文化海外传播的新途径。本案例形式适用于复习特定语言和文化知识的教学环节，待改编剧集需要涉及相关语言和文化知识，以便让学生在巩固所学知识的同时，以自己喜欢的形式开展语言表达活动，从而提高英语学习的兴趣。

4. 辅助资源

（1）相关剧集的情节概要。

（2）相关剧集的原始剧本。

（3）剧本撰写和创意写作的注意事项。

（4）《宇宙大爆炸》电视剧的幕后故事。

（七）教学案例 6-7　给陌生人写信（4 课时）

项目主题：A Letter to a Stranger

该主题属于“人与社会”范畴，涉及“良好的人际关系与人际交往”子主题。

1. 内容分析

在本案例中，学生将给陌生人写一封信或一张明信片，这个温暖人心的活动除有助于拉近人与人之间的距离外，还能培养学生的共情能力和创意写作能力。

2. 实施过程

（1）导入教学主题。

“It is the best feeling in the world getting an unexpected message from someone across the world”

Have you ever received a letter or a postcard? A real message, not an electronic one! Nowadays when we have our cell phones, laptops and WIFI whenever we want, communication became so simple, just type a message and send it in just one click. You don’t even have to follow any certain rules when composing it. Emojis replaced real emotions, we keep out thoughts and feelings inside. Now imagine you hold a pen in your hand and are going to write a letter... to a stranger! What would you write? What if this stranger’s life success depends on what you’ll write in your letter? What can you write to inspire this person?

（2）教师介绍任务概况。

Your challenge is to find a stranger and compose a letter or to choose a postcard and write on it your message according to their tastes following certain rules of letter-writing.

（3）学生在国际笔友网站任意确定一位收信人。

（4）学生可以先了解收信人的个人情况，以便向他们提出有趣的问题，或者参考以下建议：

①Express what daily life is like where you’re sending the card from by describing what you did today, your routine, etc.

②Write 5 curious facts about the place where the card is from.

③Give local traveling tips from your area! What are the must-sees around you?

④Include your favorite quote, perhaps in its original language (with translation!)

⑤What was the last thing you cooked or ate? Include a recipe!

⑥What do you have in common with the recipient of your card?

⑦Recount a childhood memory, or something you’ve learned from your grand-parents.

⑧What makes you happy? If it makes you smile, there’s a good chance others will like to hear about it.

⑨Share a local idiom or saying, in its original language, with translation of course!

⑩Did you ever travel to the place where your card is going? Recall your best memory of that place.

⑪What's the weather like as you are writing your postcard? Draw the weather forecast in detail, and don't forget to include the temperature!

⑫Share an interesting fact that you've learned, and which most people are not aware of.

⑬Got an unusual hobby or collection? Do tell!

⑭Did anything important happen in your country lately? Share an interesting news bit!

⑮Write about your favorite book, movie or band.

⑯Draw a picture of your surroundings, or your favorite object in that room.

⑰Write your favorite poem or ... make up your own poem!

⑱What are the local festivals or traditions from your area?

⑲If you're a student, what are you studying? What was the last thing you learnt in school?

(5) 学生撰写给陌生笔友的信，具体要求如下：

Each letter must have:

A Heading (you can use the school's address if you do not feel comfortable using your own)

A Greeting (Dear ________,)

A Body (3 paragraphs minimum)

The 1st paragraph should explain why you are writing to the individual. Is it a coincidence or did you choose this person because you have something in common?

The 2nd paragraph should talk about something you think is essential and interesting. Ask questions, too!

The 3rd paragraph should politely ask for a letter or a postcard in response and to wish them good luck in whatever they do。

Each of you will be required to hand in an envelope (you can decorate it) with the proper mailing address for your stranger written clearly and a stamp.

(6) 项目成果评价标准如表6-33所示。

表 6-33　教学案例 6-7 项目成果评价表

	1-待行动	2-待进步	3-合格	4-优秀	得分
问候语与结束语	缺失问候语和/或结束语	问候语和结束语存在至少 3 处错误，其中之一或二者的位置不正确	问候语和结束语几乎没有错误，位置正确	问候语和结束语的位置、标点符号和大小写均没有错误	
信的正文	很多句子碎片或连写句，没有证据表明分段	大多数句子是完整且正确的。段落缺乏组织	所有句子完整且正确，不存在句子碎片或连写句。段落基本正确	句子和段落完整正确，句子结构和词汇多变	
遵循基本写作规范	信的正文存在很多拼写和/或语法错误，内容难以理解	信的正文存在一些拼写或语法错误，干扰理解	信的正文存在 2～3 个大小写或标点符号错误，不影响理解	信的正文没有语法或拼写错误	
可辨识	很多错误干扰，难以辨认	一些错误干扰，有一部分难以辨认	书写清楚，有 1～2 个错误干扰，便于阅读	书写清楚，没有干扰性错误	
观点组织	句子之间互不关联。很难把握信的主要意思	观点组织在了一起，但不是非常清楚。需要多读几遍才能明白信的主要意思	观点表达非常清晰，但组织性有待加强	观点表达清晰且有组织。很容易明白信的主要意思	

续表

	1-待行动	2-待进步	3-合格	4-优秀	得分
遵守教室规章和指令	学生未经允许离开指定区域，干扰课堂	学生偶尔会未经允许离开指定区域	学生待在指定区域，只与同伴小声交谈	学生待在指定区域专注完成任务，安静工作，遵守项目指令和课堂指令	

（7）课程回顾与总结。

Now that your letters are mailed and you each have the ability to write an amazing letter I would like you to write one more!

Please write a one paragraph letter to me. In this letter you should evaluate yourself. Please answer some of the following questions:

Did you do your very best on this assignment?

Did you wait until the last minute to do this assignment?

How did you prepare for this task?

Do you think your stranger will write you back?

Where did you choose this person?

What grade would you give yourself on this assignment?

This is a final form of assessment for me. This will let me know if you all fully understand how to write a friendly letter and it is a chance for you to tell me why you deserve a good grade or not. Please be honest because your effort will show as I am grading the assignment.

3. 案例评析

本案例不仅适用于低年级英语专业学生的书信写作和创意写作课程，还适用于大学阶段英语课程的应用文写作。学生还可以随机接收同学写的信件，对同学的书信写作情况作出评价。自评结合他评的方式，有助于学生提高英文写作水平。

4. 辅助资源

（1）关于写信注意事项的介绍性 ppt。

（2）国际笔友网站（或教师安排笔友，也可以考虑使用自然语言处理技术撰写的回信）。

（八）教学案例 6-8　中国梦的意义（4 课时）

项目主题：What Does the Chinese Dream Mean to You?

该主题属于"人与自我""人与社会"范畴，涉及"自我认识，自我管理，自我提升"和"家乡和社会的变迁，历史的发展，对未来的畅想"子主题。

1. 内容分析

在本案例中，学生将回顾美国梦的历史变迁，并通过对比美国梦与中国梦的概念内涵，加深对中国梦的认识，培养爱国热情和民族自豪感，树立为国为民的远大理想。

2. 实施过程

（1）导入教学主题。

Newspapers, magazine articles, and blogs are talking about the end of the American Dream as the result of recent developments and events, such as the economic crisis in 2009, the shooting of Michael Brown, poverty reports, Covid-19 epidemic, etc.

In the run for presidency, Donald Trump too addresses this issue:

"The fact is, the American Dream is dead - but if I win, I will bring it back bigger and better and stronger than ever before." (Donald Trump 2016 Announcement, June 16 2015)

But what does this "American Dream" he is talking about mean? Why is it so important for the USA? And is there a German Dream? What is the Chinese dream? Why is it so important for China?

（2）教师介绍任务概况，学生分组研究美国梦和中国梦。

As experts you will be taking part in a conference about the national dreams and explain the significance to the Chinese audience.

Working with four other students in a team, you choose one of the followingroles:

Historian: The Roots of the American Dream or the Chinese Dream

Sociologist: Equality in the American Dream or the Chinese Dream

Etymologist: Definition of the American Dream or the Chinese Dream

Journalist: Today's Challenges to the American Dream or the Chinese Dream

Anthropologist: The American/Chinese Way of Life and Famous People Living the American/Chinese Dream

Before you start researching, brainstorm together in your group what you already know about the American Dream or the Chinese Dream.

（3）各组分角色阅读相应文章并记笔记。

Read the texts given for each role and take notes. Make sure you can refer back to passages of your texts if there's a question later on. Reading long and authentic texts can be difficult at times. Therefore, you should first explore the article (get an overview of the whole text by scrolling through, previewing the main idea, etc.). Next, you start with intensive reading. Keep the guiding questions (see below) for your summary in mind. They will help you to distinguish between important and secondary information.

Guiding questions are as follows:

Etymologist

• How has the meaning of the American Dream or the Chinese Dream changed over the decades? What is today's understanding of the American Dream or the Chinese Dream? To what extent does the modern understanding differ from the vision of the founding fathers?

Historian

• On the basis of the historical background, what was their American/Chinese Dream about? To what extent can you link the conception of the American Dream/Chinese Dream to the key historical events? Is it correct to just talk about a "dream" in its literal sense?

Sociologist

• What is the Civil Rights Movement/Communist Manifesto about and how is it linked to the American Dream/ Chinese Dream? What does the situation look like today? To what extent can you say has equality been achieved in the US or China today?

Journalist

• What challenges the American/Chinese Dream today? What role does the low-wage income/subsistence allowance policy for the American/Chinese Dream? To what extent can a different economic policy restore the American Dream/To what extent can an economic policy impact the Chinese Dream?

Anthropologist

• What is meant by the "American Way of Life" / "Chinese Way of Life"? Are there any famous persons who are living/ lived the American/Chinese Dream? In how far is the American/Chinese Dream and the American/Chinese Way of Life connected?

（4）小组成员集中讨论各自获得的重要信息，澄清疑问，为下一步做好准备。

（5）将 American Dream 和 Chinese Dream 进行对比，并给出对 What does Chinese Dream mean to you？的回答。

（6）小组成员合作完成课堂展示的设计和幻灯片制作。

As a group you need to make these important decisions：

Who will be doing what during the presentation? Everyone must have a part in the presentation. Who should start?

What will the title for your PowerPoint presentation be? What title brings together the important aspects of each of your roles?

Do you have a computer expert in your group? Is he/she willing to take the lead for the assembly of your PowerPoint?

The gathered information of each member will be turned into a PowerPoint presentation. You should not put entire paragraphs on the PowerPoint slides, but instead only the main points. Each role should get at least one slide. Be sure to make the slides and your presentation interesting to look at and listen to. Your peers will not only be grading you on the information provided, but also on the quality of your presentation.

Your presentation should

- Be approximately 10 minutes long.
- Be interesting, informative, and creative.
- Should present all information in a clear and focused way.
- Address the answers to the guiding questions.

Assign the following roles to the team members and write down your assignments.

- Presentation Designer：You coordinate the making of the presentation. That does not mean that you have to type everything on your own! Tell the others what they can do to help you. Tip：Each member can prepare the text for their slides individually and you can assemble them afterwards.

- Grammar/Spelling Monitor：You focus on correct grammar, spelling and punctuation of the presentation.

- Time Manager：You make sure that time is used efficiently and keep track of your members' work and make sure they are on task.

- Style Police：You check the overall appearance, use of pictures, size of letters, length of texts, etc. of the slides.

• Interpersonal Manager: Be sensitive for possible problems within your group, try to mediate between group conflicts, and be the contact person for any group concerns.

（7）彩排演讲，组内成员互提意见，最后正式展示。

（8）项目成果评价标准如表 6-34 所示。

表 6-34 教学案例 6-8 项目成果评价表

小组表现			
	不可接受 1	良好 2	优秀 3
幻灯片总体印象	结构不明，内容少于 7 页幻灯片（封面页、每位专家负责的内容页、参考资源页）未包含视觉辅助或过多，连贯性不显	结构基本清楚（引言、主题、结论），幻灯片页数满足基本要求，提供视觉辅助支持，基本连贯	结构清楚，幻灯片页数满足基本要求，提供视觉辅助支持，连贯，字形字体大小适当，便于阅读
语言	存在严重的拼写和语法错误，语言不当	拼写和语法错误极少，语言表达恰当	几乎没有拼写和语法错误，语言表达出色
内容	美国梦和中国梦的相关信息不足或有误	充分阐释美国梦和中国梦	根据推荐资源充分阐释了美国梦和中国梦，还提供了相关的额外信息，拓展了主题
小组总体表现	小组未做充分准备，缺乏组织，展示有停顿，时间管理不佳，时长短于 7 分钟，未与观众保持眼神交流	小组做了准备和彩排，展示过程流畅，时长不短于 10 分钟，与观众保持眼神交流，分工明确，展示态度良好	小组做了充分准备，展示专业，时长至少 10 分钟，与观众保持眼神交流，分工明确，展示态度完美

续表

个人表现			
	不可接受 1	良好 2	优秀 3
话语呈现	不流利，表述不清晰，未阐释重要事实，演讲结构不明	基本流利，表述清晰，音量适中，强调重点，演讲结构清楚	流利，表述清楚，语音语调标准，演讲结构清晰
肢体语言	学生不看观众，不知道把手放在哪里，有些不知所措	几乎始终保持与观众眼神交流，姿态舒展，使用恰当手势	几乎始终保持与观众眼神交流，姿态舒展自信，使用专业手势，善于模仿
语言	学生使用不当语言，未使用指定的语言支撑，难于使用恰当的表达	学生使用恰当语言，用到了指定的语言内容支撑以及主题相关词汇	学生使用专业恰当的语言，用到了指定的语言内容支撑以及主题相关词汇
按角色分工的课堂展示	无明显结构	结构清楚（引言、主体、结论）	
内容			
展示的信息内容	学生未回答 guiding questions，内容缺乏基本信息	学生根据角色分工展示了所有基本信息	学生展示了所有相关信息，回答了可选问题
使用视觉辅助	学生未使用视觉辅助或使用无关的视觉辅助，并且未做相应介绍	学生使用一些相关的视觉辅助，并做简短介绍	学生使用视觉辅助支持主要信息，并详细介绍
角色相关的幻灯页的结构	无明显结构，句子过长，难以阅读	幻灯片结构清楚，基本易于阅读和跟进课堂展示的思路	幻灯片结构清楚，易于阅读和跟进课堂展示的思路，设计富有创意

续表

团队协作			
	不可接受 1-2	良好 3-4	得分
团队	不够专注，工作进展拖沓，未记录小组决议或制定工作计划，过于吵闹	专注于密切协作，立即展开工作，记录工作进展，执行工作计划，必要时及时调整计划，安静工作	
个人	学生不够专注，未与团队成员合作，工作效率不高	学生非常专注，与团队成员保持合作，工作高效	

3. 案例评析

中国梦从理想变为现实的过程同时也是社会主义核心价值观一步步落地生根的过程，美国梦则是美国社会文化不可或缺的组成部分。对二者的深入探究和对比有助于培养青年学子的批判性思维，正确认识国家意识形态之间存在的差异，增强身份认同感和文化自信。本案例通过引导学生对比中外理念，鼓励青年一代树立自己的人生理想，明确人生的奋斗目标，早日实现中华民族伟大复兴这一中国梦。

4. 辅助资源

关于美国梦和中国梦的介绍性视频和 PPT，用于引入教学主题

(九) 教学案例 6-9　世界英语（4 课时）

项目主题：English in the World

该主题属于“人与社会”范畴，涉及“世界主要国家的文化习俗与文化景观、节假日与庆祝活动”和“身份认同与文化自信”子主题。

1. 内容分析

在本案例中，学生将探究不同英语母语国家之间的文化异同，深入理解语言背后的文化现象，挖掘文化的内涵。

2. 实施过程

(1) 导入教学主题。

Do you know how many countries in the world speak Chinese or Mandarin as an official language? Can you name a few? Now, do you think they all speak the same, use the same words or eat the same food?

How about English countries, have you wondered how different they are?

(2) 教师介绍任务概况。

You are a hotel receptionist and have to find, in groups, cultural similarities and differences between two English speaking countries. These can be foods, words / sayings, traditional sports and festivities, and cultural traditions.

Once you have found and read all the information you need, you will elaborate a brochure to help clients from a different English speaking country better understand and learn about the differences and similarities both countries share.

(3) 教师介绍完成任务的提示信息。

The first thing to do is to download a brochure template, or use your own design if you want, and discuss on how you are going to present the information on it.

Now you will need to find as many countries as you can that speak English and choose four (one per member or group).

Once you have each chosen one country you will need to research traditions of it and find any variables in their way of speaking the English language.

After each member of the group has got their information, you will as a group decide which two countries you are going to use for the brochure. If needed you will then as a group look for more information on them. (Remember to keep your individual research)

Now that you have all the information needed and have decided on the countries you are going to use, you have to start designing the brochure. Remember to include pictures.

(4) 项目成果评价标准如表 6-35 所示。

表 6-35 教学案例 6-9 项目成果评价表

	1-待行动	2-待进步	3-合格	4-优秀	得分
个人研究/设计	学生做了很少的研究/在设计上投入不足	学生在手册中使用了大部分的推荐资源	学生参考了所有资源，将相关信息正确地引入手册制作	除了使用推荐资源外，学生还参考了其他资源，出色完成了手册制作	
团队协作	成员之间没有相互协调	成员之间有所协调，在一定程度上完成了任务	学生完成了任务，但组内协调情况不够理想，最终成果不够完美	在完成项目的整个过程中，学生制定并遵守有效的合作规范	
手册制作	手册未达成预期目的，设计不佳	手册总体不错，但结构缺乏组织，图片和文字不协调	手册很不错，图片和文字相互呼应，内容很好	手册堪称完美，内容、图片和信息协调都无懈可击	
语言、连贯性、结构	语言不当，知识结构欠组织	语言水平较高，文本结构存在问题	语言使用恰当，文本结构较好	语言使用得当，文本结构好，总体衔接状况好	

（5）课程回顾与总结。

Did you learn anything new while doing this brochure?

Was the English difficult?

Did your friends cooperate?

English is a very rich culture and as you have seen, there are many countries that speak it and their English is no better than others. When you travel you should always think about this and how similar and different cultures can be.

3. 案例评析

本案例适用于英语国家文化类课程的复习环节，教师可借此要求学生运用学过的重要文化概念和理论分析在自主探究过程中发现的文化现象。此外，本案例的项目形式也适合应用文本写作和技术写作课程布置学习活动。本案例还可以拓展为比较使用中文的国家的文化异同，培养跨文化交际和对外交流能力。

4. 辅助资源

（1）英语国家的标志性图片，用于做竞猜游戏，引入教学主题，提高学习兴趣。

（2）语言和文化关系的介绍性视频。

（十）教学案例 6-10 独生子女政策的社会影响（4 课时）

项目主题：The Social Impact of One-child Policy in China

该主题属于“人与社会”范畴，涉及“社会热点与国际事务”子主题。

1. 内容分析

独生子女政策一度是现代中国的热点问题之一，学生将从不同的社会角色的角度研究它的社会影响。在本案例中，学生将使用数字工具和资源收集数据、检查模式并应用信息进行决策；选择和使用适当的工具和数字资源来完成各种任务和解决问题；根据数字工具或资源的效率和有效性证明选择的合理性；确定一个复杂的全球问题，制定系统的调查计划，并提出创新的可持续解决方案；分析当前和新兴技术资源的能力和局限性，并评估它们在满足个人、社会、终身学习和职业需求方面的潜力。

2. 实施过程

（1）导入教学主题。

As family is important to the socialization of children, it plays an important role in the development of children's intellect and personality. In order to control the country's population, People's Republic of China has implemented the one-child policy for the over three decades. Today, over 90% of all urban children, and over 60% of rural children have no brothers or sisters. What is the effect of this historically rare policy? Researchers and citizens from both the East and the West have been concerned with this issue. In China, many news reports have expressed the worry that single-child families would produce self-centered "little emperors" and "empresses." Theoretically, this concern is both reasonable and probable. How does one-child policy impact children born under this policy? How are they different from the generations before them? How does this policy affect them socially, emotionally and academically? In today's lesson, we will study possible outcomes.

（2）教师介绍任务概况。

You will take on one of the following roles to investigate this social/cultural issue in China：

①Parent of the only child：

What is your view on this policy? Compare to your generation, how the children under this policy differ from you? What are some social impact of children born to this policy? What are your concerns?

②The only child：

What is your view of this policy? Compare to the generations before you, such as the generation of your older cousins, how are you different from them? What are some benefit of being the only child? What are some disadvantage of being the only child? What are your concerns of this policy?

③The policy maker：

Why is this policy necessary? What are the benefit of having this policy? What are some disadvantage of having it? Based on the data you have, what may be the concerns of the impact of this policy?

④The educator：

Compare to students born before this policy, how are students of one child policy differ from others? What are some advantage of the only child academically, socially and emotionally? What are some disadvantages? What is your view on this policy?

（3）学生选定角色，开展研究。

Choose your role from parent, child, policy maker and educator. Based on your online reading, please research the social impact of one child policy. You will use the questions under your role as a guideline.

（4）学生对问题形成自己的观点后，寻找意见相同的同学，组成小组。

Once you've done your own research. Please publish your view in a inforagphic format.

Print out your product and post it on the classroom wall. We will do a gallery walk and pay attention to people who have similar viewpoints as you.

Find the people who share similar views as you. Form a group no more than 3, compare and share your research result.

Gather all the information your group have, reflect on the guiding questions of your role. Generate a group inforgraphic presentation.

（5）各小组展示自己的研究成果，表达观点，听取其他观点，对整个过程进行回顾和反思。

Once your infographic is generated, you will sign yourself up for the group presentation. Rubric of the presentation will be provided to you.

Present your result in front of the whole class.

Listen to others' presentation and take note on the different viewpoints.

Count and reflect on all the different viewpoints on the same issue。

Summarize the possible social impact of the one child policy from different viewpoints and generate the final inforgraphic.

（6）项目成果评价标准如表 6-36 所示。

表 6-36 教学案例 6-10 项目成果评价表

	1-待行动	2-待进步	3-合格	4-优秀	得分
个人研究/设计	学生做了很少的研究/在设计上投入不足	学生在信息图中使用了大部分的推荐资源	学生参考了所有资源，将相关信息正确地引入信息图制作	除了使用推荐资源外，学生还参考了其他资源，出色完成了信息图制作	
团队协作	成员之间没有相互协调	成员之间有所协调，在一定程度上完成了任务	学生完成了任务，但组内协调情况不够理想，最终成果不够完美	在完成项目的整个过程中，学生制定并遵守有效的合作规范	
信息图制作	信息图未达成预期目的，设计不佳	信息图总体不错，但结构缺乏组织，图片和文字不协调	信息图很不错，图片和文字相互呼应，内容很好	信息图堪称完美，内容、图片和信息协调都无懈可击	

续表

	1-待行动	2-待进步	3-合格	4-优秀	得分
语言、连贯性、结构	语言不当，知识结构欠组织	语言水平较高，文本结构存在问题	语言使用恰当，文本结构较好	语言使用得当，文本结构好，总体衔接状况好	

3. 案例评析

独生子女政策以控制人口增长为目的，顺应中国国情而生，受到国外广泛关注。对本问题的深入探究有助于引导学生从不同角度全面分析重要的国内国际问题，提出解决方案并有理有据地支持自己的观点，从而培养国际视野，提高未来在国际舞台上为中国发声的能力。本案例还可拓展为研究新近出台的三孩政策的社会影响。

4. 辅助资源

（1）独生子女政策的介绍性视频，用于引入教学主题。

（2）信息图的模板和示例。

第七章

结　语

目前，网站本地化的评测研究普遍强调技术层面，致使语言文字边缘化，而语言文字是网站内容不可或缺的组成要件，也是网站实现大众传播媒体价值的重要途径。有鉴于此，本书主要关注中美两国商业组织和非营利组织的英文官网文本，比较了语言服务、电子商务、大学、市政府和旅游五个行业部门的本地化网站（中国英文网站）和非本地化网站（美国英文网站）。

本书涉及的网站文本为导航文本和内容文本，将首页文本和首页以下的一级网页文本作为研究对象。对比研究分为两个阶段，第一阶段是中美同类组织网站文本的配对比较和分组比较，根据第一阶段的定性分析结果，提出假设供第二阶段检验。第一阶段先配对比较后再扩大数据集规模，选取文本数据可比的本地化网站和非本地化网站分别集合成组，对除电子商务以外的四类行业网站进行分组比较，进行分组比较；第二阶段对其中的两类行业（语言服务和大学）网站的“关于我们”版块进一步扩大数据集规模，运用统计分析方法进行推断和预测。两个阶段的比较均仅限于同类组织网站的等效版块文本。第一阶段比较的文本特征分为词汇特征和句子特征，即导航文本标准化程度（仅限配对比较）、高频实词（仅限分组比较）、词汇密度、平均句长和第一第二人称句子所占百分比。第二阶段将后三个文本特征作为结果变量，本地化概况和组织机构类型作为预测变量，运行统计决策树工具，确定第二阶段适用的统计检验类型为双向 MANOVA，用于确定结果变量在不同预测变量之间是否存在显著差异，以及结果变量和预测变量之间是否存在相互作用。

第一阶段各个行业的本地化和非本地化网站的配对比较均涉及导航文本和内容文本的以下特征：导航文本的字数；标准化程度最高的网站版块；“Home（主页）”存在与否；导航文本中第一人称、第二人称和第三人称视角的使用；导航文本提示的网站目标受众；网站独有的版块；内容文本的词汇密度；内容文本的平均句长以及内容文本中第一和第二人称句子的相对频率。

根据五个行业部门的本地化和非本地化网站在第一阶段配对比较的汇总结果（表 7-1），就内容文本的可量化文本特征、“关于我们”版块的导航文本单词数、大学网站导航文本标准化程度、主页导航功能、定向传播策略等五方面提出假设，供分组比较检验。基于四个行业部门的本地化和非本地化网站分组比较的结果汇总，有两个假设得到支持，一是“关于我们”的导航文本单词数介于1至5之间（不限行业），二是为不同访客提供了不同网站入口的非本地化网站多于本地化网站（语言服务行业除外）。

第一阶段的定性分析完成后，第二阶段运用样本量计算器计算出执行多变量方差分析（MANOVA）所需的样本量，再据此随机选出中美语言服务行业网站和大学网站，共分四组。四组网站的描述性统计结果显示：本地化组的平均句长均高于非本地化组，而第一人称和第二人称的比重则相反，词汇密度方面未发现显著差异。网站文本呈现的特征是否受到源语言和行业这两个独立因素的影响。主体间效应检验结果显示，词汇密度未受到源语言或行业甚至二者相互作用的显著影响（*sig.* > 0.05），而平均句长及第一和第二人称句子所占的百分比则受到源语言或行业甚至二者相互作用的显著影响（*sig.* = 0.00 < 0.05）。由此可见，以服务行业和大学为代表的一些中国组织英文网站已表现出不同于美国同行业网站的文本语言特征，但由于本研究涉及的样本量有限，可比行业部门数量较少，尚无法断言我国组织的本地化英文网站存在英语变体。

目前国内关于本地化英文网站文本的对比研究主要基于本地化网站英文质量不及非本地化网站的假设前提，以非本地化英文网站为标杆，关注本地化英文网站文本存在的语言问题以及如何改进。本研究从关注我国组织本地化英文网站的语言规约出发，统计特定文本特征的出现频率，探索我国组织本地化英文网站存在英文变体的可能性。语言文字的形成依靠的是约定俗成的过程，人们反复使用语言文字成功获得预期的交际效果，经过不断核实形成最终成果，进而固化为语言文字使用的惯例和规律。本研究受到样本量和实施技术框架的制约，得出的结论普适性不足，难以推广。

鉴于当前研究存在的不足，今后将优化集成式数据处理和管理模式，改进网站文本去噪和断句方法，增大网页文本挖掘深度，高效探索更多的行业部门机构网站、更多的行业或组织特定的网站版块（如标题措辞等）及更多的文本特征变量。此外，未来针对本地化英文网站开展的对比研究还可以考虑引入其他英语非第一语言国家/地区的组织机构英文网站，增加横向比较的维度。至于网站情境中的英语变体的探索，则可以借鉴全球英语的特征研究，通过考查全球组织的英文网站，检验前人假说并提出新的假说。和评估任何面向大众的产品一样，全面评估网站需要用户的参与，用户调查研究也是另一个很有前景的研究方向。

在研究组织机构网站文本的过程中，笔者充分感受到网站是丰富生动的语言资源宝库。研究网站本地化的文本处理方式不仅能够为网站本地化实践和教学提供参考，网络世界中浩如星海的各色网站还能够为英语语言教学提供丰富的教学资料，只要教师善于甄别，紧密结合教材内容和课程目标，践行课程思政的教学理念，就能将网络作为取之不尽用之不竭的教学语料库。

本书从服务英语课程思政教学的角度出发，以学生为中心，任务为导向，训练语言输出能力为目标，引介评析了面向义务教育阶段至大学阶段的英语教育全学段的网络自主探究式教学案例。低年级学段使用教师指定的网络资源完成学习任务，高年级学段可以检索教师指定的网站，中高级水平的青年和成人英语学习者则可以独立完成网络检索工作。大部分案例需要学生课堂讨论合作和课后调研并准备作品，所以适合阶段性复习总结环节，一个学期频次不宜过多。

网站文本的学术研究和语言教学应用可以相互助益，学术研究得出的结论可以在教学活动中得到检验，教学活动中的发现可以为学术研究提供新的提示。待组织机构网站文本的研究成果进一步成熟后，可以考虑基于组织机构官网文本和相关课程标准设计适合不同学段的英语教学活动。初步设想的教学主题如表 7-1 所示。

表 7-1 基于组织机构官网文本的英语教学主题

	初级	中级	高级
职业教育（企业网站）	认识工作的意义	选择职业	最佳求职者画像 企业形象塑造
学业规划（大中小学网站）	认识大学/中学/小学	申请专业深造	联系科研导师
公民教育（政府网站）	认识政府网站	组织宣传计划 公益活动计划	选择姐妹城市 给网站提建议
文化外宣（旅游网站）	介绍景点	设计旅游路线	评价和设计网站
产品国际化（电商网站）	认识电商购物流程 角色扮演买家卖家沟通过程	宣传家乡特产 设计产品界面	宣传中国创新科技产品

由表 7-1 可知，网站文本语言特征的研究与英语课程思政教学相辅相成，前者为后者提供生动丰富、时效性强的学习资源以及需要网络现实语境检验的研究假说，后者则通过师生构建的学习共同体，不断发现新的研究问题和灵感，为前者提供进一步探索的参考方向。有理由相信，随着组织机构网站的研究进一步深入，关于其语言文本特征的发现会与思政内容和内涵紧密结合，广泛应用于英语课程思政教学，让不同学段的英语学习者在深入理解和应用语体特点的同时，丰富心灵世界，滋养中国心，淬炼中国魂。

附　录

附录 A：第一阶段第二步分组比较所选的网站列表

L-本地化网站（中国组织机构）		NL-非本地化网站（美国组织机构）	
语言服务行业（LSP）			
L1	L1-Pactera Technology International (https：//en. pactera. com/)	NL1	Lionbridge (https：//www. lionbridge. com/)
L2	CSOFT International (https：//www. csoftintl. com/)	NL2	TransPerfect (http：//www. transperfect. com/)
L3	FBC GLOBAL (http：//www. globalfbc. com/？lang=en)	NL3	LanguageLine Solutions (https：//www. languageline. com/)
L4	EC Innovations, Inc. (http：//www. ecinnovations. c om/en. html)	NL4	Welocalize, Inc. (https：//www. welocalize. com/)
L5	Lan-bridge Communications (http：//www. lan- bridge. co. uk/)	NL5	CyraCom International, Inc. (http：//www. cyracominternational. c om/)
L6	WordTech International (http：//www. wordtechintl. c om/)	NL6	Donnelley Financial Solutions (http：//www. donnelleylanguagesolut ions. com/)

续表

L7	Master Translation Services（http：//www. mts-tech. com/）	NL7	United Language Group（http：//unitedlanguagegroup. com/）
L8	LocaTran Translations Ltd.（http：//www. locatran. com/e ng/index. asp）	NL8	ManpowerGroupSolutions – Language Services（http：//www. mgslanguage. com/）
L9	Sunyu CN（http：//www. sunyu. com/ind ex. asp）	NL9	AKORBI（https：//akorbi. com/）

大学			
L1	Tsinghua University （http：//www. tsinghua. edu. cn/publish/newthuen/）	NL1	Massachusetts Instituteof Technology（MIT）（web. mit. edu/）
L2	Peking University（english. pku. edu. cn/）	NL2	Stanford University（https：//www. stanford. edu/）
L3	FudanUniversity（www. fudan. edu. cn/en/）	NL3	Harvard University（https：//www. harvard. edu/）
L4	Shanghai Jiao Tong University（en. sjtu. edu. cn/）	NL4	California Institute of Technology（Caltech）（www. caltech. edu/）
L5	Zhejiang University（www. zju. edu. cn/english/）	NL5	Universityof Chicago（https：//www. uchicago. edu/）
L6	University of Scienceand Technology of China（en. ustc. edu. cn/）	NL6	PrincetonUniversity（https：//www. princeton. edu/）
L7	NanjingUniversity（https：//www. nju. edu. cn/E N/）	NL7	Cornell University（https：//www. cornell. edu/）

续表

L8	Beijing Normal University (english. bnu. edu. cn/)	NL8	Yale University (https://www. yale. edu/)
L9	Wuhan University (en. whu. edu. cn/)	NL9	Johns Hopkins University (https://www. jhu. edu)

市政府			
L1	Shanghai (http://www. shanghai. gov. c n/shanghai/node27118/inde x. html)	NL1	New York City, NY (http://www1. nyc. gov/)
L2	Beijing (http://www. ebeijing. gov. cn/)	NL2	Los Angeles, CA (https://www. laci-ty. org/your- government)
L3	Guangzhou, Guangdong (english. gz. gov. cn/)	NL3	Chicago, IL (https://www. cityofchi-cago. org/city/ en/chicagogovt. html)
L4	Shenzhen, Guangdong (english. sz. gov. cn/)	NL4	Houston, TX (www. houstontx. gov/)
L5	Wuhan, Hubei (english. wh. gov. cn/)	NL5	Philadelphia, PA (www. phila. gov/)
L6	Dongguan, Guangdong (http:// www. dongguantoday. com/)	NL6	Phoenix, AZ (https://www. phoe-nix. gov/citygover nment)
L7	Chongqing (en. cq. gov. cn/)	NL7	San Antonio, TX (www. sanantonio. gov/)
L8	Chengdu, Sichuan (http://www. chengdu. gov. c n/english/)	NL8	San Diego, CA (https://www. sandi-ego. gov/)
L9	Nanjing, Jiangsu (english. nanjing. gov. cn/)	NL9	Dallas, TX (dallascityhall. com/govern-ment/Pag es/default. aspx)

旅游目的地城市			
L1	Beijing (http://en. visitbeijing. com. cn/)	NL1	New York City, NY (https://www. nycgo. com/)
L2	Xi'an, Shaanxi (http://www. xian- travel. com/)	NL2	Los Angeles, CA (https://www. discoverlosangeles. co m/)
L3	Shanghai (www. meet - in - shanghai. net/)	NL3	Orlando, FL (www. visitorlando. com/)
L4	Guilin, Guangxi (http://www. visitguilin. org/)	NL4	Las Vegas, NV (https://www. visitlasvegas. com/)
L5	Hangzhou, Zhejiang (http://en. gotohz. com/)	NL5	Chicago, IL (https://www. choosechicago. com/)
L6	Chengdu, Sichuan (www. gochengdu. cn/)	NL6	Washington DC (https://washington. org/)
L7	Huangshan, Anhui (http://www. huangshantour. com/english/)	NL7	San Francisco, CA (www. sftravel. com/)
L8	Lhasa, Tibet (http://www. tibet-discovery. com/lhasa-travel/)	NL8	Miami, FL (www. miamiandbeaches. com/)
L9	Suzhou, Jiangsu (en. visitsz. com/)	NL9	Denver, CO (https://www. denver. org/)

附录 B：语言服务行业企业（LSP）网站不同版块的词汇项目（L：本地化网站；NL：非本地化网站）

Communicative Section	L1	L2	L3
Company profile	Company	Our Story	About Us
Services	（多个版块）	What We Do	Product & Service
Industries served	Industries	Localization	N/A
Technology	Technology	Technology	N/A
Featured client solutions	Our Work	Case Studies	N/A
Contact us	Contact Us | Work with Us | Connect	Contact Us | Contact	Contact Us
Join us	Careers & Culture	Join Our Team	Careers
News and events	News & Press	News & Events	Newsroom
Privacy policy	Privacy Policy	Privacy	Privacy Policy
Industry blogs and resources	Insights & Trends	Knowledge Vault	N/A
Find local office	Find Locations	Global Offices	Contact Us
Sitemap	Site Index	Sitemap	SITE MAP
Home	Home	N/A	Home

续表

Communicative Section	L4	L5	L6
Company profile	Company	About Us	About Us
Services	Services	Services	Solutions
Industries served	Solutions	Some of the companies we work with	Industries
Technology	Technology	N/A	Tools & Checklists
Featured client solutions	Solutions	N/A	Case Studies
Contact us	Contact Us	Contact Us	Contact Us
Join us	Career	Working with Lanbridge	Careers
News and events	News & Blog	Blog	N/A
Privacy policy	Terms of Use	Privacy	Privacy
Industry blogs and resources	Blog | Library	Blog	Resources
Find local office	Locations	China Offices	Contact Us
Sitemap	N/A	N/A	N/A
Home	Home	Home	Home
Communicative Section	L7	L8	L9
Company profile	About Us	About Us	About Us
Services	Services	Services	Services

续表

Industries served	Industries	Industries	Localization
Technology	Technology	Technology	Advanced Technical Support
Featured client solutions	Case Studies	N/A	N/A
Contact us	Contact Us	Contact | Contact Us	Contact Us
Join us	Contact Us	Careers	Contact Us
News and events	News and Events	N/A	News & Events
Privacy policy	N/A	N/A	N/A
Industry blogs and resources	Blog	Industry Articles	N/A
Find local office	Contact Us	Contact | Contact Us	Contact Us
Sitemap	Site Map	N/A	N/A
Home	Home	Home	Home
Communicative Section	NL1	NL2	NL3
Company profile	About Lionbridge	Who We Are	Who We Are
Services	Services	What We Do	（多个版块）
Industries served	Industries	Industries	Industries
Technology	Products	Technology	N/A
Featured client solutions	Customers	Client Solutions	N/A

续表

<table>
<tr><td>Contact us</td><td>Contact Us</td><td>Get in Touch</td><td>Contact</td></tr>
<tr><td>Join us</td><td>Careers</td><td>Join Our Team</td><td>Careers</td></tr>
<tr><td>News and events</td><td>News</td><td>Press Center</td><td>News</td></tr>
<tr><td>Privacy policy</td><td>Privacy Policy</td><td>Privacy</td><td>Privacy Policy</td></tr>
<tr><td>Industry blogs and resources</td><td>Blog</td><td>Thought Leadership
Resources</td><td>Blog | Resources</td></tr>
<tr><td>Find local office</td><td>Locations |
Our Offices</td><td>Find Your
Local Office</td><td>Contact</td></tr>
<tr><td>Sitemap</td><td>N/A</td><td>Sitemap</td><td>Sitemap</td></tr>
<tr><td>Home</td><td>Home</td><td>N/A</td><td>Home</td></tr>
<tr><td colspan="4"></td></tr>
<tr><td>Communicative Section</td><td>NL4</td><td>NL5</td><td>NL6</td></tr>
<tr><td>Company profile</td><td>About Us</td><td>（主页）</td><td>About Us</td></tr>
<tr><td>Services</td><td>Solutions |
Services + Solutions</td><td>（主页）</td><td>Solutions</td></tr>
<tr><td>Industries served</td><td>N/A</td><td>Federal & GSA</td><td>Expertise</td></tr>
<tr><td>Technology</td><td>N/A</td><td>N/A</td><td>Technology</td></tr>
<tr><td>Featured client solutions</td><td>N/A</td><td>N/A</td><td>N/A</td></tr>
<tr><td>Contact us</td><td>Contact Us</td><td>Contact</td><td>Contact |
Get in Touch</td></tr>
<tr><td>Join us</td><td>Careers + Community</td><td>Contact</td><td>Careers</td></tr>
</table>

续表

News and events	Events	N/A	News
Privacy policy	Privacy Policy	N/A	Privacy Notice
Industry blogs and resources	Blog	N/A	Blog ｜ The Blog
Find local office	Locations ｜ Worldwide Locations	N/A	Locations ｜ Our Offices
Sitemap	N/A	N/A	N/A
Home	Home	N/A	N/A
Communicative Section	NL7	NL8	NL9
Company profile	About ULG（主页）	About Us	Our Company
Services	Services	Our Services	（多个版块）
Industries served	Industries	Industries	N/A
Technology	Technologies （位于 Service 之下）	N/A	N/A
Featured client solutions	Case Studies + ebooks	N/A	N/A
Contact us	Contact Us	Contact Us	Contact Us
Join us	Careers	Jobs ｜ Careers	N/A
News and events	Newsroom	Events	News ｜ Events
Privacy policy	Privacy Policy （链接无效）	Privacy Policy	Privacy Policy

续表

Industry blogs and resources	ULG Daily	N/A	Resources
Find local office	Contact Us	N/A	Contact us
Sitemap	N/A	N/A	Sitemap
Home	N/A	Home	N/A

附录 C：大学网站不同版块的词汇项目（L：本地化网站；NL：非本地化网站）

Communicative Section	L1	L2	L3
About Us	About	About PKU	About Fudan
Admissions	Admissions	Admission	Admissions
Academics	International	Academics, Research	(Admissions)
Faculty, Staff	Faculties	Administration	Faculty (under Admissions)
Research	Research	Academics, Research	Research
Campus Life	Campus	N/A	Campus Life
News	News	News	News
Join Us	Jobs	Employment	N/A
Contact Us	Contacts	N/A	Contact Us

续表

Call for Donations	Giving to TH	Giving to PKU	Giving
Terms and Conditions of Use	N/A	N/A	N/A
Privacy Policy	N/A	N/A	N/A
Home	N/A	N/A	N/A
Communicative Section	L4	L5	L6
About Us	About SJTU	About	About
Admissions	Admission	Admissions	Admissions
Academics	Academics	Academics	(Schools)
Faculty, Staff	Faculty (under Academics)	Staff	Faculty
Research	Research	Research	Research
Campus Life	Life @ SJTU	Campus Life	Services
News	News	News	News
Join Us	Join Us	Resources	Join Us
Contact Us	Contact Us (under About SJTU)	Contact	N/A
Call for Donations	Giving	(Alumni)	N/A
Terms and Conditions of Use	N/A	N/A	N/A
Privacy Policy	N/A	N/A	N/A

续表

Home	Home	Home （在面包屑导航中）	Home （在面包屑导航中）
Communicative Section	L7	L8	L9
About Us	About	About BNU	About WHU
Admissions	Admissions	Admission	Admission
Academics	Academics	Academics, Research	Academics
Faculty, Staff	Faculty, Staff	Faculty, Staff	individual subsites of schools and
Research	Research	Academics, Research	Research
Campus Life	Campus Life	Campus Life	Campus Life
News	News	University News	News, Events
Join Us	Join Us	Opportunity | Career at BNU	Careers
Contact Us	Contact Us	Contact Us	Contact Us
Call for Donations	Give	Make a Gift	N/A
Terms and Conditions of Use	N/A	N/A	N/A
Privacy Policy	N/A	N/A	N/A
Home	N/A	Home	Home
Communicative Section	NL1	NL2	NL3

续表

About Us	About MIT	About	About Harvard
Admissions	Admission	Admission	Admission, Aid
Academics	Education	Academics	Schools
Faculty, Staff	N/A	N/A	Faculty and Staff
Research	Research	Research	N/A
Campus Life	Life@M IT	Campus Life	On Campus
News	News	News	Gazette News
Join Us	Jobs	Careers	Jobs
Contact Us	Contact	Contact	Contact Harvard
Call for Donations	Give to MIT | Giving to MIT	Giving	Give
Terms and Conditions of Use	N/A	Terms of Use	N/A
Privacy Policy	N/A	Privacy Policy	Privacy Statement
Home	N/A	N/A	N/A
Communicative Section	NL4	NL5	NL6
About Us	About Caltech	About	Meet Princeton
Admissions	Admissions	Admissions, Aid	Admission, Aid
Academics	Divisions	Academics	Academics
Faculty, Staff	Staff (under About Caltech)	(Faculty and Staff)	Our Staff (under Meet Princeton)

续表

Research	(under Research, Education)	Research	Research
Campus Life	Campus Life (under Student)	Campus Life	Student Life (under One Community)
News	News, Events	Uchicago News	News
Join Us	Join Us | Careers	Job Opportunities	N/A
Contact Us	Contact Us	Contact Us	Contact Us
Call for Donations	Giving (under Alumni)	Give | Make a Gift	Giving | Giving to Princeton
Terms and Conditions of Use	N/A	N/A	N/A
Privacy Policy	Privacy Statement	N/A	N/A
Home	N/A	N/A	N/A

Communicative Section	NL7	NL8	NL9
About Us	About Cornell	About Yale	About Us
Admissions	Admissions	Admissions	Admissions, Aid
Academics	Academics	Academics	Academics
Faculty, Staff	Faculty and Staff	Faculty and Staff	Research, Faculty
Research	Research	Research, Collections	Research, Faculty
Campus Life	Student Life	Life at Yale	Campus Life

续表

News	Cornell Chronicle	News	News, Events
Join Us	N/A	Employment Opportunities	N/A
Contact Us	Contact	Contact Us	Contact the University
Call for Donations	Give ｜ Support Cornell	Giving	Give to the University
Terms and Conditions of Use	N/A	N/A	N/A
Privacy Policy	N/A	Privacy Policy	N/A
Home	Home（在面包屑导航中）	Home（在面包屑导航中）	Home（在面包屑导航中）

附录 D：市政府网站不同版块的词汇项目（L：本地化网站；NL：非本地化网站）

Communicative Section	L1	L2	L3
About us	N/A	About Us	About Us ｜ About GZ
Education	Study	Study	Education
Welcome message	welcome to www. shanghai. gov. cn	Welcome Speech	N/A

续表

News & Events	News	Official Activities | Mayor's Bulletin	City News, What's On
Feedback	Interact	Feedback	Guest Book
FAQ	FAQ	Q&A	Quick Links
Privacy policy	N/A	Services and Privacy	N/A
Terms and conditions of use	N/A	Copyright	Disclaimer
Home	Home	Home	Home
Communicative Section	L4	L5	L6
About us	Shenzhen Profile	Wuhan Overview	About Dongguan | About Us
Education	N/A	Schooling for Foreign Children	N/A
Welcome message	N/A	N/A	N/A
News & Events	Local News	Wuhan News	News and Coming Events
Feedback	Contact Us	N/A	N/A
FAQ	N/A	N/A	N/A
Privacy policy	N/A	N/A	N/A
Terms and conditions of use	N/A	N/A	Legal Notice
Home	Home	Home	Home

续表

Communicative Section	L7	L8	L9
About us	About Chongqing	About Chengdu | About Us	About Nanjing | About Us
Education	Study in Chongqing	Education (under Residents)	Study
Welcome message	Welcome to Chongqing	N/A	N/A
News & Events	News Now | Other News | Official Release	News	News and Events
Feedback	Feedback	Feedback	Contact Us
FAQ	FAQ	N/A	(designed for individual sections)
Privacy policy	Privacy Policy	N/A	N/A
Terms and conditions of use	Terms and Conditions	N/A	Legal Declaration
Home	Home	Home	Home
Communicative Section	NL1	NL2	NL3
About us	About NYC311	N/A	About
Education	Education	N/A	Education
Welcome message	N/A	N/A	N/A

续表

News & Events	News (under Office of the Mayor) ∣ Events	Public Notices	News Releases & Other City Updates
Feedback	Provide Feedback about NYC. gov	Submit feedback	Website Feedback
FAQ	(designed for individual sections)	(designed for individual sections)	(designed for individual sections)
Privacy policy	Privacy Policy	Privacy Policy	Privacy Policy
Terms and conditions of use	Terms of Use	Disclaimer	Disclaimer
Home	Home (icon)	N/A	Home (icon)
Communicative Section	NL4	NL5	NL6
About us	About Houston	N/A	How Your City Works ∣ About Phoenix
Education	N/A	Education (under Topics)	N/A
Welcome message	N/A	N/A	N/A
News & Events	News and Events	News, Events (under Mayor's Office)	City News and Information
Feedback	Your Feedback	N/A	Contact Us
FAQ	FAQs	Frequently Asked Questions	N/A

续表

Privacy policy	Privacy Policy	HIPAA	Security, Privacy
Terms and conditions of use	N/A	Terms of Use	N/A
Home	Home (icon in the breadcrumb trail)	Home (icon)	N/A
Communicative Section	NL7	NL8	NL9
About us	N/A	N/A	N/A
Education	N/A	Public Schools	N/A
Welcome message	MESSAGE FROM THE CITY	N/A	N/A
News & Events	City Spotlight	Our San Diego and Explore San Diego	News | Spotlight | Featured News | Public Notices
Feedback	Contact Us	Contact the City	Feedback
FAQ	N/A	N/A	Contact Us
Privacy policy	Privacy Policy, Disclaimer	Privacy Policy	Privacy Policy
Terms and conditions of use	Privacy Policy, Disclaimer	Disclaimers	Disclaimer
Home	sa. gov (in the breadcrumb trail home)	Home (icon)	N/A

附录 E：旅游目的地城市网站不同版块的词汇项目（L：本地化网站；NL：非本地化网站）

Communicative Section	L1	L2	L3
Recommended Activities	Things to Do	(Multiple Sections)	Highlights
Accommodation	Accommodation	Xian Hotels, Hostels	Hotels
Routes and tours	Routes, Strategy	N/A	Themed Tours | Special Tours
Neighborhoods	Around Beijing	N/A	N/A
Transportation	Transportation	Xian Transportation	Transportation
Events	Events	N/A	Events
News	News	N/A	Travel News
About Us	About Us	(homepage)	About Us
Contact Us	Contact Us (a link to email)	N/A	About Us
Home	Home	Home	Home (in the breadcrumb trail)

Communicative Section	L4	L5	L6
Recommended Activities	Sightseeing	Things to Do	Attractions
Accommodation	Accommodation	Accommodations	Stay

续表

Routes and tours	Suggested Itineraries	Tour Itineraries	Season Tour in Chengdu
Neighborhoods	N/A	N/A	N/A
Transportation	Local Transport	N/A	Traffic
Events	Events	Festivals, Events	Events
News	Travel News	E-Journals	What's New
About Us	About	N/A	About
Contact Us	About	(homepage)	Contact Us
Home	Home	Home (in the breadcrumb trail)	Home (in the breadcrumb trail)
Communicative Section	L7	L8	L9
Recommended Activities	N/A	Top Lhasa Attractions and Activities	See, Do
Accommodation	Hotels	Lhasa Hotels, Hostels	Accommodations
Routes and tours	Routes	(Multiple Sections)	Routes
Neighborhoods	China City Guide | Destinations	Other Destinations in Tibet	N/A
Transportation	Transportation	Getting to, around Lhasa	(in an article)
Events	N/A	N/A	N/A

续表

News	News Center	N/A	What's New
About Us	About Us	About Us	N/A
Contact Us	E-mail Us	Contact Us	Contact Us
Home	Home (in the breadcrumb trail)	Home (in the breadcrumb trail)	Home (in the breadcrumb trail)
Communicative Section	NL1	NL2	NL3
Recommended Activities	Things to Do | Explore	What to Do	Things to Do
Accommodation	Stay	Where to Stay	Places to Stay
Routes and tours	N/A	Itineraries, Guides	Trip-planning Ideas
Neighborhoods	N/A	Neighborhoods	N/A
Transportation	Transportation	Getting Around	Transportation
Events	Events This Month	Events	Events
News	News, Trending	Press Releases	What's New
About Us	About Us	About Us / Careers	About Us
Contact Us	(About Us)	N/A	Contact Us
Home	N/A	N/A	N/A
Communicative Section	NL4	NL5	NL6
Recommended Activities	Things to Do	Things to Do	Things to Do

续表

Accommodation	Hotels, Casinos	Hotels	Places to Stay
Routes and tours	N/A	Trip Ideas, Itineraries	Tours, Sightseeing
Neighborhoods	N/A	Neighborhoods	Neighborhoods
Transportation	Getting Around Vegas	Transportation	Getting Around DC
Events	Shows, Events	Events, Shows	Events
News	Sign Up for Newsletter	E-Newsletter	DC Insider Newsletter (for email)
About Us	About LVCVA	About Us	About Destination DC
Contact Us	N/A	Contact Us	Contact Destination DC
Home	N/A	N/A	N/A
Communicative Section	NL7	NL8	NL9
Recommended Activities	Everything to Do	Things to Do	Things to Do
Accommodation	Hotels	Where to Stay	Hotels
Routes and tours	Trip Ideas	Tours, Excursions	Itineraries
Neighborhoods	Neighborhoods	N/A	Denver Neighborhood Guide

续表

Transportation	Get Around	Getting To, Around Miami	Transportation, Maps
Events	Events	Events	Events
News	What's Happening	Press Room	(Sign-up for Newsletter)
About Us	About	About GMCVB	About Denver
Contact Us	Contact Us	(About GMCVB)	N/A
Home	N/A	N/A	N/A

附录 F：第二阶段选择的网站（L：本地化网站；NL：非本地化网站）

本地化网站（中国组织机构）			非本地化网站（美国组织机构）		
	LSP	大学		LSP	大学
L1	Xiamen Target Language Translation Service Co. Ltd. (http://www.language - trans.com/en/)	Northwest Agriculture and Forestry University (http://en.nwsuaf.edu.cn/)	NL1	Bureaucom (http://www.bureaucom.com/)	Indiana University/Purdue University, Indianapolis (https://www.iupui.edu/about/index.html)
L2	Guangzhou Synergy Translations Co, Ltd, China (http://www.synergytranslations.com/)	Nanjing Medical University (http://e - sie.njmu.edu.cn/)	NL2	NetaRose (http://www.netarose.com/)	New York University (https://www.nyu.edu/about.html)

续表

本地化网站（中国组织机构）			非本地化网站（美国组织机构）		
L3	Linearis Translations (http://linearistranslations.com/)	University of Science, Technology Beijing (http://en.ustb.edu.cn/)	NL3	Heron Language Services (http://www.heronlanguageservices.com/)	North Carolina State University (http://www.ncsu.edu/)
L4	JiangSu LanguAge Information Technology Services Co, Ltd , China (http://www.jslga.com/en/index.asp)	Shenzhen University (http://www1.szu.edu.cn/2014/en/overview.html)	NL4	EzeeTranslate (https://www.ezeetranslate.com/)	University of California Riverside (http://www.ucr.edu/about)
L5	LingoNova (http://www.lingonova.com/)	Shaanxi Normal University (http://english.snnu.edu.cn/About/In troduction_to_ SNNU.htm)	NL5	Accent Network (http://www.accentnetwork.com)	University of Miami (https://welcome.miami.edu/about- um/index.html)
L6	Chengdu Refine Translation Co, Ltd, China (http://www.m3loc.com/)	Nanjing University of Posts and Telecommunications (http://www.njupt.edu.cn/en/7873/list.htm)	NL6	U.S. Language Solutions (http://uslsolutions.com/)	University of Nebraska Lincoln (https://www.unl.edu/about/)
L7	Transn (http://www.transn.com/)	Hohai University (http://en.hhu.edu.cn/p402c343/list.psp)	NL7	BeTranslating (https://betranslating.com/)	Case Western Reserve University (http://case.edu/)
L8	1Stopasia, China (https://www.1stopasia.com/)	South China Agricultural University (http://english.scau.edu.cn/2016/1227/c1169a30289/page.htm)	NL8	Universal Translation Studio (https://www.universaltranslationstudio.com/)	University of Georgia (http://www.uga.edu/about/)
L9	SY Localization (http://www.sylocalization.com/)	University of Chinese Academy of Sciences (http://english.ucas.ac.cn/index.php/about - ucas/introduction)	NL9	Gateway Languages (http://gatewaylanguages.com/)	University of Cincinnati (http://www.uc.edu/)

续表

本地化网站（中国组织机构）			非本地化网站（美国组织机构）		
L10	Tnfast Translations (http://tnfast.com/beijing-translation-services/)	University of Jinan (http://www.ujn.edu.cn/en/About_UJN__/Introduction_to_UJN.htm)	NL10	Logrus IT (http://www.logrusit.com/)	University of Illinois Urbana Champaign (http://illinois.edu/)
L11	Takeasy Translation pp, China (https://www.itakeeasy.com)	East China Normal University (http://english.ecnu.edu.cn/1712/list.htm)	NL11	GMR Transcription (https://www.gmrtranscription.com/)	Oregon State University (http://oregonstate.edu/)
L12	Taijia Translation Company (http://www.taijiatrans.com/english/index.asp)	Jiangsu University (http://eng.ujs.edu.cn/About_JSU/Overview.htm)	NL12	Verba + + (http://www.verbaplusplus.com/about.html)	Yale University (http://www.yale.edu/)
L13	Good Enterprise Limited (http://www.gel-global.com/web/common/index.asp)	Hunan University (http://www-en.hnu.edu.cn/About_HNU/Introduction.htm)	NL13	Primatus (http://www.primatus.net/)	Northwestern University (http://www.northwestern.edu/)
L14	Star Translation Shanghai (http://www.startranslation.com/index.htm)	Nanjing Normal University (http://en.njnu.edu.cn/about-nnu)	NL14	We Translate (http://www.wetranslateinc.com/)	Tufts University (https://www.tufts.edu/)
L15	ODB Translation (http://www.odbfy.com/)	Peking University Health Science Center (http://e.bjmu.edu.cn/aboutpkuhsc/generalinformation/index.htm)	NL15	Vanan Translation (https://vanantranslation.com/)	Purdue University (http://www.purdue.edu/)
L16	Maxsun International (http://www.maxsuntranslation.com/)	China Pharmaceutical University (http://en.cpu.edu.cn/155/list.htm)	NL16	Mars Translation (https://www.marstranslation.com/)	Stony Brook University (http://www.stonybrook.edu/about/)

续表

本地化网站（中国组织机构）			非本地化网站（美国组织机构）		
L17	Xiamen Master Translation Services Co. Ltd, China (http://www.xmmaster.com/en/about_us.html)	South China University of Technology (http://en.scut.edu.cn/aboutSCUT/introducing.jsp)	NL17	We Translate USA (http://www.we-translate-usa.com/)	University of Arizona (http://www.arizona.edu/)
L18	HI-COM, China (http://www.hicom-asia.com/)	Huazhong Agricultural University (http://www.hzau.edu.cn/en/ABOUT_HZAU/General_Information.htm)	NL18	Motaword (https://www.motaword.com/)	University of New Mexico (http://www.unm.edu/)
L19	CCJK Technologies (http://www.ccjk.com/)	University of Electronic Science and Technology of China (http://en.uestc.edu.cn/index.php?m=content&c=index&a=lists&catid=72)	NL19	Lingual Consultancy	University of Rochester (http://www.rochester.edu/)
L20	Xiamen Butterfly House translation Co. Ltd, China (http://www.butterflylocalization.com/en/)	North China Electric Power University (http://english.ncepu.edu.cn/hdgk/29718.html)	NL20	iYuno Media Group (https://www.iyunomg.com/)	Wayne State University (http://wayne.edu/)
L21	DOBEST Studio (http://3135341472.wixsite.com/dobest)	Zhejiang University (http://www.zju.edu.cn/english/2016/1019/c2932a203304/page.htm)	NL21	Lingomod (https://lingomod.com/)	University of Illinois Chicago (http://www.uic.edu/)
L22	Celestone Translation (http://www.celestone.com.cn/en/Translation/index.html)	Fudan University (http://www.fudan.edu.cn/en/channels/view/34/)	NL22	Alphabet Linguistics (https://www.alphabet-linguistics.com/)	University of California Berkeley (http://www.berkeley.edu/)

参考文献

期刊论文

［1］何森梅．从目的论看中文企业网站的英译策略［J］．黎明职业大学学报，2008（01）．

［2］黄国文，肖琼．外语课程思政建设六要素［J］．中国外语，2021，18（02）．

［3］李良博，李占喜．本地化视域下网络语篇翻译的多维重构——以国内“985高校”网站的英译为例［J］．外文研究，2015（04）．

［4］李雪峰．从翻译适应选择论看陕西企业网站外宣英译［J］．教师，2016，（26）：52-53.

［5］卢小军．中美网站企业概况的文本对比与外宣英译［J］．中国翻译，2012，33（01）．

［6］马会峰．海南岛旅游网站汉英翻译研究［J］．湖北广播电视大学学报，2014，34（08）．

［7］彭金玲．功能翻译理论视角下的旅游景点网站英译探析——兼评桂林某英文旅游网站［J］．海外英语，2013（06）．

［8］宋云霞，张大伟，孙卓，韦军．以语料库为载体的实践教学模式研究［J］．实验技术与管理，2011，28（09）．

［9］汤君丽．政府外宣网站翻译失误问题探析——以遵义市人民政府网为例［J］．科教导刊，2014，（12）．

［10］张林影．大思政背景下英语翻译课程思政实施路径研究［J］．湖北师范大学学报（哲学社会科学版），2020，40（06）．

［11］甄凤超．语料库语言学研究热点追踪与思考［J］．当代外语研究，2020（06）．

［12］周红．本地化视角下的旅游网站英译标准刍议［J］．绥化学院学报，

2015，35（11）.

学位论文

［13］蒋文莎．功能翻译理论指导下的招商引资网站英译——以中国四个沿海城市为例［D］．长沙：中南大学，2013.

［14］李洁．济宁安吉国际经济技术合作有限公司网站英译报告［D］．济南：山东大学，2014.

［15］李莉．中国企业网站中企业简介英译失误及其对策［D］．武汉：华中师范大学，2012.

［16］王文．中国跨国公司网站中企业简介英译问题分析及对策［D］．长沙：中南大学，2013.

［17］邢彦娜．文本类型理论指导下的中国公司网站上企业简介英译研究［D］．长春：吉林财经大学，2012.

［18］杨成飞．湖南省政府英文网站汉语新闻英译实践报告［D］．长沙：湖南大学，2014.

［19］杨进．"平行文本"视角下的中国企业网站中企业简介英译研究［D］．上海：上海师范大学，2013.

［20］杨晓侠．文本类型论视角下企业网站的英译——九台集团网站翻译报告［D］．苏州：苏州大学，2016.

［21］张凌．湖南大学教务处网站英译实践报告［D］．长沙：湖南大学，2014.

［22］张佩．关于中国企业网站英译的研究［D］．长春：吉林财经大学，2013.

报纸

［23］张荣军，汤云晴．深化"思政课程"到"课程思政"的立德树人观［N］．贵州日报，2020-10-06（003）.

英文文献

［24］ANTONUCCI L，BASILE M，CROCETTA C，D'ADDOSIO V，D'OVIDIO F D，VIOLA D. University of Bari's Website Evaluation［J］. In Data Science and Social Research. Springer，Cham，2017.

[25] BAHRI H, MAHADI T S T. The avatars of culture in website localization. [J]. International Journal of Multicultural and Multireligious Understanding, 2015, 2 (06).

[26] BARTIKOWSKI, B, SINGH N. Should all firms adapt websites to international audiences [J]. Journal of Business Research, 2014, 67 (03).

[27] CHAO M C H, SINGH N, CHEN Y N. Web site localization in the Chinese market [J]. Journal of Electronic Commerce Research, 2012, 13 (01).

[28] CHUN W, SINGH N, SOBH, R, BENMAMOUN M. A comparative analysis of Arab and US cultural values on the web [J]. Journal of Global Marketing, 2015, 28 (02).

[29] CRYSTAL D. Internet linguistics: A student guide [M]. New York, NY: Routledge, 2011.

[30] DÍAZ J, RUSU C, COLLAZOS C. A. Experimental validation of a set of cultural - oriented usability heuristics: e - Commerce websites evaluation [J]. Computer Standards, Interfaces, 2017 (50).

[31] DUNNE K. Putting the cart behind the horse: Rethinking localization quality management [M]. In K. Dunne etal, Perspectives on Localization. Amsterdam: John Benjamins, 2006.

[32] ESSELINK B. Localization and translation [M]. In H. Somers etal, Computers and Translation: A Translator's Guide (Vol. 35). Amsterdam: John Benjamins. 2003a.

[33] ESSELINK B. The evolution of localization [J]. The Guide from Multilingual Computing, Technology: Localization, 2003b, 14 (05).

[34] FEENEY M K, BROWN A. Are small cities online? Content, ranking, and variation of US municipal websites [J]. Government Information Quarterly, 2017, 34 (01).

[35] FENTON N, LEE K K. Nicely said: Writing for the web with style and purpose [M]. San Francisco, CA: Peachpit Press, 2014.

[36] FOLARON, D. A discipline coming of age in the digital age [M]. In K. J. Dunne etal, Perspectives on Localization (American Translators Association Scholarly Monograph Series XIII). Amsterdam, Philadelphia: John Benjamins, 2006.

[37] GARCIA I. Translating and revising for localisation: What do we know?

What do we need to know? [J]. Perspectives: Studies in Translatology, 2008 (16).

[38] GÂTĂ A, PRAISLER A. Cross cultural transfer in the case of local or regional websites of transnational companies [J]. Comunicare Interculturala si Literatura, 2015 (22).

[39] HALVORSON K, RACH M. Content strategy for the web [M]. New Riders, 2012.

[40] HERRING S C. A facetedclassification scheme for computer-mediated discourse. Language@ Internet, 2007, 4 (01).

[41] JIMÉNEZ-CRESPO M. Translation quality, use and dissemination in an internet era: Using single-translation and multi-translation parallel corpora to research translation quality on the web [J]. The Journal of Specialised Translation, 2015 (23).

[42] JIMÉNEZ - CRESPO M. Translation and web localization [M]. Routledg, 2013a.

[43] JIMÉNEZ-CRESPO M. Loss or lost in localization: a corpus-based study of original and localized non-profit websites [J]. Jostrans: The Journal of Specialised Translation, 2012 (17).

[44] JIMÉNEZ-CRESPO M. To adapt or not to adapt in web localization: a contrastive genre-based study of original and localized legal sections in corporate websites [J]. Jostrans: The Journal of Specialised Translation, 2011 (15).

[45] JIMÉNEZ-CRESPO M. The future of general tendencies in translation: Explicitation in web localization [J]. Target. International Journal of Translation Studies, 2011, 23 (01).

[46] JIMÉNEZ-CRESPO M. The future of "universal" tendencies: a review of papers using localized websites [J]. In Communication au colloque international UCCTS, 2010.

[47] JIMÉNEZ-CRESPO M. Conventions in localisation: A corpus study of original vs. translated web texts [J]. Jostrans: The Journal of Specialized Translation, 2009 (12).

[48] LAW R, QI S, BUHALIS D. Progress in tourism management: A review of website evaluation in tourism research [J]. Tourism Management, 2010, 31 (03).

[49] LIMON D. Company websites, genre conventions and the role of the trans-

lator [J]. Cultus: The journal of intercultural mediation and communication, 2008.

[50] MELE E, CANTONI L. Localization of Tourism Destinations' Websites: Theory and Practices [J]. In Innovative Perspectives on Tourism Discourse. IGI Global, 2018.

[51] NAUERT S. Translating Websites [EB/OL]. In Acts of the LSP Translation Scenarios (MuTra). Conference proceedings. http: //bit. ly/2DAH0Vt, 2007.

[52] O'HAGAN M, ASHWORTH D. Translation-mediated communication in a digital world: Facing the challenges of globalization and localization [J]. Multilingual Matters, 2002.

[53] PURWANINGSIH D R. Assessing website translation quality [EB/OL]. Triannual Seminar on Literature, Linguistics, and Translation held by English Department, Faculty of Humanities, UNSOED, http: //bit. ly/2n88CXC, 2015.

[54] PYM A. Website localization [M]. The Oxford Handbook of Translation Studies, 2011.

[55] RODRÍGUEZ C V. Globalization and localization in advertising translation: a love-hate relationship? [J]. Revista de Lenguas para Fines Específicos , 2016, (22).

[56] RUSSO K E. Global English, transnational flows: Australia and New Zealand in translation [M]. Tangram Ediz. Scientifiche, 2012.

[57] SANDRINI. Website localization and translation [C]. In MuTra: Challenges of Multidimensional Translation: Conference Proceedings, 2005.

[58] SCHÄLER R. Translators and localization: Education and training in the context of the Global Initiative for Local Computing (GILC) [J]. The Interpreter and Translator Trainer, 2007, 1 (01).

[59] SCHÄLER R. Reverse localisation [J]. Localisation Focus: The International Journal of Localisation. Limerick: Localisation Research Centre, 2006, 6 (01).

[60] SCHMALBRUCH S. The 10 most-visited cities in the US this year [EB/OL]. https: //bit. ly/2ymB5Bn, 2017.

[61] SHAN X, WANG Q. A cross-cultural analysis of brand personality: Comparisons of China's and the US energy companies' English websites [J]. Journal of Language Teaching and Research, 2017, 8 (06).

[62] TENNENT M. etal. Training for the new millennium: Pedagogies for trans-

lation and interpretation [M] . Amsterdam, Philadelphia: John Benjamins, 2005.

[63] TORRES DELREY J, RODRÍGUEZ C. V. New insights into translation-oriented, technology-intensive localiser education: Accessibility as an opportunity [EB/OL] . http://bit.ly/2BpImfJ, 2017.

[64] TRUDGILL P, HANNAH J. International English: A Guide to Varieties of English Around the World [M] . Taylor, Francis, 2017.

[65] UMOH I E. A linguistic and cultural analysis of localisation practices on oil and gas company websites. [eb/OL] http://bit.ly/2Gd3NEo, 2015.

[66] VANGENABITH, J. Next generation localisation [J] . Localisation Focus, 2009, 8 (01) .

[67] VYNCKE F, BRENGMAN, M. Are culturally congruent websites more effective? An overview of a decade of empirical evidence [J] . Journal of Electronic Commerce Research, 2010, 11 (01) .

后 记

本书在笔者读博期间关于组织机构英文网站的研究基础之上，结合笔者从事英语教育工作以来的教学设计心得，探讨了网站文本研究在不同学段英语教学实践中的应用。光阴易逝，岂容我待。在编撰书稿的过程中，往日时光一幕幕地重现在眼前，过去和现在的时空交错，令人百感交集。

时光流转，初心不变。笔者始终认为，现代语言研究需要面向应用，特别是教学应用。英语教学与研究应该相得益彰。随着英语课程思政教学的不断推进，英语教学研究也获得了新的启示和方向指引。十八大以来，习近平总书记围绕“培养社会主义建设者和接班人”作出一系列重要论述，深刻回答了“培养什么人、怎样培养人、为谁培养人”这一根本性问题。英语课程思政理念的推广有助于形成具有中国特色的英语教学生态，我国英语教师将通过教学实践努力回答“什么人教英语、怎样教英语、为谁教英语”这一根本性问题。那么，以课程思政为导向的英语教学研究就是研究英语教育培养社会主义建设者和接班人的目标、方法和最终使命。

本书介绍的网络自主探究式项目教学案例，让学生有机会在教师的指导下接触网络上鲜活生动的语言学习资源，在团队合作中共同学习成长，能够激发学生运用英语的兴趣，有助于学生了解不同文化，比较文化异同，汲取文化精华，逐步形成跨文化沟通与交流的意识和能力，学会客观、理性地看待世界，树立国际视野，涵养家国情怀，坚定文化自信，形成正确的世界观、人生观和价值观，为学生终身学习、适应未来社会发展奠定基础。英语是当今世界经济、政治、科技、文化等活动中广泛使用的语言，是国际交流与合作的重要沟通工具，也是传播人类文明成果的载体之一，对中国走向世界、世界了解中国、构建人类命运共同体具有重要作用。不同学段的英语课程应体现工具性和人文性的统一，实现知识传授与价值引领的统一。本书为提高英语课程设计的丰富性和多样性引玉，期待广大英语教学实践者和研究者人同此心，众志成城，筑牢青春防线，为青春逐梦加油，为世界舞台唱响中国的“青春之歌”喝彩。

严格来看，本书推介的诸多教学案例的适用学段涉及义务教育、高中、大学（含研究生）及英语专业，实际并未真正覆盖英语教育的所有学段，例如职高、大专等。这主要是因为笔者个人的教学经历有限，只接触过本书涉及学段的英语教学工作。“实践出真知”，欢迎其他学段的英语教学实践者参考此书，设计出符合本学段实际情况的英语课程思政教学案例。需要指出的是，职业教育领域的英语教师已在英语课程思政教学方向上进行了很多有益的探索，从笔者目前接触到的职业教育英语教育研究文献来看，职业教育学段可以参考本书的高中和大学阶段教案，作出必要调整。

为上述教学应用提供学术理念支持的组织机构英文网站文本统计研究受限于样本量和实际可比网站版块数，目前尚无法对中国英语变体存在与否给出肯定的回答。对于“中国英语变体”这一提法的质疑往往源于单纯的语言使用谬误与英语变体特征之间难以区分这一问题。不同于语言使用谬误，英语变体特征应满足以下三个主要条件：一是长期存在；二是得到特定社会的英语使用者普遍认可或在英语使用者无意识的情况下广泛传播和使用；三是不同于“标准”英语语体的特征。前两个主要条件是英语变体特征和语言使用谬误的关键区别。网站的技术特点使得提取不同时间点的网站文本成为可能，今后可以通过网站文本研究探索网站文本语言特征随时间演变的过程，以期为判定英语变体提供更加充分的证据。诚然，当前研究在第二阶段统计分析过程中仅能提供全景式描述，而未列举具体案例进行定性分析，这在一定程度上体现了基于网络语料的语料库研究存在的局限性，将在今后的研究中进行修正。

在本书即将付梓之际，笔者谨对所有关心支持本书编写的师友表示由衷的敬意与谢忱。同时，感谢光明日报出版社的编辑团队在本书出版过程中提供的尽心指导和帮助，我将永远铭记他们为本书出版付出的辛劳。任何程度的感激言辞都无法道尽我在成长过程中收获的诸多不同寻常的力量，书不尽言，言不尽意。

衷心感谢东南大学及其外国语学院对青年教师的支持和帮助，今年恰逢东南大学百廿华诞，敬祝母校学术长青，桃李四方！

刘彬

2022年5月28日　南京